Recapturing
Sophocles' *Antigone*

Greek Studies: Interdisciplinary Approaches
General Editor: Gregory Nagy, Harvard University
Assistant Editor: Timothy Power, Harvard University

On the front cover: A calendar frieze representing the Athenian months, reused in the Byzantine Church of the Little Metropolis in Athens. The cross is superimposed, obliterating Taurus of the Zodiac. The choice of this frieze for books in *Greek Studies: Interdisciplinary Approaches* reflects this series' emphasis on the blending of the diverse heritages—Near Eastern, Classical, and Christian—in the Greek tradition. Drawing by Laurie Kain Hart, based on a photograph. Recent titles in the series are:

The Wrath of Athena: Gods and Men in the Odyssey, Jenny Strauss Clay, University of Virginia

Talking Trojan: Speech and Community in the Iliad, Hilary Mackie, Rice University

Poet and Audience in the Argonautica *of Apollonius*, Robert V. Albis, The Hotchkiss School

Theatrical Space and Historical Place in Sophocles' Oedipus at Colonus, Lowell Edmunds, Rutgers University

Choruses of Young Women in Ancient Greece: Their Morphology, Religious Role, and Social Function, Claude Calame, University of Lausanne, Switzerland; translated by Derek Collins and Jane Orion

Eurykleia and Her Successors: Female Figures of Authority in Greek Poetics, Helen Pournara Karydas, Boston Latin School and Harvard University

Speech in Speech: Studies in Incorporated Oratio Recta *in Attic Drama and Oratory*, Victor Bers, Yale University

Aegean Strategies: Studies of Culture and Environment on the European Fringe, P. Nick Kardulias, College of Wooster, and Mark T. Shutes, Youngstown State University

Aglaia: The Poetry of Alcman, Sappho, Pindar, Bacchylides, and Corinna, Charles Segal, Harvard University

Immortal Armor: The Concept of Alke in Archaic Greek Poetry, Derek Collins, University of Texas at Austin

Homeric Stitchings: The Homeric Centos of the Empress Eudocia, M. D. Usher, Willamette University

Recapturing
Sophocles' *Antigone*

Wm. Blake Tyrrell
and
Larry J. Bennett

ROWMAN & LITTLEFIELD PUBLISHERS, INC.
Lanham • Boulder • New York • Oxford

ROWMAN & LITTLEFIELD PUBLISHERS, INC.

Published in the United States of America
by Rowman & Littlefield Publishers, Inc.
4720 Boston Way, Lanham, Maryland 20706

12 Hid's Copse Road
Cumnor Hill, Oxford OX2 9JJ, England

Copyright © 1998 by Rowman & Littlefield Publishers, Inc.

Epigraph reprinted by permission of the University of Chicago Press, Chicago and London, © 1976
by The University of Chicago

All rights reserved. No part of this publication may be reproduced,
stored in a retrieval system, or transmitted in any form or by any
means, electronic, mechanical, photocopying, recording, or otherwise,
without the prior permission of the publisher.

British Library Cataloguing in Publication Information Available

Library of Congress Cataloging-in-Publication Data
Tyrrell, Wm. Blake.
Recapturing Sophocles' Antigone / Wm. Blake Tyrrell and Larry J. Bennett
    p.   cm. – (Greek Studies)
Includes bibliographical references (p.   ) and index.
ISBN 0-8476-9216-7 (cloth : alk. paper). – ISBN 0-8476-9217-5 (pbk. : alk. paper)
1. Sophocles. Antigone. 2. Antigone (Greek mythology) in literature. 3. Tragedy. I. Bennett,
Larry J., 1949- . II. Title. III. Series
PA4413.A7T97 1998
882'.01—dc21

                                                                98-25660
                                                                CIP

ISBN 0-8476-9216-7 (cloth : alk. paper)
ISBN 0-8476-9217-5 (pbk. : alk. paper)

Printed in the United States of America

♾™ The paper used in this publication meets the minimum requirements of American National
Standard for Information Sciences—Permanence of Paper for Printed Library Materials, ANSI
Z39.48–1984.

For our children,
Blake, Jonathon, Jessica, and Sarah

For my mother,
Bernadine M. Bennett

In memory of my beloved nephew, Thomas C. Bennett,
indigne adempti nobis

"All there is to thinking," he said, "is seeing something noticeable which makes you see something you weren't noticing which makes you see something that isn't even visible."

Norman Maclean, *A River Runs Through It*

Contents

Foreword
Gregory Nagy, General Editor

Building on the foundations of scholarship within the disciplines of philology, philosophy, history, and archaeology, this series spans the continuum of Greek traditions extending from the second millennium BCE to the present, not just the Archaic and Classical periods. The aim is to enhance perspectives by applying various disciplines to problems that have in the past been treated as the exclusive concern of a single given discipline. Besides the crossing-over of the older disciplines, as in the case of historical and literary studies, the series encourages the application of such newer ones as linguistics, sociology, anthropology, and comparative literature. It also encourages encounters with current trends in methodology, especially in the realm of literary theory.

Recapturing Sophocles' Antigone, by Wm. Blake Tyrrell and Larry J. Bennett, approaches the *Antigone* of Sophocles by concentrating on the historical context of audience reception. From this point of view, they force a reassessment of what the play is about. According to Tyrrell and Bennett, the *Antigone* is not about burying a corpse, as has been the focus of much modern criticism. Rather, it is about the consequences of Creon's exposure of Polyneices' corpse. The play becomes the catalyst for the audience to ask itself: who should control the disposition of the corpse–the Demos or the family?

Sophocles' *Antigone* makes the audience confront the tensions and emotions aroused by a public funeral that represents the intrusion of the Demos on the traditional rights of women to care for the dead of their families. The wording used by Sophocles evokes the conventions of the public funeral oration, delivered by statesmen over the bodies of those who died for the State. The dialogue between Antigone and Ismene and the kommos of Antigone and the Coryphaeus are especially pertinent. The rituals of funeral intersect with those of marriage, and these intersections deepen the tragedy. By corrupting funeral rites and exposing the corpse of Polyneices, Creon allows the pollution to spread. With the loss of ritual purity comes the loss of fertility. The deaths of the bride and groom lead to the destruction of the house. Furthermore, the *Antigone* reproduces for the tragic stage the myth of the Theban dead, which was not only part of the orator's repertoire of myths but also belonged to an overall mythical armature that casts Thebes as an "anti-Athens" (in the words of Froma Zeitlin). In Athenian "state myth," Thebes represents the opposite of Athens, as here highlighted by the roles of Creon, Ismene, and even Antigone. Creon as a Theban leader is impious for denying burial from the outset. Athenians, by opposition, are surely "civilized": they bury their dead. As an anti-Athenian, Creon could only expose the corpse or give it its last rites improperly.

Tyrrell and Bennett contrast this perspective with modern critical views of tragedy and the tragic hero that feature Creon as the good man who tragically turns into a tyrant. Similarly, Ismene is not the foil for Antigone that modern readers have created. She refuses to oppose a painful decree of the State against tending her brother's corpse, but she willingly offers herself to die for her near-and-dear ones, and she defends the marriage of Antigone and Haemon. All of these stances are desirable attributes in the women of the Athenians who are the audience. The headstrong Antigone who is bent on a single deed–to bury her brother and, on failing that, to perform over him a symbolic burial–is a modern invention, according to Tyrrell and Bennett. No Athenian audience would unambiguously admire a woman who competed with men for *aretê* and caused them such shame by not acting in accordance with their instructions.

This book places the *Antigone* in the context of fifth-century Athens, returning the play to the way it may have been received by an audience of contemporary Athenians. It allows the play to set its own agenda. It is not a commentary, nor do the authors engage the innumerable polemics occasioned by modern interpretations. Notably, the book views the events at Polyneices' grave by referring primarily to the Homeric treatment of the theme of the exposed corpse, not to the question of a "double burial," which derives from a formulation devised by Richard Jebb on line 423 of his commentary. The latter question–as well as other questions–will not go away because of this book, but the hope remains that still other questions, especially those that were demonstrably essential to fifth-century Athenians, will have their day in the sun. This book raises precisely those kinds of questions.

Preface

Sophocles' *Antigone* was the most popular Greek tragedy among European poets, composers, and intellectuals during the nineteenth century, and although surpassed in popularity in the early twentieth century by Sophocles' *Oedipus the King*, it is still widely studied, taught, and performed. An extensive body of critical opinion has therefore grown up around the play so that it now seems familiar and well understood. Yet, there are portions of the text that refuse to be integrated into the received interpretations. Often seen as vexing passages in an otherwise smooth voyage through the play's thirteen hundred and fifty-two lines, they are rather buoys, as it were, that mark those places where the readers' desires for the text to respond to their interests and expectations have been thwarted.

In this reading, we have tried to return the *Antigone* to its setting among Athenians of fifth-century Athens. We do not claim, of course, to know how Athenians of Sophocles' original audience reacted to and experienced his play, but the circumstances that conditioned and formed their opinions and Sophocles' were social and can be known as well as anything can be known about fifth-century Greece. In contextualizing the play in the dynamics of fifth-century Athens, we have benefited from recent developments in the study of Greek antiquity and tragedy and have taken full advantage of the views and insights of others, but we have not attempted a summation of scholarly opinion on his play. Instead, we have followed the play's progress from beginning to end in an effort to understand how it might have functioned in its contemporary setting and how the spectacle might have unfolded before its audience. This approach has brought new insights to the text, challenged the validity of long-standing critical problems, and we hope, resolved some difficulties in its interpretation. The effect has been not only to "defamiliarize" and enliven a well-known "classic of the canon" but also to reveal the mechanisms within and without the play that disallow modern accretions to its words. Since the Aristotelian action of the *Antigone* is exposure of the dead, Creon, who forbade burial of Polyneices' body, became prominent in our reading of the play. Paradoxically, as Creon claimed more of our attention, the voices of the women, Ismene, Antigone, and Creon's wife, Eurydice, demanded to be heard. In particular, Antigone's lines 904ff., in which she renounces a husband's or son's rotting corpse, have moved from the margins, where most opinion on the play has banished them, to the center of our reading. Antigone speaks these lines as the representative of Athenian women whose traditional care for the dead had been usurped when the *dêmos* seized control over those killed in its wars. Women who once mourned and prepared their dead for burial within the confines of their own houses had to submit to the new rituals of the state funeral. By saying she would yield the corpses of husband and child to the citizens, Antigone confers upon their men a charter and their women's blessings for the public funeral. A passage that has been an anathema in modern critics reemerges as the *anathêma* (ornament) we believe Sophocles intended it to be. For this reason, we have entitled our study of Sophocles' play *Recapturing Sophocles'* Antigone.

Unless otherwise indicated, all translations are our own. For the Greek text, we have generally followed and drawn line numbers from H. Lloyd-Jones and N. G. Wilson's *Sophoclis Fabulae* (Oxford 1990). We have often preferred the reading of the manuscripts over modern emendations. References to the Scholiast on Sophocles' *Antigone* are cited from Richard François Brunk, *Scholia Graeca in Sophoclem ex Editione Brunckiana,* 2d ed. Oxonii: E Typographeo Clarendoniano, 1810. All ancient dates are B.C. except where noted. Abbreviations for ancient authors and texts follow those of Henry George Liddell, Robert Scott, and Henry Stuart Jones, *A Greek-Lexicon*, 9th edition (Oxford: Oxford University Press, 1940).

We would like to express our gratitude to our friend and colleague, Frieda S. Brown, Professor Emeritus of Romance Languages and Literature at Michigan State University, for her careful reading of our manuscript.

While we were working on this book, our children, like Antigone and Haemon, underwent their own rites of passage. They were much in our thoughts. Our common dedication reflects those times of concern and wonderment.

1. Introduction: Insight, Contexts, Methods

In the epigraph to this book, the speaker, Paul Maclean, is thinking about why his brother has not caught any fish. This thought leads him to see the absence of stone flies, something he had not noticed before, and to realize what cannot be seen, drowned flies: "Since I couldn't see them dead in the water, I knew they had to be at least six or seven inches under the water where I couldn't see them. So that's where I fished."[1] There is more to Paul's thinking than thinking. There is the background knowledge about rivers, fish, flies (real ones and camouflaged hooks); there is also the methodology that organizes background with present conditions to arrive at an interpretation, in this case, the whereabouts of fish.

Exposed amid the corpses of his fellow warriors, Polyneices is more than Antigone's brother. He is one of the Seven slain before Thebes. Scholars have noted this, but its significance for reading Sophocles' *Antigone* has not been fully explored. In attempting to bury Polyneices, Antigone is reprising a wondrous deed claimed for Athenians by their orators at public funerals since at least the 460s.[2] During the violent decades that preceded the *Antigone,* Athenians were being educated in a revisionist version of the ancient tale of the Seven Against Thebes. The champions of aristocratic mythmaking were suppressed in favor of nameless Argive soldiers as the conflict was recast as occurring between *poleis* (city-states).[3]

---

1. Norman Maclean, *A River Runs Through It and Other Stories* (Chicago and London: The University of Chicago Press, 1976), 93.

2. The public funeral could not have existed before Cleisthenes' reforms (last decade of the sixth century B.C.) since the chests holding the remains were displayed according to the tribal system he devised (Thucydides 2.34.3). The actual time of its inauguration is likely much later, during the 470s (Christoph W. Clairmont, *Patrios Nomos: Public Burial in Athens during the Fifth and Fourth Centuries B.C.* [Oxford: B. A. R., 1983], 7-15) or the 460s (F. Jacoby, "*Patrios Nomos*: State Burial in Athens and the Public Cemetery in the Kerameikos," *Journal of Hellenic Studies* 64 [1944], 37-66; Nicole Loraux, *The Invention of Athens: The Funeral Oration in the Classical City*, trans. Alan Sheridan [Cambridge: Harvard University Press, 1986], 56-72).

3. Similarly, when the orators adapted the myth of the Amazons' invasion of Attica, Theseus' rape of an Amazon, which occasioned the invasion, and the role of his Amazon in

Sophocles alludes to these "Theban Dead" whose mangled bodies lie before Thebes:

ἔχθρᾳ δὲ πᾶσαι συνταράσσονται πόλεις
ὅσων σπαράγματ' ἢ κύνες καθήγνισαν
ἢ θῆρες, ἤ τις πτηνὸς οἰωνός, φέρων
ἀνόσιον ὀσμὴν ἑστιοῦχον ἐς πόλιν.

Antigone 1080-1083

All the cities are being stirred up in enmity,
whose torn bodies the dogs have consecrated
or beasts or some winged bird, carrying
the unhallowed stench into a hearth-having city.[4]

In a victory ode composed around 474 (*Nemean* 9.24) B.C. and another around 468 (*Olympian* 6.15), the Boeotian poet Pindar tells how the Thebans themselves observe piety by burning the bodies of the Seven. Thebans of Aeschylus' lost *Eleusinians* concede to Theseus' entreaties and relinquish the bodies to his care (Plutarch *Theseus* 29.4).[5] On the other hand, Thebans in the speeches of funeral orators scorn their obligations to the dead and scruples before the gods and, refusing to surrender the bodies for burial, leave them exposed as carrion before their city. A speech Herodotus attributes to the Athenians on the fields of Plataea illustrates how orators he probably heard told the myth:

τοῦτο δὲ 'Αργείους τοὺς μετὰ Πολυνείκεος ἐπὶ Θήβας ἐλάσαντας,
τελευτήσαντας τὸν αἰῶνα καὶ ἀτάφους κειμένους, στρατευσάμενοι
ἐπὶ τοὺς Καδμείους ἀνελέσθαι τε τοὺς νεκρούς φαμεν καὶ θάψαι τῆς
ἡμετέρης ἐν 'Ελευσῖνι.

Herodotus 9.27.3

When the Argives with Polyneices came against Thebes and, perishing there, lay unburied, we say that we made an expedition against the Cadmeians [i.e., Thebans], picked up the corpses, and buried them in Eleusis in our own land.

---

defending Athens were omitted. See Wm. Blake Tyrrell, *Amazons: A Study in Athenian Mythmaking* (Baltimore and London: The Johns Hopkins University Press, 1984), 13-19.

4. Richard Jebb, *Sophocles: The Plays and Fragments*, vol. 3, *The "Antigone"* (Cambridge: Cambridge University Press, 1900), 191, identifies the cities as those "which had furnished contingents to the Argive expedition against Thebes." He also finds in "evils of enemies" (Sophocles *Antigone* 16) "a hint" of denial of burial to others (192). Lines 1080-1083 have been thought spurious but on no convincing grounds (J. C. Kamerbeek, *The Plays of Sophocles*, vol. 3, *The "Antigone"* [Leiden: E. J. Brill, 1978], 182). All translations are our own.

5. For these myths, see Otto Schroeder, *De laudibus Athenarum a poetis tragicis et ab oratoribus epidicticis excultis* (Göttingen: Officina Hubertiana, 1914), 40-43; Ludwig Preller, *Griechische Mythologie*, vol. 2, pt. 2: *Die Nationalheroen*, 4th ed. (Berlin: Weidmann, 1921), ed. Carl Robert (Zurich: Weidmann, 1967), 751-752; Christopher Collard, *Euripides:"Supplices,"* (Groningen: Bouma's Boekhuis, 1975), 5-6.

The conflation of Polyneices with the Theban Dead led, in our reading, first to the presence and effects of funeral oratory in *Antigone,* then to things we had not noticed before and to trolling the stream, as it were, of critical opinion.[6] Maclean was successful because he thought the river through, with the instincts of a fish in mind. Although the meaning or meanings of *Antigone* may be more elusive than even fish, we sought them by trying to reconstruct, through the normative codes of Athens of the 430s, an audience for whom Sophocles might originally have intended his play.[7] Paul could interpret the river that day because he had done it many times before and, before that, had learned from his father who probably learned from somebody else. The insights of others into tragedy, into *Antigone,* and into the ancient world brought us to our insight, and our insight, in turn, identified the background information about the ancient world and relevant scholarship that we needed in order to envision a Sophoclean audience of the sort we had in mind.

The last years of the 440s have traditionally been considered the historical context for the first performance of *Antigone.* Aristophanes, scholar and head librarian of the Alexandrine Library, contends in his *Life of Sophocles* that the Athenians elected Sophocles to a generalship in the Samian War out of appreciation for his play. Since the war broke out in the early summer of 441/440 B.C., the play would, then, have been produced in the spring of that year.[8] But elections for the year's generalships had already been held in Boedromion (roughly September) of 441, months before the festival of the City Dionysia. Unless the elections were postponed, and there is no evidence for such an irregularity, the first performance of *Antigone* must be moved back at least to 442/441. In this year, the first prize went

---

6. Larry J. Bennett and Wm. Blake Tyrrell, "Sophocles' *Antigone* and Funeral Oratory," *American Journal of Philology* 111 (1990), 441-456.

7. Christiane Sourvinou-Inwood ("Assumptions and the Creation of Meaning: Reading Sophocles' *Antigone,*" *Journal of Hellenic Studies* 109 [1989], 134) remarks: "[I]f we wish to read a text such as the *Antigone* as closely as possible to the ways in which its contemporary audience did, we must reconstruct in detail their cultural assumptions, by means of which meaning was created, and try to read through perceptual filters created by those assumptions."

8. In accepting 438 B.C. as the year of the first performance of the *Antigone,* we are following the reconstruction of events surrounding the play proposed by R. G. Lewis in "An Alternative Date for Sophocles' *Antigone,*" *Greek, Roman, and Byzantine Studies* 29 (1988), 35-50. For 443 B.C. as the date of *Antigone,* see Ulrich von Wilamowitz-Moellendorff, *Aristoteles und Athen* (Berlin: Weidmann, 1893), 2.298; for 442, see Wilhelm von Schmid and Otto Stählin, *Die griechische Literatur in der Zeit des attischen Hegemonie vor dem Eingreifen der Sophistik,* vol. 2 of *Geschichte der griechischen Literatur* (Munich: C. H. Beck, 1959), 317; for 442 or, probably, 441, see Jebb, *Antigone,* xlii-xlvii. For a discussion of the traditional dating, see also Andrew Brown, *Sophocles:"Antigone"* (Warminster: Aris and Phillips, 1987), 1-2; Mary R. Lefkowitz, *The Lives of the Greek Poets* (Baltimore: The Johns Hopkin University Press, 1981), 81-82. For the Samian War, see N. G. L. Hammond, *A History of Greece to 322 B.C.* (Oxford: Oxford University Press, 1959), 314-316. The Athenian year extended from the fall to the summer. In modern terms, a year began in 442 B.C. and ended in 441, and so the year is marked as 442/441 B.C.

to Euripides for a series of plays that included the *Alcestis*. Since the competitive Athenians were not likely to reward Sophocles for second place, a premier performance in 442/441 is improbable as is one in the previous year, 443/442. During the latter year, Sophocles was serving as a treasurer and financial overseer for the Delian League and was surely deeply involved in official duties. On the other hand, a later year, 440/439, finds Sophocles serving as a general with Pericles in the Samian War, and his service probably continued to the end of the war in late spring or early summer of 439 B.C. Sophocles, it would seem, did not have the leisure necessary for composing and producing his plays until the Samian War ended in the spring or early summer of 439 B.C. Therefore, *Antigone* was performed in the year after the war, 438 B.C., in the archonship of Theodorus, and did not gain a generalship for its author. Although Sophocles composed *Antigone* about the time of the Samian War, Aristophanes was mistaken in assuming Sophocles was awarded a generalship as a result of the *Antigone*.

In the year following the expulsion of the Persians (478/477), the Athenians assumed leadership over a league of Greek cities and islands whose purpose was to punish the Persians and seek reparations. While championing the league's interests, the Athenians had converted the alliance into an empire and made subjects of their allies. Even after they concluded peace with the Persians in 449 B.C., they did not stop their tyranny. They continued to exact tribute, monies that they used to implement Pericles' program for glorifying Athens with the Parthenon, the magnificent temple of Athena Parthenos, and other public buildings. Tribute also funded ships for the fleet that secured their control over subjects flung far and wide over the Mediterranean Sea. According to the founding treaty of the alliance, the allies were individually allied with Athens but not with one another. They remained independent states under their own laws and were free to go to war against each other. But when war broke out between the Milesians and Samians, both allies, over Priene, a strategic city between their territories on the Ionian mainland, the Milesians appealed to the Athenians as leader of the alliance. The Athenians, lacking authority to intervene, nonetheless ignored the treaty arrangements and ordered the Samians to cease hostilities and accept their arbitration. When the Samians refused, asserting their independence and rights under the treaty, the Athenians declared war, subdued the island, and set up a democratic government. Those Samians who escaped to the mainland enlisted the aid of the Persian satrap Pissuthnes, returned to the city, and drove out the Athenians. At this time, Byzantium revolted against the Athenians and blockaded the Bosporus, endangering the trade routes to the Black Sea. The situation was serious in that it threatened the existence of the empire in the eastern Mediterranean. Pericles acted with dispatch and with force. Hostilities settled into a siege of the city that lasted nine months. At its end, Pericles reportedly brought the commanders of the Samian ships and the marines over to the marketplace of the Milesians in Miletus. There he had them bound to boards and exposed until they were nearly dead. Next he had them clubbed to death and their bodies thrown away without benefit of funeral rites. Plutarch, who names the Samian historian and sensationalist Duris as his source, does not believe the story because other prominent historians do not mention it (*Pericles* 28.2). Yet the punishment resembles *apotympanismos*, "binding on planks," which Athenians inflicted upon citizens guilty of heinous crimes.[9] Pericles, it may be argued, treats the Samians as disloyal citizens. In that light, their revolt is equivalent to *stasis*, factional discord among citizens, and analogous to the quarrel between Oedipus' sons, Eteocles and Polyneices, each of whom claimed the kingship of Thebes for himself.

The connection between the aftermath of the Samian War and *Antigone* is further secured by the fact that Pericles delivered the oration at the public funeral for those killed in subduing Samos (Plutarch *Pericles* 28.4-7). The subtext of funeral oratory in a play about exposing corpses could well be addressing covertly the suffering and savagery of the war that Pericles' funeral oration and the public funeral were meant to soothe. When Pericles was descending from the bema, women praised him as if "he were an athletic victor" (ὥσπερ ἀθλητὴν νικηφόρον 28.5) and crowned him with garlands and ribbons. But Cimon's sister Elpinike derided him sardonically for accomplishing "marvelous deeds ... worthy of garlands" (θαυμαστά ... ἄξια στεφάνων 28.6) in killing "many brave ... citizens" (πολλοὺς καὶ ἀγαθοὺς ... πολίτας 28.6) in a war against "an allied and kindred city" (σύμμαχον καὶ συγγενῆ πόλιν 28.6), unlike her brother who defeated Phoenicians and Medes. What is noteworthy for the historical context of *Antigone* is the mixed reception of Pericles' speech by women, some of whom praise him, in effect, for usurping their lamentations with his prose, while Elpinike blames him for causing the deaths of Athenian men in a bitter war against allies, another example of the *dêmos'* imperialism under the generalship of Pericles.

Greek tragedies are usually held to have addressed topical events, concerns, and issues in only the most remote manner. To be sure, the plots of the dramas are drawn almost exclusively from the mythic past, and efforts to find in them the political views of their authors have had little and dubious success. Yet, even if *Antigone* were not intended to be seen and heard in the context of 438 B.C.—which we do not believe for a moment—the audience would be hard-pressed not to make connections between the plot and language of the play and the recent events in the eastern Mediterranean and in the Kerameikos where the public funeral had been held only a few months before. The issues that must be explored as necessary background for approaching *Antigone* are, then, those of the public funeral and its effects on women and their traditional care for the dead of the family.

Sometime before *Antigone* was presented, the Athenians adopted the custom of bringing home the bones and ashes of those Athenians killed outside Attica and

9. See Lysias, *Against Agoratus* 56, 68; Aristotle *Rhetoric* 1385 A; Demosthenes *On the Affairs in the Chersonese,* 61; Philip A. Stadter, *A Commentary on "Plutarch's Pericles"* (Chapel Hill and London: The University of North Carolina Press, 1989), 258-259.

burying them with the pomp and ceremony of a funeral paid for at public expense. Soldiers may already have been bringing home the remains of kinsmen and others, as ChristophW. Clairmont has suggested.[10] In this event, the action of the *dêmos* would have formalized a custom (*nomos*) carried on privately by individuals. The *dêmos* now assumed the responsibility for all those killed in its wars. Henceforth, its generals were obligated to secure the remains of the dead and return them to Athens, and the polemarch "arranged funeral games and did the customary offerings for those killed in war" (Aristotle *Constitution of the Athenians* 58.1). Later, another legislator added the *epitaphios logos* (funeral oration) (Thucydides 2.35.1), and the prose of the *dêmos'* orator entered into competition with the aristocratic praise of the individual in the poetic forms of epigram and *thrênos* (song of grief) and with the age-old lamentations of women.[11] The *locus classicus* for the public funeral is the thirty-fourth chapter of Thucydides' second book:

ἐν δὲ τῷ αὐτῷ χειμῶνι Ἀθηναῖοι τῷ πατρίῳ νόμῳ χρώμενοι δημοσίᾳ ταφὰς ἐποιήσαντο τῶν ἐν τῷδε τῷ πολέμῳ πρώτων ἀποθανόντων τρόπῳ τοιῷδε. τὰ μὲν ὀστᾶ προτίθενται τῶν ἀπογενομένων πρότριτα σκηνὴν ποιήσαντες, καὶ ἐπιφέρει τῷ αὐτοῦ ἕκαστος ἤν τι βούληται· ἐπειδὰν δὲ ἡ ἐκφορὰ ᾖ, λάρνακας κυπαρισσίνας ἄγουσιν ἄμαξαι, φυλῆς ἑκάστης μίαν· ἔνεστι δὲ τὰ ὀστᾶ ἧς ἕκαστος ἦν φυλῆς. μία δὲ κλίνη κενὴ φέρεται ἐστρωμένη τῶν ἀφανῶν, ὃι ἂν μὴ εὑρεθῶσιν ἐς ἀναίρεσιν. ξυνεκφέρει δὲ ὁ βουλόμενος καὶ ἀστῶν καὶ ξένων, καὶ γυναῖκες πάρεισιν αἱ προσήκουσαι ἐπὶ τὸν τάφον ὀλοφυρόμεναι. τιθέασιν οὖν ἐς τὸ δημόσιον σῆμα, ὅ ἐστιν ἐπὶ τοῦ καλλίστου προαστείου τῆς πόλεως, καί αἰεὶ ἐν αὐτῷ θάπτουσι τοὺς ἐκ τῶν πολέμων, πλήν γε τοὺς ἐν Μαραθῶνι· ἐκείνων δὲ διαπρεπῆ τὴν ἀρετὴν κρίναντες αὐτοῦ καὶ τὸν τάφον ἐποίησαν. ἐπειδὰν δὲ κρύψωσι γῇ, ἀνὴρ ᾑρημένος ὑπὸ τῆς πόλεως, ὅς ἂν γνώμῃ τε δοκῇ μὴ ἀξύνετος εἶναι καὶ ἀξιώσει προήκῃ, λέγει ἐπ' αὐτοῖς ἔπαινον τὸν πρέποντα· μετὰ δὲ τοῦτο ἀπέρχονται.

Thucydides 2.34

In this same winter [431/ 430 B.C.], in accord with ancestral custom, the Athenians conducted at public expense the burial of the first men killed in the present war. They set up a tent where they displayed the bones of the departed for two days. Individuals confer upon their own whatever they wish. When it is time to carry the bones out for burial, wagons bring chests of cypress wood, one for each tribe. The bones are deposited in the tribe's box. One bier is carried out, empty and spread with covers, for the missing, those who could not be found at the taking up of the dead. Whoever

---

10. Clairmont, *Patrios Nomos*, 11.

11. For the relationship between the *thrênos* and the *epitaphios logos* in the public funeral, see Loraux, *Invention*, 42-50. See also Donovan J. Ochs, *Consolatory Rhetoric: Grief, Symbol, and Ritual in the Greco-Roman Era* (Columbia: University of South Carolina Press, 1993), 61-79.

wishes of the citizens and foreigners joins in the procession. The women relatives are present, mourning and wailing on the route to the cemetery. The Athenians place the bones in the public tomb, which is located in the city's most beautiful suburb. They always bury the dead from the wars there except for those at Marathon. Because they judged their bravery exceptional, they buried them on the plain. After they hid the bones with earth, a man, selected by the city, who is not devoid of sense and is of fitting repute, speaks a suitable eulogy over them. Then they depart.

Athenian burial practice, like so much of their imperialistic culture during the fifth century, was unique among Greeks. Thucydides thought it an ancestral, that is, traditional, practice.[12] Athenians were buried at public expense outside Attica as early as 507/506. An epigram for the Athenians slain by Euboeans states that "a marker mound over us is thrown up near the Euripos Strait at public expense (σῆμα δ' ἐφ' ἡμῖν/ἐγγύθεν Εὐρίπου δημοσία κέχυται Page, p.191).[13] But burial of the war dead at home does not fit the conditions of warfare during the sixth century or during the Persian Wars. In those days, men died defending their borders or in the territories of fellow Greeks. After 478 B.C., when Athenians undertook the leadership of the alliance of Athenians and Ionians sworn to punishing the retreating Persians and gaining reparations, things changed. Engaged at first in the business of the alliance and then in pursuing their own goals of conquest, Athenians began losing men heavily. They left their dead in the soil of foreign, even non-Greek, lands. Deprived of their women's care and customary rites, interred in strange, remote places, these dead must have rent a deep chasm in the continuity of life from and back to the earth. Athenians particularly, because of their belief in their birth from the earth, would have felt the inability of the family to tend its dead.[14] They responded by founding a public funeral that stepped into the void created by successive restrictions upon the funerals of aristocratic families.[15]

---

12. A. W. Gomme (*A Historical Commentary on Thucydides*, vol. 2, *The Ten Years' War* [Oxford: Oxford University Press, 1956], 94-98) believes that, by using the phrase *patrios nomos* (ancestral custom), Thucydides dates the origin of the public funeral to the time of Solon in the early sixth century. See also Jacoby, *Patrios Nomos*, 39-40, 58; Martin Ostwald, *Nomos and the Beginnings of the Athenian Democracy* (Oxford: Oxford University Press, 1969), 75.

13. See Clairmont, *Patrios Nomos*, 88, for a discussion of the epigram as "inscribed on the polyandrion of the Athenians."

14. Belief in their autochthony, or birth from the earth (*khthon-*) itself (*aut-*), is found in the earliest stratum of Athenian mythology (Apollodorus *The Library* 3.14-15.6 *passim*) and is a commonplace of funeral oratory (Lysias *Funeral Oration* 17; Plato *Menexenos* 237 B-C). See Schroeder, *De laudibus*, 5-9; Nicole Loraux, *The Children of Athena: Athenian Ideas about Citizenship and the Division between the Sexes*, trans. Caroline Levine (Princeton, NJ: Princeton University Press, 1993), 37-71.

15. For legislation on funeral rites and lamentation, see Margaret Alexiou, *Ritual Lament in Greek Tradition* (Cambridge: Cambridge University Press, 1974), 14-23; Robert Garland, "The Well-Ordered Corpse: An Investigation into the Motives behind Greek Funerary Legislation," *Bulletin of the Institute of Classical Studies of the University of London* 36 (1989), 1-15; H. A. Shapiro, "The Iconography of Mourning in Athenian Art," *American Journal of Archaeology* 95 (1991), 630-631; Gail Holst-Warhaft, *Dangerous Voices: Women's Laments and Greek*

Families of wealth and distinction celebrated the wake (*prothesis*), procession to the cemetery (*ekphora*), and rituals at the tomb with as much ostentation and opulence as could be mustered. Among their purposes was the desire to confer heroic status upon their dead and manipulate the community into feeling their loss as its own. For generations, legislators had been trying to control or at least restrain such funerals.[16] Their laws regulated the numbers of participants and the expense aristocratic families could lavish upon the funerals and had the effect of curbing the display of wealth and importance and tempering the intrusion of funeral processions upon the townspeople. Legislation designed to minimize what was conducted in public also aimed at shifting control to the *polis* over what transpired in the streets of the city. According to Cicero (*Laws* 2.63-65), a law of Solon limited the size and adornment of tombs, diminishing their splendor and impact as *sêmata* (markers) of the deceased's honor and prestige, and disallowed praise of the dead in public except by an orator officially chosen for the task. Other motives were as important, however, and these concerned women directly. Women had always managed the care and mourning for the dead of their families. To judge from the influence women of modern Greece derive from these responsibilities, lamentation may have afforded Athenian women status among themselves for skills in creating and performing laments.[17] Among men and the community at large, laments provided women with a public medium to voice their views and, in particular, to stir their men to exact vengeance for perceived wrongs.[18] The legislators' purposes seem to have been as much to free the men from being shamed by their women's censures and emotional displays as to check the women themselves. In any case, the men do not appear comfortable with the behavior of women in mourning, perhaps because of its tendency to arouse deep emotions, physical violence, and madness.[19] Laments

Literature (London and New York: Routledge, 1992), 114-119.

16. Concerning motives impelling funeral legislation, see Garland, *Well-Ordered Corpse*; Holst-Warhaft, *Dangerous Voices*,114-119; Richard Seaford, *Reciprocity and Ritual: Homer and Tragedy in the Developing City-State* (Oxford: Oxford University Press, 1994), 78-86.

17. This assumption is suggested by Anna Caraveli's research ("The Bitter Wounding: The Lament as Social Protest in Rural Greece," in *Gender and Power in Rural Greece*, ed. Jill Dubisch [Princeton, NJ: Princeton University Press, 1986], 169-194) into the function of lament as a means of bestowing social worth and expressing social comment by women in the Zagori area of Epiros of modern Greece and in the village of Dzermiades in Crete. See also the classic study of Greek lament by Margaret Alexiou, *Ritual Lament*, and a recent survey of the relationships between ancient and modern Greek laments in Holst-Warhaft, *Dangerous Voices*.

18. Alexiou (*Ritual Lament*, 21-22) comments: "In the inflammable atmosphere of the blood feud between the families of Megakles and Kylon that was still raging in Solon's time, what more effective way could there be to stir up feelings of revenge than the incessant lamentation at the tomb by large numbers of women for 'those long dead'?"

19. Anna Caraveli-Chaves, "Bridge Between Worlds: The Greek Women's Lament as Communicative Event," *Journal of American Folklore* 93 (1980), 129-157; Holst-Warhaft, *Dangerous Voices*, 20-35.

were not banished from the public funeral. Instead, women participated in the *dêmos'* ritual on its terms and in a space never their own.

The public funeral exacerbated the antagonism of the *dêmos* and the family over funeral celebrations by separating the dead from their families. Women had brought the dead into the world in the company of women, and they or other women of the family should have prepared the bodies for burial and mourned them. Bones and ashes brought home by family members could be tended in the house, but the public funeral replaced the body of the deceased and moved the place of grieving from the house with its familiar things and smells to the open sunny spaces of the men's agora. Although the public ritual allotted two days for the family to mourn its loss, twice that allowed for private funerals, such concessions paled before the splendor of the third day, when the civic values underlying the ceremony came to the fore.

On the dawning of this day, no longer were the bones distinguished by the names, identities, economic, and social differences that separated individuals in life. Now they were "the dead," an expression virtually synonymous with the city as shown by the organization of the remains in chests according to Cleisthenian tribes. The empty bier indicated the importance of honoring those slain as an anonymous group, for which purpose actual remains were not needed. Wagons carrying the chests formed a procession more elaborate than any family could mount and wended their way in broad daylight toward the Dipylon Gate and the Kerameikos, "the city's most beautiful suburb." The procession was perhaps escorted by hoplites in full armor.[20] Anyone could join. Thucydides uses the same formula, *ho boulomenos* (whoever wishes), that allowed access to the democracy for citizens in full standing. In this instance, the formula also opened the procession to foreigners who, probably being allies, were invited to lament their suppressors. The high-pitched keening of the women filled the air, soon to be superseded by the sonorous voice of the orator. When the dead arrived at the public cemetery, the mourners sought renewal through an oration that replaced not only the familial rites of fertility and purification but also the praise and laments sung for individual heroes by their poets.

Tending the body and a final intimacy with the deceased were not all that the *dêmos* took from the Athenian women. The death of a man, particularly one of standing, property, and dependents, necessitated changes within the family. New relationships had to be established; the dead man's will or his oral instructions and bequests had to be implemented. Funeral arrangements had to be made and paid for, relatives and friends invited, and provisions obtained for entertaining them.[21] These were anxious times. The reshaping of kinship ties and the transferring of

---

20. Loraux, *Invention*, 20.
21. S. C. Humphreys, *The Family, Women, and Death: Comparative Studies* (London: Routledge and Kegan Paul, 1982), 144-150.

wealth frequently ruptured family structures, leading to unseemly squabbles in the house or at the tomb, protracted hostilities, and even litigation. During these days, women could exert considerable influence through their control over lamentation and mourning. Since only those allowed to mourn the dead could inherit from him, women indirectly played a prominent part in redistributing wealth among the male heirs.[22] Such power over the family's property, residing as it did with women, became the target of the legislator's restrictions because it ran counter to the rise of the family based upon "father-right."[23] But the public funeral took the trend one step further. It not only deprived women of control over the mourning group; it also complicated the reorganization of the family's finances and property by aborting *prothesis* and *ekphora*, the institutions central to identifying legitimate kin.

Pericles alone among extant orators alludes to the women who were participating in the ceremony:

τῆς τε γὰρ ὑπαρχούσης φύσεως μὴ χείροσι γενέσθαι ὑμῖν μεγάλη ἡ δόξα καὶ ἧς ἂν ἐπ᾽ ἐλάχιστον ἀρετῆς πέρι ἢ ψόγου ἐν τοῖς ἄρσεσι κλέος ᾖ.

Thucydides 2.45.2

Great will be your glory by not proving inferior to your given nature, and hers is the greatest glory whose fame, whether for excellence or blame, spreads least among males.

His caution comes, of course, from the funeral oration written by Thucydides who recalls the eulogy delivered by Pericles for the dead of the first year of the Peloponnesian War. It is generally admitted that Thucydides intended Pericles' oration as a statement of the meaning of Athens itself with wider connotations than that of a eulogy over the dead of one year. Accordingly, Pericles' admonition to the women should not be restricted to the dramatic situation of the last day of the funeral but should be understood in the context of Thucydides' purposes for the funeral oration. In that context, it addresses the role of lamenting women in Athenian society.[24] Although famous, it may still yield an unnoticed clue to the relations between men and women over the care of the dead, relations that came into sharper focus during those days of a public funeral.

For the first two days, when families lamented their dead as they wished, the agora must have been filled with women wailing and lamenting the bones and ashes of their kin in ways traditionally practiced over bodies. (Thucydides observes that the women wailed in the procession to the cemetery [2.34.4]; that they remained

---

22. Alexiou, *Ritual Lament*, 21.

23. Alexiou, *Ritual Lament*, 21.

24. Pericles' caution to women has broader implications than the moment as imagined, for example, by Nicole Loraux (*Invention*, 24) who suggests that Pericles was giving the women "a word of warning, just enough to remind them to behave with due decorum and reserve" during the third day.

silent in the presence of the dead for two days is unlikely.) Athenian women may have performed laments competitively for recognition and merit (*aretê*) in invention, adaption of known laments, and emotional intensity in singing.[25] Laments provided women with a vehicle to declare their grievances as well as to incite men to violence in rectifying wrongs done to the family. During the public funeral, women surely were constantly reminded of how the *dêmos* had intruded upon their privileges and ancestral duties to the dead. It is altogether possible that they would express their resentment and air their complaints, all to their men's discomfiture. Whereas men conceded that it was woman's nature to lament, excessive lamentation consistently invited their censures.[26] By admonishing the women not to be less than their natures, Pericles grants them lamentation while trying to keep them from exploiting laments as a way of calling attention to themselves and causing the men to notice them for praise or blame for what they are singing. A.W. Gomme dismisses Pericles' advice by claiming "most of it not called for by the occasion."[27] But Thucydides evidently wanted the occasion to be considered, since he describes it in detail. As is characteristic of his history, he omits any unnecessary mention of women, but every Athenian would know they were present for the whole ceremony, not merely its last day.

Familiar patterns of mourning had to have come forth during the first days of the ceremony, even under the trying circumstances of the agora, because the ways that women mourned could not be changed or set aside. They had no choice because they knew no other way; they had to sing in the old ways, one woman to another in antiphony. Someone would sing a solo song for her dead, and other women would respond to her, each mourning for her own dead by joining in the suffering and pain of the lead woman.[28] "Briseis weeps for Patroclus, and the women about her grieved, ostensibly for Patroclus, but each for her own sorrows" (ἐπὶ δὲ στενάχοντο

---

25. See Caraveli, *Bitter Wounding*, 171-178. To aid in restoring the voices of Athenian women as reflected in the characters of Sophocles' play, we have consulted anthropological studies of traditional Greek villages and families in modern Greece and other Mediterranean countries. Of particular use have been works of Alexiou (*Ritual Lament* 4-23), Loring M. Danforth (*The Death Rituals of Rural Greece*, photography by Alexander Tsiaras [Princeton NJ: Princeton University, 1982]), and C. Nadia Seremetakis (*The Last Word: Women, Death, and Divination in Inner Mani* [Chicago and London: The University of Chicago Press, 1991]). These studies strongly suggest the existence of such female discourse in lamenting the dead and the bride. Moreover, they alert the reader of *Antigone* to implications in the text that otherwise might have gone unnoticed.

26. Pollux' redundancy (*Onomasticum* 6.202) exemplifies this: γυναικεῖον γένος ἐστι θρηνῶδες καὶ φιλόθρηνον καὶ φιλόδυρτον καὶ θρηνητικόν (womanly nature is fit for the dirge and fond of mourning and fond of wailing and given to lamenting).

27. Gomme, *Thucydides*, 143.

28. This idea combines the antiphony that characterizes ancient Greek lament (Alexiou, *Ritual Lament*, 13) with Seremetakis' observation (*Last Word*, 99) on the role of the soloist: "The *koriféa* is the soloist in pain and the *moiroloyistres* are the chorus: their responses to the *koriféa* validate her pain with their own pain."

γυναῖκες, / Πάτροκλον πρόφασιν, σφῶν δ' αὐτῶν κήδε' ἑκάστη Homer
Iliad 19. 301-302). In weeping for Patroclus, however, Briseis recalls her life before
the coming of Achilles, the destruction of her family, and the loss of her betrothal to
Achilles that results from Patroclus' death.[29] Similarly, in weeping for their dead,
the women of the Athenians might have alluded more or less directly to the loss of
their rights and privileges or to their removal from their houses. Spread out across
the agora, they could have fallen into competition with one another in improvising
their laments about what was on all their minds. The men standing by and listening
would be embarrassed by having their actions cast in their teeth. Pericles' words go
beyond appealing for decorum to revealing the anxieties felt by the *dêmos* that the
women's bottomless woe might escalate into altercations and rivalries among them
and disrupt the solemnity and harmony of the occasion. Further, women's voices,
by mediating between the living and the dead, could inspire uneasiness and worse
among the men. Women could not overthrow the social structure, but they could
expose the glorious vision of Athens held forth by the *dêmos* and its orators as a
fragile invention of fallible men. Hence, in lieu of silencing the women, Pericles tries
to mute their menacing sounds.

The public funeral for the dead of the Samian War was one among others that the
Athenians had been celebrating for twenty or thirty years before the *dêmos* produced
Sophocles' *Antigone*. They could see the stelae, monuments recording the names
of the dead, expanding along the road leading to the Academy (Pausanias 1.29.4).
The public funeral was not unique in focusing attention on the cost of the empire,
but it alone put that cost in the currency of the dead. It opened a breach in Athenian
culture that endured long after the last line of Sophocles' play had been spoken.
Consequently, when the *dêmos'* generals failed to retrieve the dead and shipwrecked
in 406 B.C. off the Arginousae islands, the Athenians held the generals responsible
for the loss of the dead and shipwrecked and turned a stunning victory into perhaps
the ugliest moment of the Peloponnesian War.[30] The six generals who returned
home to Athens were condemned *en bloc* and executed (Xenophon *Hellenica*
1.7.35). Illegal and murderous actions by the Athenians were driven by their outrage
over the leaders' failure to rescue the kinsmen, alive and dead, a rage fueled not
only by the loss of life but also the loss of burial promised. Thus, with the parodist's
acumen, Plato flouts the *dêmos'* culpability in the form of a lament for those lost at
sea:

οἰομένων γὰρ ἤδη αὐτὴν καταπεπολεμῆσθαι καὶ ἀπειλημμένων ἐν
Μυτιλήνῃ τῶν νεῶν, βοηθήσαντες ἑξήκοντα ναυσίν, αὐτοὶ ἐμβάντες
εἰς τὰς ναῦς, καὶ ἄνδρες γενόμενοι ὁμολογουμένως ἄριστοι, νικήσαντες

---

29. For women's mourning in Homer, see Holst-Warhaft, *Dangerous Voices*, 108-113.
30. On the battle of Arginousae and its aftermath, see A. Andrewes, "The Arginousai Trial,"
Phoenix 28 (1974), 112-122.

μὲν τοὺς πολεμίους, λυσάμενοι δὲ τοὺς φιλίους, ἀναξίου τύχης
τυχόντες, οὐκ ἀναιρεθέντες ἐκ τῆς θαλάττης κεῖνται ἐνθάδε.

Plato Menexenos 243 C

When the enemy thought that the city was exhausted by the war, and its ships were
blockaded in Mitylene, our men embarked and came to the rescue with sixty ships,
thus proving their bravery beyond question. They defeated the enemy and freed their
friends, but encountering an undeserved fortune, they were not picked up from the
sea and lie there now.

Over fifty years earlier, Aeschylus in *Agamemnon* seemed to allude to the emotions
surrounding the public funeral:

τὸ πᾶν δ' ἀφ' "Ελλανος αἴας συνορμένοισι πέν-
θεια τλησικάρδιος
δόμῳ 'ν ἑκάστου πρέπει.
πολλὰ γοῦν θιγγάνει πρὸς ἧπαρ·
οὓς μὲν γὰρ ⟨τις⟩ ἔπεμψεν
οἶδεν, ἀντὶ δὲ φωτῶν
τεύχη καὶ σποδὸς εἰς ἑκά-
στου δόμους ἀφικνεῖται.

ὁ χρυσαμοιβὸς δ' "Αρης σωμάτων
καὶ ταλαντοῦχος ἐν μάχῃ δορὸς
πυρωθὲν ἐξ 'Ιλίου
φίλοισι πέμπει βαρὺ
ψῆγμα δυσδάκρυτον ἀντ-
ήνορος σποδοῦ γεμί-
ζων λέβητας εὐθέτους.

Aeschylus Agamemnon 429-444

Throughout the city, for those who set forth from Hellas' land,
there was a conspicuous sorrow
patiently endured in the house of each.
But many things still touch the heart.
Those whom someone sent out
he knew, but in return for them
urns and ashes arrive
at the houses of each.

Ares, the exchanger of gold for bodies,
wields the scales in the spear battle
and sends to *philoi* [31]
the heavy golden powder,

---

31. Because of the difficulty in conveying their varied connotations, we have retained the
Greek adjectives *philos/philoi* (masculine singular and plural, respectively) and *philē/philai*

refined in the flames of Troy and
bitterly wept over,
filling jars easily stored in ships
with dust that used to be a man.

Aeschylus is addressing an audience of Athenians in 458 B.C. who had suffered
dreadful losses in the campaigns of the previous year.[32] He probably did not need
to look far for this image as urns of bones and ashes were arriving at the city's
harbors in place of sons and husbands. Their remains were "golden," as valuable to
their kin as the "gold" they sent them forth to win. The public funeral cut deeply
into the *nomoi*, the customs and practices established too long ago to remember.
As the aftermath of Arginousae reveals, the wounds to the family caused by the
dêmos' appropriation of the dead were clearly still suppurating long after Aeschylus'
Agamemnon and Sophocles' *Antigone*. On this fault line in Athenian society, we
have located *Antigone*.

The issues and passions aroused by the public funeral were congruent with
other issues born of the conflicts of families with one another and with the collective
that constituted the *polis*. However, Athenians developed, not always purposefully,
informal ways and formal institutions to avoid succumbing to these forces that
shaped and, at the same time, vitiated their society and sometimes threatened its

---

(feminine singular and plural, respectively) as well as their noun *philotês*. The latter is usually
translated "friendship, love, affection," and its adjectives, "friendly" or "loved," or when used
as substantives, "friend" or "loved one." David Grene (trans., *Antigone* in *Complete Greek
Tragedies: Sophocles I*, ed. David Grene and Richmond Lattimore [Chicago and London: The
University of Chicago Press], 165), for example, has Ismene say "your friends are right to love
you," thus choosing to avoid the equally possible "your loved ones are right to love you." These
meanings may be subsumed under another, more deeply rooted idea. *Philotês* in its earliest ·
known form expresses the obligations a member of a community has toward a *xenos* (stranger/
guest). Emile Benveniste (*Indo-European Language and Society*, trans. Elizabeth Palmer
[London: Faber and Faber, 1973], 280) has shown that "the behaviour expressed by *philein*
[verbal form] always has an obligatory character and always implies reciprocity; it is the
accomplishment of positive actions which are implied in the pact of mutual hospitality." This
is the behavior expected of a host toward his guest or the head of the house toward its members,
particularly his wife (*Indo-European Language and Society*, 278-282). Such relationships
easily extend beyond their institutional basis in hospitality or marriage to bonds of friendship,
affection, and love, but these emotions are not essential to the bonds of *philotês*. Consequently,
philotês need not indicate friendship, only an agreement concerning an action binding on its
partners. When Hector and Ajax break off their duel in *Iliad* 7, they agree to exchange weapons
and gifts. Their action constitutes a *philotês* between them: "They parted, having joined in
philotês" (Homer *Iliad* 7.302). They separate still enemies but now *philoi*, men obligated by an
agreement. For a discussion of the origins of *philos* and its relationship to *echthros* (enemy) in
Antigone, see Simon Goldhill, *Reading Greek Tragedy* (Cambridge: Cambridge University Press,
1986), 79-106.

32. Eduard Fraenkel, *Aeschylus: "Agamemnon,"* 3 vols. (Oxford: Oxford University Press,
1950), 2.227.

existence. One such institution, fraught with contradictions, was the democracy itself. Another was the festival of the City Dionysia and its showpiece, tragedy. In addition to its conjunction with the public funeral and disruption of burial practices, *Antigone* belongs in the context of the theater of Dionysus Eleuthereus.

The plays presented on the tragic stage probed the makeup of Athenian society as an entity through plots derived from heroic times. They also entertained their audiences through performances that engaged them emotionally and aimed at imparting lessons on living in Athenian society.[33] In this sense, tragedy itself and *Antigone* as the example at hand may be understood as instrumental in alleviating an ongoing "social drama" analogous to that described by Victor Turner. Turner divides the social process into four phases: "(1) breach; (2) crisis; (3) redressive action; (4) re-integration or recognition of schism."[34] The breach occurs by "the public breach or non-fulfilment of some crucial norm regulating the intercourse of the parties." With its public funeral, the *dêmos* trespassed upon areas of death reserved for families. In practice, the families were those of the aristocracy and elite whose interests were not always those of the *dêmos*.[35] The wide-ranging associations of death with life extended the intrusion to all areas of Athenian society. This first phase is then followed by a "mounting crisis" that, unless diffused, has the tendency "to widen and extend until it becomes co-extensive with some dominant cleavage in the widest set of relevant social relations to which the conflicting parties belong." Although evidence for this stage is minimal, Pericles' caution in Thucydides' *Funeral Oration* and the aftermath of Arginousae indicate, it would seem, the presence of a "crisis" caused by the public funeral. That the intrusion of *hoi polloi* of the assembly into the *mukhoi* (innermost parts of the house) where the women reside should continue to fester among the women and be felt by their men is reasonable, especially during the days of the public rituals. As we have suggested, this was the

---

33. For tragedy as a medium of social inquiry and thought, see Jean-Pierre Vernant, "Greek Tragedy: Problems of Interpretation," in *The Structuralist Controversy: The Languages of Criticism and the Sciences of Man*, ed. Richard Macksey and Eugenio Donato (Baltimore and London: The Johns Hopkins University Press, 1972,) 273-289, and Vernant and Pierre Vidal-Naquet, *Myth and Tragedy in Ancient Greece*, trans. Janet Lloyd (New York: Zone Books, 1990), 29-48; Segal, *Tragedy and Civilization*, 48-59; Goldhill, *Reading Greek Tragedy*, 57-78. For tragedy as performance, see Oliver Taplin, *The Stagecraft of Aeschylus: The Dramatic Use of Exits and Entrances in Greek Tragedy* (Oxford: Oxford University Press, 1977) and *Greek Tragedy in Action* (Berkeley and Los Angeles: University of California Press, 1978). For an attempted synthesis of tragedy as theater of ideas and as performance, see David Wiles, "Reading Greek Performance," *Greece and Rome* 34 (1987), 136-151.

34. V. W. Turner, *Schism and Continuity in an African Society: A Study of Ndembu Village Life* (Manchester: University of Manchester Press, 1957), 92. The quotations in this paragraph are found in Turner, *Schism*, 91-92.

35. See Robin Seager, "Elitism and Democracy in Classical Athens," in *The Rich, the Well Born, and the Powerful*, ed. Frederic Cople Jaher (Urbana: University of Illinois Press, 1973), 7-25; Josia Ober, *Mass and Elite in Democratic Athens: Rhetoric, Ideology, and the Power of the People* (Princeton, NJ: Princeton University Press, 1989), 192-247.

division in Athenian society that Sophocles and his patron, the *dêmos*, faced with *Antigone*. Therefore, the "redressive action" that "leading members of the relevant social group" brought to bear involving Sophocles proved to be the presentation of his dramas, including *Antigone,* in the theater of Dionysus.[36] One performance of Sophocles' play did not end the crisis; we imagine, rather, that the whole experience in the theater confronted it in a roundabout way and for a time at least made this rupture of the "old ways," like so many others brought on by the empire, appear tolerable.

Dionysus, the god of the *polis*, as Richard Seaford has astutely observed, wields a violence that restores order by destroying a household, usually the ruling household, which is threatening the community.[37] The action of the god and the performance in his honor overlap in *Antigone*. With the tools of his art, Sophocles creates a representation of an intrusion *like* that of the *dêmos* but *not identical* to it, namely, Creon's action in denying burial rites to Polyneices' corpse. Sophocles depicts Creon as a ruler of a city who acts impiously toward one of its citizens and as a *kyrios* (master) who refuses the obligations of *philotês* and who cannot control the women of his family. These failures bring about the destruction of his household and his own ruin with the implied victory of the *polis* of the Thebans on the stage and of the Athenians in the audience. Dramatic performance reproduces, touches upon, and may even have given shape to, the concerns of those Athenians in the theater. That is, the performance projected outside everyone the crisis that all had been thinking and talking about and feeling not just during the days of the public rituals.[38] In this way, *Antigone* was itself a tool to promote reintegration and head off the sort of schism that occurred after Arginousae.

Both the festival of the City Dionysia and its tragedies were long in place by the time of *Antigone*. If the upheaval caused by funeral restrictions and the results of the Samian War contextualize the play in terms of its reception by the audience, the milieu of the tragic theater constitutes the medium through which the messages are delivered. In these contexts and others affected by disruption in one area of society overflowing into others, *Antigone* itself played a part in redressing the flaws caused by the *dêmos*' intrusion into women's territory. At the same time, it was an organ of

---

36. Nothing is known about the other two tragedies and the satyr play produced with *Antigone*.

37. Seaford, *Reciprocity and Ritual*, 344-362. Seaford (344) recognizes that his formulation for how tragedy effects "a *historical* transition—from the self-destruction of the ruling family, marked by reciprocal violence and perverted ritual, to the communal cohesion of *polis* ritual," does not apply as well to Sophocles as to Aeschylus because of Sophocles' focus "on the self-destruction rather than the transition." Such a transition, in this case, from Creon's exposure of the dead to the treatment of the dead during the public funeral may be glimpsed in *Antigone* 904ff.

38. V. W. Turner, "Liminality and the Performative Genres," in *Rite, Drama, Festival, Spectacle: Rehearsals Toward a Theory of Cultural Performance,*" ed. John J. MacAloon (Philadelphia: Institute for the Study of Human Issues, 1984), 22-23.

the very institution that was intruding and so contributed to the usurpation of the prerogatives of the family and its women, a function also of other tragedies in the theater of Dionysus. By performing laments and rituals in the make-believe of the theater and by voicing them through the masks of male actors and the lyrics of male choristers, tragedy, as Gail Holst-Warhaft explains, assisted the *dêmos* in diffusing the power and potential violence inherent in women's lamentation. For Holst-Warhaft, tragedies like *Antigone* provide "men with an outlet for the potential violence of grief while denying women any public role in the artistic ritual drama they customarily controlled."[39] Since women likely attended the tragic contests, *Antigone* invited the women of the audience to grieve for their dead through a medium invented by men.[40] In this way, theater replicated and competed with the public funeral as a way of imposing the *dêmos'* conception of mourning upon the *polis*. The process, first visible among extant plays in Aeschylus' *Persians*, was ongoing in the works of Sophocles and Euripides and, doubtless, in the plays of other tragedians.[41]

Antigone began when Sophocles first thought of making a play on the house of Labdacus and became social when he applied to the archon eponymous for funding for a chorus. Sophocles stands at the beginning of the communicative process as the originator of the *Antigone* of the script, choreography, and song. His task demanded skill and talent; he brought to it genius. But Athenians also admired him for how those qualities gave him something to teach the audience, that is, they admired him, without necessarily realizing it, for his mastery of the normative codes of their society.[42] In this role, Sophocles put into theatrical expression images, ideas, beliefs, prejudices, anxieties, and hostilities already known to his audience.[43] Drawing upon social codes he acquired as an Athenian and adapted as a dramatist, he served as a bridge and a mediator among Athenians. He did not invent these codes. They were part of his culture and formed him as well as all who deemed themselves Athenians. He composed a vehicle for exploring the ramifications of an

39. Holst-Warhaft, *Dangerous Voices*, 129.

40. For a recent review of the evidence for women's participation in the tragic festivals, see Jeffery Henderson ("Women and the Athenian Dramatic Festivals," *Transactions of the American Philological Association* 121 [1991], 133-147) and his note 2 (page 133) for further bibliography. Henderson concludes (144): "[T]he fact that the audience was conventionally addressed or otherwise referred to as male reflects a normative distinction between a notional audience of men (political) and an actual audience that included women (festive)."

41. For the "taming of lament" by tragedy, see Holst-Warhaft, *Dangerous Voices,* 127-170, and for this effect in *Antigone*, 161-166.

42. Roland Barthes, "The Death of the Author," in *Image, Music, Text*, trans. Stephen Heath (New York: Hill and Wang, 1977), 142.

43. As Ober (*Mass and Elite*, 38) states: "Each member of any given community makes assumptions about human nature and behavior, has opinions on morality and ethics, and holds some general political principles; those assumptions, opinions, and principles which are common to the great majority of those members are best described as ideology."

action, specifically, the exposure of a corpse, that casts such codes and the values they support into conflict. He wanted his play to entertain, but he undoubtedly intended to teach his audience about how to live their lives, for that had been the function and claim of poets since Homer.[44] He stirred his spectators to think about their society, to experience its problems and conflicts, and to release their resentments and hostilities in the constructive violence of Dionysus Eleuthereus. But for his message to be received and his teaching accepted, the viewpoints expressed in *Antigone* could not become equivocal. By being the one who exposes the corpses of Polyneices and the others, Creon acts impiously, and although Antigone acts piously in attempting to confer rites upon her brother's body, her deeds entail defying a man in authority and are censured in favor of Ismene's concession to those in power and willingness to die for her *philê* after her sister's actions no longer threaten the social stability of the *polis*.

In teaching Athenians of his audience how to live piously, Sophocles was not depicting or probing the personalities of his characters. Although modern audiences, with decades-long experience of interpreting stage figures psychologically, have read a personal identity into Antigone and Creon, for Sophocles' audience, Antigone and the others embodied social roles and gender expectations. Antigone acts not as Antigone qua individual but qua *philê* and as a nubile young woman. Characters of this kind are misread by construing their actions and words as those of a fully formed personality with past experiences, sense of self-identity, and an inner life.[45] Antigone represents a woman who suddenly finds herself deprived of the care of

---

44. John Herington (*Poetry into Drama: Early Tragedy and the Greek Poetic Tradition* [Berkeley and Los Angeles: University of California Press, 1985], 71) points out: "[E]ven in the period of the final disintegration of the song culture there were still well-informed Greeks who recognized its [poetry's] claim to teach the art of living as true, or if not true, still as centrally important. This claim, too, was directly inherited by Attic tragedy from the song culture, and perhaps we should not neglect it if we are to see that art in its proper historical, social, and literary perspective."

45. R. G. A. Buxton (*Sophocles* [Oxford: Clarendon Press for the Classical Association, 1984], 3) explains: "We have . . . learned to think twice before giving a psychological answer to a question of the type, 'Why does such-and-such a character say such-and-such?' An example is the question, 'Why does Ajax, in the "deception speech," say that he will give way?' The assumption behind this is that Ajax's words should be interpreted in the light of the motives and intentions his words enable us to reconstruct. But it may be that a more sensible question is 'Why does Sophocles have Ajax make this speech?'" Similarly, we should not ask why Antigone accepts responsibility for the dust placed upon Polyneices' body at 245ff., when nothing in the play places her at his body before line 423, but rather what Sophocles gains by having her accept the responsibility. On character in tragedy generally, see John Jones, *On Aristotle and Greek Tragedy* (London: Chatto and Windus, 1971), 31-38; Christopher Gill, "The Question of Character and Personality in Greek Tragedy," *Poetics Today* 7 (1986), 251-273; in Sophocles, see P. E. Easterling, "Character in Sophocles" in *Greek Tragedy*, ed. Ian McAuslan and Peter Walcot (Oxford: Oxford University Press, 1993), 58-65; Sourvinou-Inwood, "Assumptions," 135-136. Matt Neuburg ("How Like a Woman: Antigone's 'Inconsistency'," *Classical Quarterly* 40 [1990], 63-66) observes: "an important component of the poet's conception of character is

her dead kinsman by a man who intends to expose his body as carrion for the dogs and birds. She responds to the dead Polyneices in the ways expected of a woman, and what she experiences follows, on the one hand, from her defiance of male and public power and, on the other, from her condition as a nubile woman upon whom her family places demands for the next generation.

While *Antigone* was new in that it had not been seen or heard before its first performance, much about it was also old. Sophocles did not create out of whole cloth; he adapted traditional poetic language and dramatic conventions elaborated over time by other poets.[46] Athenians in his audience were versed in what was required to comprehend the messages of his play because they were products of the same society as he.[47] Tragedian and audience shared a time, place, and culture. Sophocles and his sponsor, the *dêmos,* could depend upon those in the theater to make sense of what they saw and heard for the first time. All that remains of the original performance of Sophocles' play is the script, the words as they have survived through the vagaries of the manuscript tradition. They are paramount, and all that can be said about the play ultimately derives from them. Thus, our first and primary method is the close reading of the text. But reading alone is insufficient. It will not reveal, for instance, the ramifications of the *monos* (alone) commonplace or the significance of a man's taking a woman by the wrist (Sophocles *Antigone* 916) in Athenian culture.[48] When the Watchman compares Antigone to a bird crying out over its nest bereft of nestlings, readers commonly construct meanings in the similarity of sound and circumstance. The bird as augury would not readily come to mind. Athenians, at least when listening to the tales of singers and poets, were always alert to birds coming to humans as vehicles of the divine will. Sophocles could expect his original audience to seek meaning through this connotation, while, in the reading process, the bird as conveyor of divine will opens new avenues for interpreting Antigone's role in the scene.

The play, Hamlet tells us, is the thing, but in most of what has been said about a Greek tragedy, the words have been everything. Yet *Antigone* watched by Sophocles' original audience was far more than words. That audience, after all, heard the words in harmony with the voices of the actors and choristers and within the context of all the phenomena of theater and culture. More happened than what was said. To recapture Sophocles' *Antigone*, even in a limited way, we must go beyond the

---

to have the characters give expression, not to their inner psychological story, but to the social conflicts and pressures upon them which are being treated at that point in the play" (66).

46. For a study of the poetic tradition influencing the prologue of *Antigone*, see J. F. Davidson, "The Parados of the *Antigone*: A Poetic Study," *Bulletin of the Institute of Classical Studies of the University of London* 30 (1983), 41-51; for allusions in *Antigone* to Homer and Aeschylus, see Richard Garner, *From Homer to Tragedy: The Art of Allusion in Greek Poetry* (London and New York: Routledge, 1990), 78-90.

47. Vernant, "Greek Tragedy," 274.

48. For New Criticism, associated with close reading, in classics, see Frederic William Danker, *A Century of Greco-Roman Philology* (Atlanta: Scholars Press, 1988), 204-212.

words of the written text on the understanding that the play undoubtedly did so in its original performance. Much has been lost but not all, since the script holds clues, "stage directions," as it were, to what transpired before the audience. The reader attentive to these clues can surmount the written page to become a spectator in the "theater of the mind."[49] The movement of a hand or modulations of the voice that go unnoticed by the script are lost. By the same token, the gesture or vocal shift that it records warrants serious consideration, since Sophocles had his actor point them out even though the audience could see or hear without that aid. To loosen, if not escape, the stifling grasp of the written word on the imagination, our method in reading *Antigone* includes a reconstruction of the spectacle of the script in performance.

Sophocles' Athenians did not receive the messages conveyed by his dialogue, singing, and choreography passively. Taking in information constantly, they formed and rejected inferences, constructed and abandoned hypotheses, experienced a gamut of emotions, and left the play in a babble of commentary.[50] All along, they were trying to normalize, or "naturalize," Sophocles' play as something new and different and yet familiar.[51] How spectators reacted to his play was ultimately beyond Sophocles' control, but as its author, he had to have some conception of how his audience would respond. While he could not compel them to accept one meaning, he could guide and direct his audience to goals and reactions he and the *dêmos* were looking for. Throughout the play, Sophocles provides the spectators with clues that signal how they are to contextualize what is going on before them in what they already know. In turn, they must work at deciphering his clues, an activity that demands effort and the necessary background knowledge. Ideally, the exchange directs interpretative activity toward a socially desirable range of agreement and

---

49. The concept of theater of the mind and the pioneering efforts in applying it to the study of Greek tragedy are those of Oliver Taplin, *Greek Tragedy in Action*, 1-8. Taplin's expression, "theatre of the mind," is found on page 3.

50. Our approach, which generally follows that of reader-response criticism, allows the audience to participate in the process, to think along with the playwright rather than having the meaning "dumped in its lap." For reader-response criticism, see Jane P. Tompkins, "The Reader in History: The Changing Shape of Literary Response," in *Reader-Response Criticism: From Formalism to Post-Structuralism*, ed. Jane P. Tompkins (Baltimore and London: The Johns Hopkins University Press, 1980), 201-232; Elizabeth Freund, *The Return of the Reader: Reader-Response Criticism* (London and New York: Methuen, 1987). For communication as a two-way channel, see Michael J. Reddy, "The Conduit Metaphor: A Case of Frame Conflict in Our Language about Language," in *Metaphor and Thought*, 2d ed., ed. Andrew Ortony (Cambridge: Cambridge University Press, 1993), 164-201; for such communication specifically in the theater, see Keir Elam, *The Semiotics of Theatre and Drama* (London and New York: Methuen, 1980), 32-38.

51. Jonathan Culler (*Structuralist Poetics: Structuralism, Linguistics, and the Study of Literature* [Ithaca, NY: Cornell University Press, 1975], 138) elucidates: "[T]o naturalize a text is to bring it into relation with a type of discourse or model which is already, in some sense, natural and legible."

granted disagreement. In probing the social fabric, Sophocles could not rend it irreparably or perplex the spectators and thereby risk alienating them by being too different. The public and religious functions of tragedy predicated such a limit on meanings; to suppose otherwise assumes the chaos of any meaning being valid as well as a *dêmos* so foolish as to confuse and outrage itself.

Antigone is set in Thebes, but it is about Athenian realities. It belongs to a mythmaking about Athens presented through a Thebes that Froma Zeitlin has called an "anti-Athens" or a mirror image of Athens.[52] Zeitlin explains in her seminal article of 1986 that Athens "portrays a city on stage that is meant to be dramatically 'other' than itself. Thebes . . . provides the negative model to Athens's manifest image of itself with regard to its notions of the proper management of city, society, and self." Anti-Athens mythmaking consists of "clusters of ideas, themes, and problems" that, by occurring throughout the mythmaking in separate instances or utterances, became conventional. They interrelate by a mode of referentiality analogous to Ferdinand de Saussure's dialectic of *parole* and *langue.*[53] As one utterance (*parole*) refers to another through language (*langue*), one instance in the mythmaking, for example, Creon's refusal of Haemon's advice, may be interpreted as referring to another, say, Oedipus' acceptance of advice from Antigone in the *Oedipus at Colonus*, through the continuum or language of the mythmaking. This continuum, although created diachronically, acted in individual Athenians at any given time synchronically. They learned its form and conceits by virtue of their acculturation and could recognize new variations on the old. For those outside their culture, the continuum is available in representative historical expressions in tragedy and other media that may be studied and compared synchronically. No individual message contains all that can be said or imagined about anti-Athens, but one message may treat a particular theme or commonplace more openly and so be useful in deciphering that theme or commonplace in another utterance.

In anti-Athens mythmaking, whatever belongs to an Athenian qua Athenian is absent in a Theban qua anti-Athenian. What Athenians claim to be true of themselves is not true of Thebans. What they assert of Thebans, they repudiate as true of themselves. Since such mythmaking depends upon differences, mediation or sharing of attributes imperils its effectiveness. Generally speaking, a narrative told from an Athenian viewpoint, one like Euripides' *Suppliant Women* that includes an Athenian hero or one that takes place on Attic soil such as Sophocles' *Oedipus at Colonus*, represents the positive aspects—what Athenians deem normal and orderly—of the polarity Athens/anti-Athens. This Athenian presence accentuates the oppositions, because it illustrates what Athenian culture esteems as proper in

---

52. Froma I. Zeitlin, "Thebes: Theater of Self and Society in Athenian Drama," in *Greek Tragedy and Political Theory*, ed. J. Peter Euben (Berkeley and Los Angeles: University of California Press, 1986), 101-103. The quotations that follow are found on page 102.

53. Ferdinand de Saussure, *Course in General Linguistics*, trans. Wayne Baskin (New York, Toronto, and London: McGraw-Hill, 1966), 8-15.

clear-cut contrast to Thebans acting improperly. A narrative of this sort is straightforward and may be used to interpret the more complex situations of a narrative set in Thebes, the *Antigone*, for instance, or Aeschylus' *Seven Against Thebes*. The latter kind of narrative tells Athenians who they are by showing them who they are not. In a Theban setting on stage, because characters reflect in varying degrees negative aspects of the polarity, they are all flawed in some manner, but they may also verge in certain respects toward the positive aspects reserved for Athenians. Thus, criteria and categories opposing the cities are expressed less directly, and the characters are drawn less negatively to avoid their becoming caricatures. It follows, then, that a Theban can bury the dead—but never properly. Despite her piety, Antigone is prohibited from even the symbolic burial that some have claimed for her,[54] and Creon is blatantly impious in exposing, and negligent in interring, Polyneices' corpse.

Most of those in Sophocles' audience had seen plays set in Thebes before. They were experienced in this way of depicting anti-Athenians and would therefore realize as soon as they heard of Creon's edict (Sophocles *Antigone* 21ff.) that things were going to turn out badly for him. The audience, of course, would have no way of predicting the appearance of Tiresias or Eurydice, so that to approach *Antigone* with knowledge of the play as a whole rather than as an unfolding and constantly changing situation misuses Sophocles' words and precludes the reader as an authorial audience.[55] However, members of Sophocles' original audience and his later readers are in the same situation once the play has finished; both groups may range throughout the play to build and support interpretations. Whereas the spectator must remember lines and references or secure them from other spectators,

---

54. Jebb (*Antigone*, 86) was first to propose "symbolical burial." On this nagging question, see, for example, W. H. D. Rouse, "The Two Burials in *Antigone*," *Classical Review* 25 (1911), 42; Minnie Keys Flickinger, "Who First Buried Polynices?" *Philological Quarterly* 12 (1933), 130-136; Edward J. Messemer, S.J., "The Double Burial of Polynices," *The Classical Journal* 37 (1942), 515-526; Ivan M. Linforth, "Antigone and Creon," *University of California Publications in Classical Philology* 15 (1961), 194; A. T. von S. Bradshaw, "The Watchman Scenes in the *Antigone*," *Classical Quarterly* 12 (1962), 200-211; A. O. Hulton, "The Double-Burial of the *Antigone*," *Mnemosyne* 16 (1963), 284-285; Holger Friis Johansen, "Sophocles 1939-1959," *Lustrum* 7 (1962), 186; Gerhard Müller, *Sophokles:"Antigone"* (Heidelberg: Winter, 1967), 72-73; William M. Calder III, "Sophokles' Political Tragedy, *Antigone*" *Greece and Rome* 9 (1968), 394-398; Joseph S. Margon, "The First Burial of Polyneices," *The Classical Journal* 64 (1969), 289-295; D. A. Hester, "Sophocles the Unphilosophical: A Study in the *Antigone*," *Mnemosyne* 24 (1971), 25; Marsh McCall, "Divine and Human Action in Sophocles: The Two Burials of the *Antigone*," *Yale Classical Studies* 22 (1972), 103-117; Borimir Jordan, *Servants of the Gods* (Göttingen: Vandenhoeck and Ruprecht, 1979), 92 n. 151; Ruth Scodel, "Epic Doublets and Polynices' Two Burials," *Transactions of the American Philological Association* 114 (1984), 50-52; Richard M. Rothaus, "The Single Burial of Polyneices," *The Classical Journal* 85 (1990), 209-217.

55. For a parallel observation, see Sourvinou-Inwood, "Assumptions," 135-136. The term "authorial audience" denotes a hypothetical audience that an author has in mind in composing

the reader has the advantage of going back over the text any number of times. Thus, we imagine the reader as someone who has seen and heard the whole play many times and has its entirety readily available but must as an authorial audience use foreknowledge sparingly and with awareness of its perils. Nevertheless, any experienced audience, whether Athenian or modern, of a play about the myth of the unburied dead in Thebes would know the outcome. What keeps Sophocles' audiences in their seats is not the plot, but Sophocles' dialogue, lyrics, and choreography in bringing Creon to his appointed end. An analogous situation in American mythmaking is an experienced audience about to watch a version of Billy the Kid or the gunfight at the OK Corral. Although actors, characterization, dialogue, scenery, costumes, and properties are new, the audience knows beforehand that Sheriff Pat F. Garrett catches and kills Billy and that Wyatt Earp survives the gunfight.

Sophocles' audience and its *Antigone* no longer exist. Both have been replaced by audiences of modern readers who may have different expectations from those of the poet and by *Antigone*s received through manifold cultural heritages distinguished by different times and places.[56] Modern audiences react, in approaching the play on stage or on the printed page, as what they are: modern spectators and readers rooted in their own time and formed by phenomena, categories and modes of thought, and traditions of *Wissenschaft* unknown to the ancients.[57] They may, of course, read *Antigone* for their own purposes, for, in one important way, they are no different from Sophocles' original audience in that both respond to the text from what they know. Neither the modern nor ancient audience passively receives or merely decodes what is before them. Both interact with what they are experiencing by contributing to the text, the drama enacted or read, from their own background knowledge.[58]

Sophocles wrote for an audience of mostly Greeks and mainly Athenians. We cannot share the reactions of Sophocles' audience that day in Elaphebolion, but that does not prohibit us from attempting a reading of his text in terms of the ancients' experience of it. We seek to recapture an *Antigone* that might have been possible for those in the *dêmos*' theater. The social and public circumstances that conditioned the formations of their interpretations are well known to students of ancient Greece and cannot be ignored. To postulate a reading of the *Antigone* that could have been available to the ancients, to pick up the clues and catch the allusions intended, the reader must approximate as closely as possible the audience

his work. For the term and further explanation, see Peter J. Rabinowitz, "Shifting Sands, Shifting Standards: Reading, Interpretation, and Literary Judgment," *Arethusa* 24 (1986), 115-134.

56. See George Steiner, *Antigones* (Oxford: Oxford University Press, 1984).

57. Steiner (*Antigones*, 304) concludes his interpretation of *Antigone* "across time": "New 'Antigones' are being imagined, thought, lived now; and will be tomorrow."

58. E. D. Hirsch Jr., *Cultural Literacy: What Every American Needs to Know* (Boston: Houghton Mifflin, 1987), 33-69.

Sophocles had in mind, the audience to whom he and the *dêmos* addressed the play.[59] As PeterJ. Rabinowitz explains:[60]

> This audience [the authorial audience] is always hypothetical. Because of the ineradicable individuality of actual readers, an author can never really be sure about the characteristics of the people who will pick up his or her book. Yet s/he must still design that book rhetorically for some more-or-less specific audience: it is impossible even to begin to write without making assumptions about the potential reader's values, knowledge, and understanding of conventions. Authors thus imagine presumed audiences for their texts. Since textual decisions are consequently made with the authorial audience in mind, the actual readers must come to share its characteristics as they read if they are to understand the text as the author wished.

Plato lamented that the father of a composition could not come to its defense when it was being unfairly reviled:

> ὅταν δὲ ἅπαξ γραφῇ, κυλινδεῖται μὲν πανταχοῦ πᾶς λόγος ὁμοίως παρὰ τοῖς ἐπαΐουσιν, ὡς δ' αὔτως παρ' οἷς οὐδὲν προσήκει.

Plato Phaedrus 275 D-E

> When a narrative is put in writing, it is tossed about in the same way among those who understand as among those who have no business with it.

A modern author, faced with a great diversity of readers, needs to compose his work with a chosen audience in mind. However, no such modern reader confronted Sophocles. He knew who would be sitting on the slope of the Acropolis and could depend upon the homogeneity of his society.[61] To listen to Sophocles from a contemporary perspective, modern readers must found their interpretations upon questions they deem relevant, important, and interesting to Sophocles' fifth-century Athenian audience. By "making sense" of an ancient work through their own

---

59. To be sure, scholars have long read *Antigone* with knowledge of Sophocles' Athens. But during the nineteenth century when it was the most popular tragedy among European intellectuals, poets, and composers, foundations for interpreting the play were laid down that did not always concur with the interpretative environment of Athens in the 440s. Antigone as sister and her sisterly love for her brother captivated Wordsworth and Byron in ways that have little or no connection with Sophocles' audience (Steiner, *Antigones*, 12-14). Moreover, since the issues it explores have seemed timelessly relevant, the play has been open to supplementation by the reader's assessment of that relevance to his or her situation. One's notions of "family" and "marriage" could readily be substituted for Antigone's. This is the case with "family" in Hegel's influential comments on *Antigone*, for which, see A. C. Bradley, *Oxford Lectures on Poetry*, 2d ed. (London: Macmillan, 1909), 69-95; reprinted in Anne Paolucci and Henry Paolucci, *Hegel on Tragedy* (Garden City, NY: Doubleday, 1962), 367-388; Brian Vickers, *Towards Greek Tragedy: Drama, Myth, Society* (London: Longman, 1973), 526-546; Steiner, *Antigones*, 27-42.

60. Rabinowitz, "Shifting Sands," 117.

61. On the audience at tragedies, see Arthur Pickard-Cambridge, *The Dramatic Festivals of Athens*, 2d ed., rev. John Gould and D. M. Lewis (Oxford: Oxford University Press, 1986), 263-278; Henderson, "Women," 133-147.

knowledge and/or by restricting themselves to the words on the page, they can miss implications that may have enriched the play for the ancients.

Both Sophocles and his authorial audience were engaged in making meanings through the *Antigone*. Sophocles initiated the process by prompting his audience to recall those elements of their common background knowledge of both the mythmaking continuum and their experiences as Athenians. He encouraged them to adopt his perspectives, which often engendered conflicts and contradictions among members of the audience. Such conflicts, in turn, promoted the questioning of values. In theory, at least, a work as rich and suggestive as Sophocles' can generate an indefinite number of meanings. With the addition of his modern readership, it has spawned more than he could ever have imagined. In the context of the theater at Athens, however, the proliferation of meanings was limited to those the audience as a whole was willing to grant or tolerate. It was a reflection of their society and their ways of caring for the dead that Sophocles put before them with *Antigone*. The majority presumably cooperated with him in rehearsing its dynamics, glorying in its strengths, and facing its flaws. Under these circumstances, only so many meanings were likely to emerge with any significance. To ascertain those meanings as precisely as possible, we have imposed two "frames" that respond to Sophocles' clues. Each frame creates a particular perspective on the programmatic question, "Who controls the corpse, the *dêmos* or the family?"

The "outer frame," which consists of knowledge relevant to the public life of Athenians, examines Creon's action through the claims of the *dêmos* and the family upon those killed in the city's wars. This background includes the rites of the public funeral and the vocabulary, commonplaces, and themes of the funeral oration. The most extensive version of the myth of the Theban Dead comes from the eulogy of Athenians killed in the Corinthian War (395-387/386 B.C.) written by Lysias. Since he was a metic, Lysias could not have delivered the speech. Released from the restraints imposed by an actual funeral, he passes quickly over the war (*Funeral Oration* 67-68) in favor of a rhetorical display that gives a fair idea of the medium itself:[62]

Ἀδράστου δὲ καὶ Πολυνείκους ἐπὶ Θήβας στρατευσάντων καὶ ἡττηθέντων μάχῃ, οὐκ ἐώντων Καδμείων θάπτειν τοὺς νεκρούς, Ἀθηναῖοι ἡγησάμενοι ἐκείνους μέν, εἴ τι ἠδίκουν, ἀποθανόντας δίκην ἔχειν τὴν μεγίστην, τοὺς δὲ κάτω τὰ αὑτῶν οὐ κομίζεσθαι, ἱερῶν δὲ

---

62. The eulogies (Thucydides 2.34.6) of "suitable" speakers disappeared with the spoken word. Those funeral orations that remain are by the famous: besides Lysias, there are Gorgias (fragment 6 Diels-Kranz), Thucydides (2.35-46), Demosthenes, Plato, in the form of the parody *Menexenos*, and Hyperides. The orator's version of the Theban Dead myth may also be found in Isocrates' *Panegyricus* (58), and the tragic poet's in *Panathenaecus* (168-171). Schroeder (*De laudibus*) and John E. Ziolkowski (*Thucydides and the Tradition of Funeral Speeches at Athens*, Salem, NH: The Ayer Company, 1985, c. 1981) provide useful collections of the funeral orator's commonplaces.

μιαινομένων τοὺς ἄνω θεοὺς ἀσεβεῖσθαι, τὸ μὲν πρῶτον πέμψαντες
κήρυκας ἐδέοντο αὐτῶν δοῦναι τῶν νεκρῶν ἀναίρεσιν, νομίζοντες
ἀνδρῶν μὲν ἀγαθῶν εἶναι ζῶντας τοὺς ἐχθροὺς τιμωρήσασθαι,
ἀπιστούντων δὲ σφίσιν αὐτοῖς ἐν τοῖς τῶν τεθνεώτων σώμασι τὴν
εὐψυχίαν ἐπιδείκνυσθαι· οὐ δυνάμενοι δὲ τούτων τυχεῖν ἐστράτευσαν
ἐπ’ αὐτούς, οὐδεμιᾶς διαφορᾶς πρότερον πρὸς Καδμείους
ὑπαρχούσης, οὐδὲ τοῖς ζῶσιν Ἀργείων χαριζόμενοι, ἀλλὰ τοὺς
τεθνεῶτας ἐν τῷ πολέμῳ ἀξιοῦντες τῶν νομιζομένων τυγχάνειν πρὸς
τοὺς ἑτέρους ὑπὲρ ἀμφοτέρων ἐκινδύνευσαν, ὑπὲρ μὲν τῶν, ἵνα μηκέτι
εἰς τοὺς τεθνεῶτας ἐξαμαρτάνοντες πλείω περὶ τοὺς θεοὺς
ἐξυβρίσωσιν, ὑπὲρ δὲ τῶν [ἑτέρων], ἵνα μὴ † πρότερον εἰς τὴν αὐτῶν
ἀπέλθωσι πατρίου τιμῆς ἀτυχήσαντες καὶ Ἑλληνικοῦ νόμου
στερηθέντες καὶ κοινῆς ἐλπίδος ἡμαρτηκότες. ταῦτα διανοηθέντες, καὶ
τὰς ἐν τῷ πολέμῳ τύχας κοινὰς ἁπάντων ἀνθρώπων νομίζοντες,
πολλοὺς μὲν πολεμίους κτώμενοι, τὸ δὲ δίκαιον ἔχοντες σύμμαχον
ἐνίκων μαχόμενοι. καὶ οὐχ ὑπὸ τῆς τύχης ἐπαρθέντες μείζονος παρὰ
Καδμείων τιμωρίας ἐπεθύμησαν, ἀλλ’ ἐκείνοις μὲν ἀντὶ τῆς ἀσεβείας
τὴν ἑαυτῶν ἀρετὴν ἐπεδείξαντο, αὐτοὶ δὲ λαβόντες τὰ ἆθλα ὧνπερ
ἕνεκα ἀφίκοντο, τοὺς Ἀργείων νεκρούς, ἔθαψαν ἐν τῇ αὐτῶν Ἐλευσῖνι.
περὶ μὲν οὖν τοὺς ἀποθανόντας τῶν ἑπτὰ ἐπὶ Θήβας τοιοῦτοι
γεγόνασιν.

Lysias *Funeral Oration* 7-10

When Adrastus and Polyneices marched against Thebes and were defeated in battle,
the Cadmeians would not allow the burial of the corpses. The Athenians judged that
those men, if they had done some wrong, paid the utmost penalty by dying, that the
gods below were not receiving their due, and that as long as the shrines were being
desecrated, the gods above were being treated with impiety. Thus, they first sent
heralds, requesting that the Cadmeians allow them to take up the corpses, believing it
characteristic of brave men to avenge enemies who are living but of those who have no
faith in themselves to show courage toward the bodies of the dead. When they could
not obtain their request, they marched against the Cadmeians, although no previous
quarrel existed with the Cadmeians, nor were they pleasing the living Argives. Rather,
considering it right that those killed in war receive the customary rites, they underwent
dangers against others for the sake of both parties: for the [Cadmeians], that they no
longer would outrage the gods by transgressing against the dead, and for the [Argives],
that they would not return to their own land, having failed to obtain traditional honors
[for the dead], and leave robbed of Greek custom and cheated out of the common
hope. With these thoughts in mind and believing that the fortunes of war are common
to all men, although their enemies were many, they fought and gained victory with
justice as their ally. Urged on by their success, they refrained from lusting for greater
retribution from the Cadmeians. To them, in return for impiety, they displayed their
bravery and, taking up the corpses of the Argives, prizes for which they had come,
they buried them in their own Eleusis. In regard to the dead of the Seven Against
Thebes, they proved themselves to be such men.

Framed by the orator's myth, Creon's action is one of impiety that recalls Theban impiety in funeral oratory. However Creon defends and rationalizes exposure of Polyneices' corpse, denial of burial is fundamentally wrong before gods and men. This conclusion cannot be circumvented or mitigated *in this frame*. From the start, he is an impious, hubristic Theban made familiar by funeral orators and tragedians. Nevertheless, Creon's action resembles that of the Athenian *dêmos*; both deprive women of the care of their war dead. Seen through the outer frame, then, his action gains complexity by interacting with the audience's feelings and emotions toward the *dêmos*' public funeral and its treatment of women. While the difference between what Creon intends and what the *dêmos* does remains, it might have been tempered by the fact that both deny to women their rights in caring for the dead, and strike at the women's place in society.

Antigone is about Theban inability to bury the corpse with due rites. For this reason, Creon enjoys most of the stage time and dialogue and was probably played in first performance by the protagonist. Unless Athenians are to be imagined as ennobling the straw men of their propaganda, he should not be construed as a hero.[63] Creon does not merely oppose burial; he actively intercedes with an edict and watchmen to prevent burial.[64] His interdiction is the action driving the play, the Aristotelian praxis of the play (*Poetics* 1449 B 24-28). In a word, Sophocles' plot explores the consequences and repercussions stemming from Creon's exposure of Polyneices.

Polyneices viewed from the outer frame becomes more than Antigone's brother; he is one of the Theban Dead. In turn, by attempting to bury him, Antigone becomes like the Athenians in that she is reprising a deed from the glorious time of the Athenians' past. To some extent, Athenians had to have admired what she was doing, since Creon's impiety was apparent to them from the start. Even so, Antigone goes to war against her city, an effect of imagery discussed below, thus verging on another figure of the orator's mythmaking, the Amazons. These warrior women assaulted the Acropolis with an army in hope of replacing the men in power and turning the city topsy-turvy (Lysias *Funeral Oration* 4-6), which is precisely what Creon thinks Antigone is doing. Athenians displayed the battle against the Amazons on the Theseion and Stoa Poikile, and, at the time *Antigone* was being produced, Pheidias was finishing the Parthenon's west metopes and its cult statue of Athena

---

63. For the issue of the tragic hero of *Antigone*, see James C. Hogan, "The Protagonists of the *Antigone*," *Arethusa* 5 (1972), 93-100.

64. After inviting the elders of the chorus to be *skopoi* (215), "watchers, guardians," of his orders, he describes the men assigned to Polyneices' body as *episkopoi* (217). The intensifying prefix *epi-* on *skopoi* seems to imply not so much "watchers" as "lookouts," scouts in search of anyone who invades the domain Creon has asserted over the body.

Parthenos, both of which display the Amazon myth.[65] It was a potent myth for the men of Athens to justify their dominance over Persians in war and their own women in marriage.[66] An Amazon-like Antigone complicates the Athenian-like Antigone because the latter's action in emulating a feat of men is inappropriate for her sex. In effect, a woman exerts her own will and employs force, if only in imagery, to maintain her sex's traditional control over burial of the dead. Such a woman, in refusing to surrender one of her own (Sophocles *Antigone* 48) to a man who holds public power, does more than merely protest the usurpation of her sex's traditional care of the dead that enables the public funeral. She also withholds from the rituals of the public funeral the righteousness, longed for by men, of acceptance by the women of the community.

Whereas the Argives Creon exposes are enemies (Sophocles *Antigone* 10), Polyneices, whatever his deeds, is a kinsman. Creon, who assumes power over Thebes through nearness of kin (174), repudiates the obligations of kinship by casting out his nephew's body as carrion for the beasts. Because his action intrudes upon, indeed, usurps women's prerogatives concerning the family's dead, it draws resistance from Antigone who views Polyneices solely as kinsman. Knowledge of private life, our "inner frame," consists of information from the inner world of the house, family, and women. Women wielded considerable influence and power in the household and, indirectly, upon the community. Their lives centered around the birth and nurture of children, overseeing the transition to adult status through wedding rituals, preparing the bodies of the dead for burial, and mourning their loss. Much remained unsaid about the women of those Athenians who celebrated the public funeral in the 430s. Their men preferred not to talk about them, and women, conspiring with their men's posturing and prescriptions, consented to be muted, at least in public. Yet they evolved for themselves social practices and discourses as fully complex as those of the men but apart from the men. What traces remain, however, must be sought through the voices and activities of men who have appropriated them for their own purposes.

---

65. For the Amazon myth and the Parthenon, see Page DuBois, *Centaurs and Amazons: Women and the Pre-History of the Great Chain of Being* (Ann Arbor: The University of Michigan Press, 1982), 63-64; Tyrrell, *Amazons*, 19-21; David Castriota, *Myth, Ethos, and Actuality: Official Art in Fifth-Century B.C. Athens* (Madison: The University of Wisconsin Press, 1992), 143-151. For the Amazons on the Theseion and Stoa Poikile, see Tyrrell, *Amazons*, 10-13; Castriota, *Myth*, 43-58, 80-85. For the Parthenon generally, see R. E. Wycherly, *The Stones of Athens* (Princeton, NJ: Princeton University Press, 1978), 105-139.

66. Tyrrell, *Amazons*, 125-128.

2. Ismene's Choice
Prologue (1-99)

How *Antigone* began was evident to Sophocles' spectators, but modern audiences have imagined the opening in various ways. Richard Jebb, for example, has Antigone call Ismene from the house, while Richard Emil Braun places her at the altar in front of the house, waiting for Ismene to come forward from the house. Robert Fagles, on the other hand, has Antigone emerge from the house, followed by Ismene, and David Grene has them "meet in front of the palace gates in Thebes."[1] Modern stage directions depend upon two pieces of information supplied by the script: Antigone "kept fetching" or "sending for" Ismene (ἐξέπεμπον Sophocles *Antigone* 19), and Antigone knows what happened in the city. Except for Antigone's "as they say" (ὡς λέγουσι 23), how she learns about Creon's decree is left unstated. Ismene, who has remained in the house, knows nothing about it.[2] The theater of Dionysus Eleuthereus had no curtain to open to show Antigone before the house. Fagles' description is possible in that both actors could emerge from the house together and exit separately. But "I kept fetching you out" indicates that Antigone had to summon Ismene repeatedly, which gives the edge to having her come from the outside and somehow signal Ismene to come out. Moreover, there are other reasons to suppose that the actor playing Antigone entered by one of the gangways the spectators used to enter the theater not long before. In this way, everyone in the theater—officials, spectators, and actors—comes from the same place, the city, to reflect on its common concerns, both real and imagined. Sophocles begins his *Ajax* with a silent scene: Odysseus enters, his eyes glued to the ground and the tracks he

---

1. Jebb, *Antigone*, 8; Richard Emil Braun, trans., *Sophocles: "Antigone"* (Oxford: Oxford University Press, 1973), 21; Robert Fagles, trans., *The Three Theban Plays* (New York: Viking Press, 1982), 59; Grene, *Antigone*, 161.

2. The audience is free to speculate about Antigone's sally into the city, but such speculation remains just that without textual support. On the other hand, Sophocles needs to have someone know what has happened in the city in order to begin the drama and to set up Creon's entrance in the first episode. That it is Antigone who knows is predicated on the Antigone role in this myth.

is following. The scene, visible to the audience, is described in the text (*Ajax* 1-8). Although not as certain as the silent entrance of Odysseus, the sisters' separate entrances make a visual statement about who they are before they react to the news about their brothers. Separate entrances also offer a clue to the initial reaction Sophocles may have hoped to elicit from his audience. Christiane Sourvinou-Inwood remarks that the women are not where they are supposed to be and that "This frames them negatively."[3] However, if only Antigone is outside and Ismene must be summoned, the scene reflects negatively on Antigone alone. Antigone arrives by the gangway from the city, summons Ismene, and, after speaking with her briefly before the courtyard gates of the house, leaves by the other ramp to the country, not to reenter the house until under arrest shortly before being escorted to her death cave. She moves horizontally, so to speak, across the cavea, while, by contrast, Ismene moves perpendicularly from and back into the house.

Creon's action affects Antigone first. Learning of his decree, she seeks out her sister, Ismene. She enters, prepared to defy Creon's orders. Defiance of men and their *polis* in this mythmaking constitutes the "Antigone" character. Euripides' Antigone responds to Creon's "Rest assured, this man will be unburied" (ἄταφος ὅδ᾽ ἀνήρ, ὡς μάθης, γενήσεται *Phoenician Women* 1656) with "I will bury him, even if the *polis* forbids it" (ἐγὼ σφε θάψω, κἂν ἀπεννέπῃ πόλις 1657). A threatened Creon replies: "You will bury yourself next to this corpse" (σαυτὴν ἄρ᾽ ἐγγὺς τῷδε συνθάψεις νεκρῷ 1658), and the confrontation between them is established. Sophocles' Antigone declares: "It is no business of his to keep me from what is mine" (οὐδὲν αὐτῷ τῶν ἐμῶν <μ᾽> εἴργειν μέτα *Antigone* 48). What she means by "mine" exceeds the boundaries of normal kinship as her first words reveal:

῍Ω κοινὸν αὐτάδελφον ᾽Ισμήνης κάρα,
ἆρ᾽ οἶσθ᾽ ὅ τι Ζεὺς τῶν ἀπ᾽ Οἰδίπου κακῶν
ὁποῖον οὐχὶ νῷν ἔτι ζώσαιν τελεῖ;

                                                                    Sophocles *Antigone* 1-3

O common one of the same womb, head of Ismene
do you know of any suffering of those from Oedipus
that Zeus is yet to fulfill for us two yet living?

Antigone's language is difficult, her emotions perhaps confusing her grammar, and both—language and grammar—have led to textual uncertainties.[4] She addresses Ismene with a fulsome expression of their blood relationship that *koinon*

---

3. Sourvinou-Inwood, "Assumptions," 138.
4. Concerning the text of lines 2-3, see Jebb, *Antigone*, 8-9, 241-243; H. Lloyd-Jones and N. G. Wilson, *Sophoclea: Studies on the Text of Sophocles* (Oxford: Oxford University Press, 1990), 115.

(common) by itself would establish.[5] By being redundant, *autadelphon* (of the same womb) refines and emphasizes her concept of blood relationship. Kinship is a shared or common thing among kin, but, for Antigone, it is further limited to those of the self- (*aut-*) same (*a-*) womb (*delph-*). Charles Segal observes how Antigone defends herself by limiting kinship to "a function of the female procreative power: she defines kinship in terms of the womb (*splankhna*)."[6] The rest of the line is given to an endearment that follows from the first part: Ismene is dear to Antigone because she comes from the same womb. Indeed, Sophocles' avoidance of a usual word for sister may also point to Ismene as less important to Antigone in that capacity than as "wombmate." Antigone later refers to Polyneices and Eteocles as uterine kin, literally, "those of the same womb" (τοὺς ὁμοσπλάγχνους Sophocles *Antigone* 511). Family loyalty to her wombmates motivates her defiance of Creon's edict and her seeking out of Ismene. Her description of Ismene implies something more than their consanguinity as sisters and the surviving children of Oedipus. It suggests the excessive closeness brought about by Oedipus, their common father and brother.

Dominant male discourse affixes responsibility and blame for the incest upon Jocasta. Odysseus tells the Phaeacians that he saw Oedipus' mother, Epikaste, "who accomplished an enormous deed in her mind's ignorance when she married her own son" (ἢ μέγα ἔργον ἔρεξεν ἀϊδρείῃσι νόοιο, / γημαμένη ᾧ υἷι Homer *Odyssey* 11.272-273). Oedipus of Sophocles' *Oedipus Tyrannus* calls for a sword with which to search out his "wife not wife where he found the double maternal field of himself and his children" (γυναῖκά τ' οὐ γυναῖκα, μητρῴαν δ' ὅπου / κίχοι διπλῆν ἄρουραν οὗ τε καὶ τέκνων 1256-1257). Similarly, Aeschylus' chorus of maidens bemoans:

παῖδα τὸν αὑτᾶς πόσιν αὑ-
τᾶι θεμένα τούσδ' ἔτεχ', οἱ δ'
ὧδ' ἐτελεύτασαν ὑπ' ἀλλαλοφόνοις
χερσὶν ὁμοσπόροισιν.

Seven Against Thebes 928-931

Having made her own son
a husband for herself, she bore these [Eteocles and Polyneices],
and they perished by hands murdering one another,
hands from the same sowing.[7]

---

5. Kamerbeek, *Antigone*, 37.

6. Segal, *Tragedy and Civilization*, 183. John D. B. Hamilton ("Antigone: Kinship, Justice, and the Polis," in *Myth and the Polis*, ed. Dora C. Pozzi and John M. Wickersham [Ithaca, NY: Cornell University Press, 1991], 94) also notes: "In honoring Polyneikes, she honors the womb." For this reason, the paraphrase of the first line, "Ismene, my dear sister, whose father was my father" (Grene, *Antigone*, 161), seems particularly ill-chosen, not to say wrong.

7. The young Theban women of Aeschylus' chorus also see Oedipus' responsibility: "He dared sow his mother's sacred field, where he was nurtured, with a bloody root" (ματρὸς ἀγνὰν

"It is as if *she* were the pollution," exclaims Page DuBois, "that must be eliminated because she received both him and his father."[8] Antigone reverses the emphasis. She never acknowledges the hostility her wombmates felt toward one another and does not hold her mother's womb as the source of pollution of incest and kin murder (Sophocles *Antigone* 863-865). Her mother was unlucky; she had her bed ruined by Oedipus. The father and head of the normal family is, in Antigone's family, the source of the evils Zeus is fulfilling. But Antigone's is not a normal family; Oedipus is her brother as well as her father as she insinuates:

ἐλθοῦσα μέντοι κάρτ' ἐν ἐλπίσιν τρέφω
φίλη μὲν ἥξειν πατρί, προσφιλὴς δὲ σοί,
μῆτερ, φίλη δὲ σοί, κασίγνητον κάρα.
ἐπεὶ θανόντας αὐτόχειρ ὑμᾶς ἐγὼ
ἔλουσα κἀκόσμησα κἀπιτυμβίους
χοὰς ἔδωκα· νῦν δέ, Πολύνεικες . . ..

Sophocles *Antigone* 897-902

Still, I nourish hope of going there
philê to my father, and especially *philê* to you,
mother, and *philê* to you, brother-head,
since all of you in death with my own hands
I washed and dressed, and gave
liquid offerings at your tomb.[9] And now Polyneices. . ..

Brother and father do not ordinarily exist in the same man, so that the implication is readily dismissed. After mention of her father and mother and before mentioning Polyneices, a reference to Eteocles would be expected, as the Scholiast assumes, and Sophocles capitalizes upon that expectation while, at the same time, allowing uncertainty. Antigone, who was not present at Eteocles' "burial," could not have cared for his body. It may occur to the spectator who remembers this that Antigone is referring to Oedipus qua brother. Sophocles created a similar ambiguity a few lines earlier:

/ σπείρας ἄρουραν ἵν' ἐτράφη / ῥίζαν αἱματόεσσαν / ἔτλα *Seven Against Thebes* 752-756).

8. DuBois, *Centaurs and Amazons*, 77.

9. Sophocles' original audience could not compare these lines from the fourth episode to those of Antigone in the prologue. Modern readers of Sophocles must be careful not to base their interpretations primarily on material not yet available to an ancient audience, and lines 869-871 have their own purpose in context. Later readers of Sophocles do, however, resemble his original spectators after the latter had seen the play. Since it would be artificial, to say the least, to pretend that we do not know the ending, we have anticipated the characters at times as if Athenians were engaged in discussing the play afterwards.

ἰὼ δυσπότμων κασί-
γνητε γάμων κυρήσας,
θανὼν ἔτ' οὖσαν κατήναρές με.

Sophocles Antigone 869-871

Alas, brother, by attaining ill-
fated marriages,
dead though you be, you slew me still alive.

Antigone may have Polyneices' marriage in mind, as did the Scholiast, but Oedipus' marriage with Jocasta has also directly affected her, since it produced the wombmate for whom she forfeits her life. She ignores the generation separating her from Oedipus when she considers him as brother. Seth Bernardete is right about Antigone: she is "antigeneration, the true offspring of an incestuous marriage."[10]

Antigone's family is not analogous to the patriarchal household of Athens of the 430s; it is not even the incestuous family of father Oedipus. It is a family headed by her mother, and kinship, as already noted, is determined by the mother's womb rather than the father's phallus. With her family, Sophocles approximates a construct of Athenian mythmaking about conditions before King Cecrops institutes marriage, when men, ignorant of their role in sexual intercourse, do not know their sons.[11] Women therefore give their names to the children, thus determining membership in the family. All that changes when the men, aroused by Poseidon's rage, strip the women of their public privileges and seize mastery over their procreativity and children. Antigone champions a family that is precivilized and savage in being headed by a woman. This form of the family sets up her conversion, as we shall see, through her marriage to Hades, after which she adopts the values imposed by marriage in general and by the public funeral in particular.

Antigone comes to Ismene for aid in lifting Polyneices' body. Ismene refuses her helping hands, and Antigone swears that Ismene will never do anything amiably with her again (Sophocles *Antigone* 69-70). But she has a second need for Ismene; she needs her voice. Along with preparing the dead for burial, mourning and lamentation belonged to women. These activities in large part defined women as social beings and contributed importantly to the welfare of the community. They were done in concert with many women. In her study of modern funeral practices among the Inner Mani, C. Nadia Seremetakis relates the incident of an old woman who had been living in the city and, upon her death, was returned to her natal

---

10. Seth Bernardete, "A Reading of Sophocles' *Antigone*," *Interpretation: A Journal of Political Philosophy* 5 (1975), 11.

11. Varro in Augustine, *City of God*, 18.9; Simon Pembroke, "Women in Charge: The Function of Alternatives in Early Greek Tradition and the Ancient Idea of Matriarchy," *Journal of the Warburg and Courtauld Institutes* 30 (1967), 26-27; Pierre Vidal-Naquet, *The Black Hunter: Forms of Thought and Forms of Society in the Greek World*, trans. Andrew Szegedy-Maszak (Baltimore and London: The Johns Hopkins University Press, 1986), 216-217.

village for burial. The woman had no living relatives in the village, and only one niece from the city to mourn her:[12]

> [T]he collective mourning was minimal. The urban relatives appeared ignorant and/or indifferent to any local ethics. The rural women who attended did not make any declarations of shared substance. The entire weight of the ceremony was taken by an urban niece of the deceased who had retained all the skills of lamentation, appropriate body gestures and behavior. She was mourning, wailing, and talking to the dead for at least seven hours in an incredible effort to create and maintain a center for the ceremony. She wanted to avoid a "silent" death, so her aunt would "not go discontented," alone and unscreamed.

The village women hummed and nodded and often apologized for not being able "to help her out," "'to take the song' from her." They would not step over the boundary, Seremetakis attests, "defined by the absence of past reciprocity, the absence of close kin, biological or fictive." Evidently, after the deceased left for the city, and her kinfolk in the village died, she had no contact with anyone there. She had, in ancient Greek terms, no *philotês* with those left behind, and no one in the village felt obligated by ties of reciprocity or kinship to mourn her.

These mourning practices are structured by the equation: mourning: relation = silence: absence of relation. The women of the village could not join in with the niece of the deceased because they were outsiders. Seeing his mother in what to him is unbefitting mourning, a shocked Theseus importunes:

μῆτερ, τί κλαίεις λέπτ' ἐπ' ὀμμάτων φάρη
βαλοῦσα τῶν σῶν; ἆρα δυστήνους γόους
κλύουσα τῶνδε; κἀμὲ γὰρ διῆλθέ τι.
ἔπαιρε λευκὸν κρᾶτα, μὴ δακρυρρόει
σεμναῖσι Δηοῦς ἐσχάραις παρημένη.

Euripides Suppliant Women 286-290

Mother, why have you put your finely spun dress
over your eyes? Why are you crying? from hearing
their pitiable laments? Yes, they struck me, too.
Lift up your white head. Do not shed tears
while sitting at august Deo's altars.

Appeal to religious scruples unheeded, Aethra breaks out into mourning and bewailing with the wretched women. Theseus admonishes her: "You must not grieve for their plight. . . .You are not related to them" (τὰ τούτων οὐχὶ σοὶ στενακτέον. . . .οὐ σὺ τῶνδ' ἔφυς 291-292). Aethra surprises Theseus by passing over the boundary separating kin from outsiders and by joining in the mothers' mourning for their sons. Vase paintings of the *prothesis* rarely show a single woman beside the deceased.[13] Mourning and keening were carried out antiphon-

---

12. Seremetakis, *Last Word*, 101. The quotations in this paragraph are found on page 101.
13. See plates 3334, 3335, and 3339 in Paul Monceaux, "Funus," in *Dictionnaire des*

ally between two groups of kinswomen and close friends.[14] Every woman who deemed herself entitled or obligated would insist on participating. Funeral legislation was based on this assumption, and legislators could not exclude women as remote as children of first cousins (Demosthenes *Against Macartatus* 62).[15] What woman, then, would shame herself by repudiating these obligations? What woman would incur excommunication from the family by denying these obligations? That Antigone expects Ismene to join her is affirmed by what is known about the bonds of mourning *philotês* and about mourning in the lives of women of classical Athens.

When Ismene remains silent like an outsider, Antigone will have nothing further to do with her: "If you think it best, you hold in dishonor the gods' honored things" (σὺ δ' εἰ δοκεῖ / τὰ τῶν θεῶν ἔντιμ' ἀτιμάσασ' ἔχε Sophocles *Antigone* 76-77). She expels Ismene from the family for shrinking from her burial arrangements for their brother. Because Ismene does not rise in Antigone's estimation to the duties of a *philê*, she is no longer *philê*, no longer a member of the burying group that is synonymous with the family.[16] When Ismene cautions silence over her exploit, Antigone erupts: "No, shout it out loud! You'll be more hostile if you keep silent and do not proclaim this to everyone" (οἴμοι, καταύδα· πολλὸν ἐχθίων ἔσῃ / σιγῶσ', ἐὰν μὴ πᾶσι κηρύξῃς τάδε 86-87). Creon has announced his proclamation. Now Antigone wants Ismene to issue another declaring aloud her burial rites/rights.

Without Ismene, Antigone has no one to answer her cries of mourning. Polyneices is doomed to the silent death that the niece was so desperately trying to avert at her aunt's burial. "Silent death is a bad death," Seremetakis explains, because "it implies the deceased was alone, without clan, without 'numbers,' without appearance . . . or screaming."[17] Aeschylus' Agamemnon received a silent, "bad death" from Clytemnestra:

---

antiquités grecques et romaines, vol. 2, ed. Ch. Daremberg and Edm. Saglio (Paris: Librairie Hachette, 1896), 1371-1374. Plate 3332, a closeup of the head of the deceased, shows one woman, apparently the wife. See also the plates in John Boardman, "Painted Funerary Plaques and Some Remarks on *Prothesis,*" *The Annual of the British School at Athens* 50 (1955), 51-66; Donna C. Kurtz and John Boardman, *Greek Burial Customs* (Ithaca, NY: Cornell University Press, 1971), 120, figures 33-35; Shapiro, *Iconography,* 630-640, figures 1, 3-4, 5, 8-13.

14. Alexiou (*Ritual Lament,* 13) has traced the origin of laments to "the antiphonal singing of two groups of mourners, strangers and kinswomen, each singing a verse in turn and followed by a refrain sung in unison." The *kommos* (sung lament) in Aeschylus' *Libation Bearers* (306-478), Alexiou points out, reproduces the form in an exchange between the deceased Agamemnon's children and slave women ordered to join them. For an analysis of antiphonal structure and formulaic expressions in laments, see Alexiou, 131-184.

15. Solon was determined to exclude professional singers of dirges, who would be women (Plutarch *Solon* 21.6).

16. It is not insignificant, as Alexiou (*Ritual Lament,* 20) indicates, that "[t]here is evidence that throughout Greek antiquity the right to inherit was directly linked with the right to mourn."

17. Seremetakis, *Last Word,* 76.

πάντολμε μᾶτερ, δαΐαις ἐν ἐκφοραῖς
ἄνευ πολιτᾶν ἄνακτ'
ἄνευ δὲ πενθημάτων
ἔτλας ἀνοίμωκτον ἄνδρα θάψαι.

Libation Bearers 430-433

All daring mother, in hostile procession
without citizens your lord,
and without lamentations your husband,
unmourned, you dared to bury.

Silent death expresses for Clytemnestra the hatred she harbors for the husband and father who sacrificed her daughter like a young female goat (Aeschylus *Agamemnon* 232). For a woman who wants to mourn her dead, a silent death must hold emotions of deprivation and alienation as grievous as Clytemnestra's are hostile. Antigone needs Ismene's screams to proclaim the death to the community. Ismene's silence deepens the silence surrounding Polyneices' body. Burial customs add another dimension to Antigone's not wanting Ismene to be silent. Since Ismene is no longer a *philê* in Antigone's eyes, she will not permit Ismene's silence, for even that would confer upon her a part in the burial rites.

Antigone is left a solitary mourner in a silent death, as she sets out to heap a mound over her *philos* (Sophocles *Antigone* 80-81). She declares her intention to give her *philos* the kind of burial men in epic and the Archaic Age might have given their slain fellows.[18] "She speaks as if she hoped to give him regular sepulture," Jebb comments, citing *Iliad* 7.336: τύμβον δ' ἀμφὶ πυρὴν ἕνα χεύομεν [Let us heap one mound over the burnt spot], and 24.799: σῆμ' ἔχεαν [They heaped up a marker mound].[19] This is exactly what Antigone says she intends to do—the definitiveness of her future participle of purpose *khôsous[a]* (to heap up) belies Jebb's attenuating "as if she hoped to." The hapless Elpenor entreats Odysseus for such a rite: "Burn me with what armor as is mine, and heap a marker mound for men on the shore of the gray sea" (με κακκῆαι σὺν τεύχεσιν, ἄσσα μοί ἐστι, / σῆμά τέ μοι χεῦαι πολιῆς ἐπὶ θινὶ θαλάσσης Homer *Odyssey* 11.74-75). On returning to Circe's island, Odysseus carries out his promise to Elpenor:

φιτροὺς δ' αἶψα ταμόντες, ὅθ' ἀκρότατος πρόεχ' ἀκτή,
θάπτομεν ἀχνύμενοι, θαλερὸν κατὰ δάκρυ χέοντες.
αὐτὰρ ἐπεὶ νεκρός τ' ἐκάη καὶ τεύχεα νεκροῦ,
τύμβον χεύαντες καὶ ἐπὶ στήλην ἐρύσαντες
πήξαμεν ἀκροτάτῳ τύμβῳ εὐῆρες ἐρετμόν.

Homer *Odyssey* 12.11-15

---

18. See Kurtz and Boardman, *Greek Burial Customs*, 71-84, 105-108, for the classical period.

19. Jebb, *Antigone*, 24.

Quickly cutting wood where the shore jutted out farthest,
we performed his burial rites, grieving and shedding tears profusely.
But after the body and the body's armor were burned,
we heaped a mound and, dragging a grave stele,
we affixed on top of the mound a handy oar.

Humble by comparison with Patroclus' or Hector's, Elpenor's cremation lies beyond the means of a single person. Burial mounds in epic and the construction of grave mounds require the hands of many men and are clearly beyond the capacity of a single woman.[20] Ismene replies pragmatically when she points out to her sister that she lusts for the impossible (Sophocles *Antigone* 90). Antigone's plan is "bad counsel" (δυσβουλίαν 95), and she is "senseless" (ἄνους 99) for undertaking it.

Antigone challenges Ismene: "You will soon demonstrate whether your are wellborn or born base from good stock" (καὶ δείξεις τάχα /εἴτ' εὐγενὴς πέφυκας εἴτ' ἐσθλῶν κακή Sophocles *Antigone* 37-38), and with these words, Creon's action comes home to Ismene. The charge is couched in terms of patriliny and generation, the terms specifically used by men of high birth (*eugeneia*) and worth (*esthlon*) derived from their fathers.[21] Antigone insists that Ismene prove the nobility of her birth from her mother by acting as a man would in evincing his *eugeneia* from his father. To her sister's demand phrased in the vocabulary of men's preoccupations, Ismene answers with an image from women's art of weaving: "You poor thing, if things are in this state, what more can I add by loosening or tightening the knot?" (τί δ', ὦ ταλαῖφρον, εἰ τάδ' ἐν τούτοις, ἐγὼ / λύουσ' ἂν εἴθ' ἅπτουσα προσθείμην πλέον; 39-40). Her language recalls a scene familiar in every Athenian household—that of women walking to and fro before the loom with the fabric growing at their skilled hands.[22] Weaving was an intensely female occupation, long polarized from men's war by epic poetry (Homer *Iliad* 6.490-493).[23] Ismene's question sets the tone for evaluating Antigone's request: "See whether you will join in the toil and the deed with me" (εἰ ξυμπονήσεις καὶ ξυνεργάσῃ σκόπει 41).

---

20. Reading of Homer and even a cursory look at the grave mounds pictured in Kurtz and Boardman (*Greek Burial Customs*, 73, 76) for the Archaic period, a form of burial practiced in the classical period "virtually unchanged, except for a noticeable tendency towards simplification" (98), show that the construction of such a mound could not be done by one person.

21. Walter Donlan, *The Aristocratic Ideal in Ancient Greece: Attitudes of Superiority from Homer to the End of the Fifth Century B.C.* (Lawrence, KS: Coronado Press, 1980), 134.

22. Jebb (*Antigone*, 17) thinks that "though the phrase may have been first suggested by the loom, it was probably used without any such conscious allusion." It is true that the spectator or reader cannot be certain of the degree of consciousness behind the allusion on either Ismene's or Sophocles' part, but given it is spoken by Ismene, a woman prepared to accept traditional gender roles, it does not seem far-fetched to assume a conscious reference to weaving.

23. For an exposition of weaving and weaving techniques, see Eva C. Keuls, "Attic Vase-Painting and the Home Textile Industry," in *Ancient Greek Art and Iconography*, ed. Warren G. Moon (Madison: The University of Wisconsin Press, 1983), 209-230; E. J. W. Barber, "The

Critics have been harsh with Ismene who pales for them before Antigone.[24] She refuses to join her sister, they say; she is but a foil for her heroic sister. But Ismene, no less than Antigone, has been forced by Creon's action to make a decision. She chooses her *polis* over her *philoi* and, with this decision, she silences herself as a mourner. The Scholiast on line 47 writes that "the one [Ismene] follows the situation; the other [Antigone], kinship" (ἡ μὲν . . . τῷ πράγματι, ἡ δὲ τῇ οἰκειότητι ἀκολουθεῖ). Ismene recognizes *to pragma*, "the matter," "affair," "*res*." Ismene knows Oedipus' responsibility as father and describes Jocasta as both mother and wife, delimiting a patriarchal, albeit incestuous, family structure (Sophocles *Antigone* 49-54). It is Ismene who responds appropriately to things as they are, while Antigone, dismissing all but kinship, acts outside her means. Ismene knows how her *philoi* died and how her sister and she came to be alone. She is keenly aware of the weakness of women before men and of the necessity to submit to the force of law and the authority of rulers (58-64). At the same time, she realizes her obligations to the dead as well as the pain that would be incurred in honoring them, knowledge which prompts her to beg forgiveness of the dead for relinquishing Polyneices to "those in authority" (τοῖς ἐν τέλει 67). Acting beyond the practicalities, she concludes, is foolhardy.

Ismene abides by the social norms, and returns at the end of the prologue to the house. She demonstrates a woman's nature according to Xenophon's description:

τῇ δὲ γυναικὶ ἧττον τὸ σῶμα δυνατὸν πρὸς ταῦτα [ῥίγη . . . καὶ θάλπη καὶ ὁδοιπορίας καὶ στρατείας] φύσας τὰ ἔνδον ἔργα αὐτῇ . . . προστάξαι μοι δοκεῖ ὁ θεός.

Xenophon *Oeconomicus* 7.23

Since he endowed the woman by nature with a body less capable with respect to these [cold and head and travel and military service] . . . the god seems to me to have assigned to her the indoor tasks.

Sophocles' Ismene and the fourteen-year-old wife of Xenophon's Ischomachus illustrate the same ideological prescriptions for the dutiful, subservient woman in Greek society. Ismene is "incapable" (ἀμήχανος Sophocles *Antigone* 79) of violence against men and their law because she lives the funeral orator's prescriptions for women. The orator repeatedly praises men for noble birth and *aretê* (bravery/ skill).[25] Men seek *kleos* (reputation); they want to hear talk about themselves

---

Peplos of Athena," in *Goddess and Polis: The Panathenaic Festival in Ancient Athens*, ed. Jenifer Neils (Hanover, NH: Hood Museum of Art, Dartmouth College; Princeton, NJ: Princeton University Press, 1992), 103-117.

24. For a survey of opinions, see Steiner, *Antigones*, 144-145

25. For *aretê*, see Thucydides 2.35.1, 36.1, 42.2, 43.1, 45.1, 46.1; Lysias *Funeral Oration* 1, 2, 6, 10, 20, 23, 25, 26, 33, 40, 42, 43, 44, 47, 50, 54, 57, 61, 63, 66, 69, 71, 74, 76, 80, 81; Plato *Menexenos* 236 E, 237 A, 239 A, B, 240 D, 241 C, 243 D; Gorgias fragment B, 6 (Diels-

among others in the community. With a notable oxymoron—a woman's glory is great when *kleos* about her is least heard—Pericles reverses male values to impose values on women. For women, no reputation, whether for courage or cowardice, is best. The absence of *kleos*, that is, silence among males, confers upon them great glory. Ismene conforms and allows herself to be silenced by men. Creon in the play and the funeral orator in the subtext compel her to betray her womanly nature which is "fit for the dirge and fond of mourning and fond of wailing and given to lamenting."[26] She surrenders her *philos* to the dictates of the citizens and their leaders, abandoning her sister and her obligations to family. Yet, as she throttles her voice out of respect for the *polis*, she is neither cold-hearted nor uncaring. She knows her place but feels profound grief. Her "begging those below for pardon" (αἰτοῦσα τοὺς ὑπὸ χθονὸς / ξύγγνοιαν ἴσχειν 65-66), her desire to join Antigone in dying for "this rite" (τοῦδε τοῦ τάφου 534) performed by her *philê,* and her "madness" are so many indications of her conflict. Creon testifies to her madness; he saw her, he says, "possessed by frenzy and not in possession of her senses" (λυσσῶσαν αὐτὴν οὐδ᾽ ἐπήβολον φρενῶν 492). However, it is not Ismene's mental condition per se but the role played by Creon's intrusion upon the mourning privileges and responsibilities of his women that interests us here. To understand fully the significance of that intrusion, we must examine Ismene's madness through the inner frame of mourning rituals. The dynamics of grieving enacted by Homeric men and women will help us construct the inner frame.

Homer's men give themselves over immediately to extravagant displays of mourning. "A black cloud of sorrow covered over [Achilles]" (τὸν δ᾽ ἄχεος νεφέλη ἐκάλυψε μέλαινα Homer *Iliad* 18.22), when he learned of Patroclus' death. He succumbs so violently to grief that Antilochus, although weeping himself, grasps Achilles' hands for fear he will kill himself (18.32-34). Weeping is condoned, but a man relies upon his companions to restrain him "lest it become dangerous or morbid."[27] Achilles himself calls Priam back from weeping for Hector so that they may have supper together (24.523-524; 549-550). In contrast, Andromache transforms the outward signs of her grief from fainting and tearing her hair to leading a *goos* before the other women. As opposed to the *thrênos*, a formal dirge performed by a professional, the *goos* is an improvised song that relatives sing in response to the

---

Kranz); Demosthenes *Funeral Oration* 2, 3, 6, 12, 17, 20, 36; Hyperides *Funeral Oration* 8, 9, 18, 23, 24, 27, 29, 30, 40.

26. Pollux 6.202, quoted with translation, above, Introduction, n. 26. See also Loraux, *Invention*, 45.

27. Holst-Warhaft (*Dangerous Voices*, 107) elaborates: "Giving way to loud and uncontrolled weeping is not only normal, it seems, in the world of the knightly heroes, but gives a certain pleasure. On the other hand it is not to be indulged in alone or too long, lest it become dangerous or morbid. In the heat of passionate grief, a man may indulge himself in lament almost to the brink of death without incurring shame, but he relies on his comrades to pull him back to himself."

immediate situation.[28] Andromache begins her first *goos*: "Hector, I grieve for you" ("Εκτορ, ἐγὼ δύστηνος 22.477), but both her *gooi* concern the sufferings that await the living as a result of Hector's death (22.477-514, 24.725-745), and both are sung before other women who join with her in mourning (22.515, 24.746).

In this dynamic, men and women lament in the company of others; solitude is dangerous, for it threatens violence or mental breakdown. While men appear to give themselves to emotions aroused by the death itself, women channel their feelings and release them in songs about their own loss and futures, where the patterning and discipline of the song act to alleviate the pain and render it socially constructive.[29] Underlying the women's behavior may be a preference similar to that Loring M. Danforth encountered among the women of the village of Potamia in northern Thessaly:[30]

> The women of Potamia generally agree that the singing of laments is preferable to wild shouting and wailing as a means of expressing grief at death rituals. Many women believe that such shouting is physically harmful and may cause illness.

Homeric men and women have communal, socially bound customs for releasing their sorrows. Ismene has neither a companion to restrain her grief and summon her back to herself nor a kinswoman to respond antiphonally to her *goos*.[31] With no outlet or recourse to action, her emotions take over, and Ismene's grief has no boundaries or channels to shape it. She goes mad. Her silence prefigures that of Creon's wife, Eurydice, who mutes her voice when Creon most needs her laments for the son whose death he has caused (Sophocles *Antigone* 1269).

Seen through the outer frame, Creon's action of exposing Polyneices presents Ismene and Antigone with the same choice that confronts the Athenians of the funeral oration, for Polyneices represents the Theban Dead in this framework. The rituals and ideology of the public funeral convey associations and meanings to the choices made by Polyneices' *philai*, meanings that do not obtain for the characters. Ismene's inability to act against the citizens appears through the outer frame as comparable to the actions of the "others" in the *epitaphios logos*. These "others" function as a foil for Athenians, someone to be different from and superior to as defined by Athenians. Thus, for example, Lysias boasts of the Athenians:[32]

---

28. Alexiou, *Ritual Lament*, 11-13.

29. Holst-Warhaft, *Dangerous Voices*, 108-114.

30. Danforth, *Death Rituals*, 73.

31. Alexiou (*Ritual Lament*, 13) points out that "In Homer the antiphonal element is becoming obscured, and even the refrain has been reduced to a perfunctory formula." The latter, it seems, is ἐπὶ δὲ στενάχοντο γυναῖκες (and then the women mourned), repeated after both Andromache's *gooi* (Homer *Iliad* 22.515, 24.746). Eurydice, Ismene's aunt, enters in the *exodos*, but she has no presence or part to be played until the *exodos*.

32. Other examples include: "We [Athenians] govern . . . being ourselves a model for some rather than imitating others" (χρώμεθα . . . πολιτεία . . . παράδειγμα . . . μᾶλλον αὐτοὶ

αἰσχυνόμενοι ὅτι ἦσαν οἱ βάρβαροι αὐτῶν ἐν τῇ χώρᾳ, οὐκ ἀνέμειναν πυθέσθαι οὐδὲ βοηθῆσαι τοὺς συμμάχους, οὐδ᾽ ᾠήθησαν δεῖν ἑτέροις τῆς σωτηρίας χάριν εἰδέναι, ἀλλὰ σφίσιν αὐτοῖς τοὺς ἄλλους Ἕλληνας.

Lysias *Funeral Oration* 23

Feeling shame that the foreigners were in their country, the Athenians did not wait for the allies to find out and come to their aid, nor did they condone having to thank others for their freedom but supposed that others ought to thank them.

These "others" are men in rivalry for *aretê* with the Athenians. Women, Pericles insists, should not emulate men; they are supposed to be "other." The negative connotations attached to the "others" in the outer frame do not pertain to Ismene because she is a woman. On the contrary, since the city needs the men of its families for the *polis* to survive, Ismene unites the positive aspects of both the inner and outer frames: she surrenders Polyneices as *philos* of father Oedipus' family and as war dead to Creon, a man in charge. While conforming to the Athenians' conception of how women were expected to react when men asserted power over them, Ismene violates what that same conception has reared her to accept as her nature as a woman. The contradiction results in madness. Ismene's decision is, in effect, that forced upon Athenian women. By yielding up their war dead, the women make the city's public funeral possible but at a cost to everybody, themselves most of all.

Polyneices, lying among the slain Argives, represents all the corpses exposed before Thebes. Antigone's effort to heap a mound over his body consequently invites comparison to the effort of ancestral Athenians as related by funeral orators. Hers is a deed that, when carried out by men, defends piety toward the gods above and below, but when attempted by a woman, imperils the gender differences and structures of male-dominated society. Sophocles associates Antigone with the Athenians through the language of funeral oratory. She undertakes a "dangerous act" (κινδύνευμα Sophocles *Antigone* 42), a word reminiscent of the orator's commonplace "danger" (κίνδυνος).[33] Like the Athenians, she is alone and seeks to die nobly carrying out a noble deed.[34] Antigone's mimesis of the Athenians'

ὄντες τισὶν ἢ μιμούμενοι ἑτέρους Thucydides 2.37.1); "Who of the other Greeks could have rivaled them in counsels, numbers, and bravery?" (τίνες ἂν τούτοις τῶν ἄλλων Ἑλλήνων ἤρισαν γνώμῃ καὶ πλήθει καὶ ἀρετῇ; Lysias *Funeral Oration* 42); "These men . . . exacted vengeance for wrongs the foreigners had done others" (οὗτοι . . . τιμωρίαν ὑπὲρ ὧν τοὺς ἄλλους ἠδίκουν ἐπέθηκαν Demosthenes *Funeral Oration* 11); Our earth "did not begrudge her fruits but distributed them even to others" (τούτου δὲ τοῦ καρποῦ οὐκ ἐφθόνησεν, ἀλλ᾽ ἔνειμεν καὶ τοῖς ἄλλοις Plato *Menexenos* 238 a).

33. For *kindunos* and the related verb *kinduneuô*, see Thucydides 2.39.1, 4, 40.3, 42.4, 43.4; Lysias *Funeral Oration* 9, 12, 14, 20, 23, 25, 26, 33, 34, 47, 50, 63, 68; Plato *Menexenos* 246 c; Demosthenes *Funeral Oration* 11, 26, 29, 30; Hyperides *Funeral Oration* 17.

34. Examples of the *monos* (alone) commonplace include: "This city alone of those now in existence comes to the test more powerful than its reputation" (μόνη . . . τῶν νῦν ἀκοῆς

famous deed echoes subtextually in the very language of the text and can be of no concern to Creon who does not hear it. On the other hand, from her entrance, Antigone speaks in military imagery (8-10) that portrays her as a woman at war: "I will not betray [Polyneices] and fall into enemy hands" (οὐ γὰρ δὴ προδοῦσ' ἁλώσομαι 46).[35] Her native city is the enemy and its general, Creon. Antigone does not literally take up arms against Creon or her city, but Sophocles builds up the image of a conflict between the sexes that recalls the myth of the Amazons. These warrior women invaded Attica and threatened to displace men as leaders of the family and *polis*. The myth was portrayed on the Theseum and Stoa Poikile and was rehearsed as part of the orator's catalog of mythic exploits.[36] Creon hears the language of war and finds Antigone threatening his manhood (484-485). But in the final analysis, it is his actions that transform Antigone into an image of the Athenians themselves and a female bogey of their mythmaking.

κρείσσων ἐς πεῖραν ἔρχεται Thucydides 2.41.3); "Nevertheless, we were again left alone" (ὅμως δ' οὖν ἐμονώθημεν πάλιν Plato *Menexenos* 245 D). For the language of oratory in the prologue of *Antigone*, see Bennett and Tyrrell, "Funeral Oratory," 446. For the "noble death" in funeral oratory, see Loraux, *Invention*, 98-118.

35. On military imagery, see Robert F. Goheen, *The Imagery of Sophocles' "Antigone"* (Princeton, NJ: Princeton University Press, 1951), 19-20.

36. Tyrrell, *Amazons*, 10-19; Castriota, *Myth,* 43-58, 83-86.

3. The Dust
Parodos and First Episode (100-331)

No sooner has the door to the house closed behind Ismene than the choristers begin to dance their way into the orchestra. The military-like cadences of their movements contrast with costumes identifying them as elderly men. In the middle of the left line, occupying its third position, the Coryphaeus, or chorus leader, stands out in his more resplendent robe. The elders' song reflects the joy of all Thebans over their rescue from the Argives. Significantly, the elders say nothing about the dead lying before the city. They are fixed on the living, and it is as a living man that Polyneices comes into their song. The elders discover in Polyneices' name (He of Many Quarrels) the nature of the man whose "contentious quarrels" (*neikeôn . . . amphilogôn* 111) brought the Argive foe upon Thebes. But the quarrels themselves are "disputed," containing words (*-logôn*) that may argue on both sides (*amphi-*). These ambiguities leave open the question of who is the traitor. The elders know that Eteocles and his brother hated one another and died at one another's hand in the fighting; they are

τοῖν στυγεροῖν, ὦ πατρὸς ἑνὸς
μητρός τε μιᾶς φύντε καθ' αὑτοῖν
δικρατεῖς λόγχας στήσαντ' ἔχετον
κοινοῦ θανάτου μέρος ἄμφω.

Sophocles Antigone 144-147

the pair filled with hate who, of one father
and one mother born, leveled mutually
victorious spears against one another and gained,
both of them, a share in a common death.

Eteocles and Polyneices are enemy brothers, that is, they are alike in spite of the difference erected by being on opposite sides of the Theban battlements.[1] By uniting them with the dual number in the description of their deaths, Sophocles has

---

1. For the symmetry of Eteocles and Polyneices in Aeschylus' *Seven Against Thebes*, see Froma I. Zeitlin, *Under the Sign of the Shield* (Roma: Edizioni dell' Ateno, 1982), 135-145. For

the elders speak of them as indistinguishable in their hatred, spear work, and deaths. These brief allusions did not invent the brothers' sameness but rather called upon the audience's previous knowledge of it. Oedipus' curse and the death of his sons had been part of the epic tradition surrounding Thebes for generations.[2] While eschewing direct borrowings, Sophocles drew upon previous models and traditional language so that his audience could hardly fail to appreciate the parallels between Oedipus' sons. Still, the symmetry remains incomplete without an awareness of what remains unsaid in the play; by not abiding by his agreement with Polyneices to abdicate the Theban throne in Polyneices' favor after a year, Eteocles, too, brought the Argives upon his native city and, although less obviously, is also a traitor.

In this study, our focus is upon the function of the choral sections as a *sêmantôr,* or guide, in clueing the audience about the ensuing episode. The elders allude gnomically to a prideful man: "For Zeus exceedingly hates the boasts of a big mouth" (Ζεὺς γὰρ μεγάλης γλώσσης κόμπους / ὑπερεχθαίρει Sophocles *Antigone* 127), which aphorism they then illustrate with the man whom Zeus strikes with a thunderbolt as he drew near the top of the city's battlements.[3] The man swung outward as if on a ladder and crashed to the ground. In that man, many in Sophocles' original audience probably recognized the unnamed Capaneus.[4] He alone in the Argive army suffered such a death for boasting that he would lay waste to Thebes with or without the gods' consent. Perhaps Capaneus was so well known in this myth that Sophocles saw no need to name him in order for his fate to illustrate the paradigm. In any case, designating, albeit tacitly, the boastful man as Capaneus asks the audience to remember him as an illustration from the *parodos,* and leaving his identity open allows him to prefigure a man yet to be identified and encourages the audience to assess the boastfulness of anyone who utters the name of Zeus. Once someone is seen to be boastful, Zeus's "brandished fire" should not be long in following. Creon speaks of Zeus only moments later and several times thereafter. In fact, no character speaks of Zeus more often than Creon. The chorus has prepared the audience for receiving his discourse about the god.

---

the motif of "enemy brothers," see René Girard, *The Violence and the Sacred,* trans. Patrick Gregory (Baltimore and London: The Johns Hopkins University Press, 1977), 44-47, 59-64.

2. Davidson ("Parodos," 41) maintains that direct links or verbal echoes from an earlier poet to a later one, although possible, give a false impression of the complexity of poetic borrowing, but that sources such as battle scenes in the *Iliad* or Pindar's *Nemean* 9 are to be regarded as "representative of the types of poetic writing that directly or indirectly influenced the spirit and shape of the Sophoclean passage."

3. R. W. B. Burton (*The Chorus in Sophocles' Tragedies* [Oxford: Oxford University Press, 1980], 92) describes the anapests (127-133) and second strophe (134-137) as "a miniature of so much Greek choral lyric," to wit, a maxim illustrated by a myth.

4. For Capaneus, see Aeschylus *Seven Against Thebes* 423-434; Euripides *Suppliant Women* 496-499 and *Phoenician Women* 1172-1186; Apollodorus, *The Library* 3.6.7.

The elders have assumed their station in the orchestra when a man enters from the city. The actor wears a bearded mask and represents a man of obvious importance, which the splendor of his costume would reflect. He is attended by slaves, played by *doryphorêmata* ("spear carriers"), who betoken his stature and remain unrecognized until needed (Sophocles *Antigone* 491). The Coryphaeus identifies him as "the king of the land, Creon, son of Menoeceus" (βασιλεὺς χώρας, / Κρέων ὁ Μενοικέως 155-156). A word has evidently dropped out of line 156, perhaps one meaning "ruler," but the context makes clear that Creon is at once familiar and new to the audience. He is someone whose individual persona is unknown, but as one in power over Thebes, he embodies the stereotype of the Theban leaders in anti-Athens mythmaking who, by definition, mistreat corpses. The audience has heard how he has denied burial to the Argives and Polyneices with evils that befit the enemy (10). Polyneices, however, is a Theban and Creon's *philos*. Creon is not a foreigner to Polyneices and, more importantly, owes his corpse the obligations of kinship. Whereas the funeral orator casts the myth in polar terms of "us" and "them," Sophocles undermines the polarity by the sameness of blood kinship.

"The chorus is disposed toward [Creon] in the best and generous way" (ἄριστα καὶ μεγαλοφρόνως διεσκεύασται αὐτῷ ὁ Χορός), observes the Scholiast, capturing the elders' disposition. The Coryphaeus calls Creon a *basileus*, a word that usually denotes an hereditary monarch. Yet the son of Menoeceus does not belong to the dynasty of Theban kings that Oedipus enviously recounts (Sophocles *Oedipus Tyrannus* 267-268), nor is he a ruler of long-standing. The elders know this, but they choose to flatter him. Creon has summoned them for an extraordinary conference, counting on their loyalty to the house of Labdacus for support. They watch him approach; he obviously has something to say. It is a moment that many in Sophocles' original audience surely experienced often: a man steps out of the throng and moves forward in the assembly or law court to be heard. Josiah Ober imagines what Sophocles' audience may have been wondering:[5]

> he who thrust himself forward to the bema, abandoning his place in the mass had, by that act, declared an individuality that was potentially suspect. His motive in choosing to address the people might be self-interest, rather than a desire to further the interests of the state as a whole. The skilled and trained speaker who used his *isêgoria* [freedom of debate] to address the Assembly might mislead the people into voting against the good of the state by employing the power of rhetoric.

Athenians in the theater did not leave at the entrance their skills in listening to public speakers. On the contrary, the stage provided a "playful" opportunity to hone those abilities.[6] How, then, might Creon have struck them?

---

5. Ober, *Mass and Elite*, 296-297.
6. Ober, *Mass and Elite*, 153-155.

At first, Creon asserts that both Eteocles and Polyneices equally polluted themselves with kin murder, that he is related to both, indeed, that his claim to power depends upon kinship with both and upon the fact that both are dead (Sophocles *Antigone* 170-174). He draws no distinctions between them and so would seem to know what Athenians know—that they must both be buried. To this point, Creon might perhaps have struck the audience as a man of sense. He next declares his ruling principles:

ἐμοὶ γὰρ ὅστις πᾶσαν εὐθύνων πόλιν
μὴ τῶν ἀρίστων ἅπτεται βουλευμάτων,
ἀλλ᾽ ἐκ φόβου του γλῶσσαν ἐγκλῄσας ἔχει,
κάκιστος εἶναι νῦν τε καὶ πάλαι δοκεῖ·
καὶ μείζον᾽ ὅστις ἀντὶ τῆς αὑτοῦ πάτρας
φίλον νομίζει, τοῦτον οὐδαμοῦ λέγω.
ἐγὼ γάρ, ἴστω Ζεὺς ὁ πάνθ᾽ ὁρῶν ἀεί,
οὔτ᾽ ἂν σιωπήσαιμι τὴν ἄτην ὁρῶν
στείχουσαν ἀστοῖς ἀντὶ τῆς σωτηρίας,
οὔτ᾽ ἂν φίλον ποτ᾽ ἄνδρα δυσμενῆ χθονὸς
θείμην ἐμαυτῷ, τοῦτο γιγνώσκων ὅτι
ἥδ᾽ ἐστὶν ἡ σῴζουσα καὶ ταύτης ἔπι
πλέοντες ὀρθῆς τοὺς φίλους ποιούμεθα.

Sophocles Antigone 178-190

In my opinion, whoever, in guiding the whole city,
does not adhere to the best counsels, but
from fear of something keeps his tongue locked,
that man seems to me now and before this to be most evil.
Whoever deems a *philos* more important
than his fatherland, this man I say is nowhere.
I for one—may Zeus who always sees all know this—
never would I keep silent on seeing ruin
approaching the citizens instead of safety,
neither would I ever regard as my *philos*
an enemy of the land, since I am aware that
this land is the one who carries us safely and,
sailing on her upright, we make our *philoi*.

In 343 B.C., some hundred years after Sophocles' actor delivered these lines, Demosthenes quoted them during his prosecution of Aeschines for misconduct of the embassy to Macedonia (346 B.C.). The lines were a ready weapon against Aeschines because he played the role of Creon on stage. "None of these lines did Aeschines say to himself on the embassy . . . having bid farewells-a-many to wise Sophocles " (τούτων οὐδὲν Αἰσχίνης εἶπε πρὸς αὑτὸν ἐν τῇ πρεσβείᾳ . . . ἐρρῶσθαι πολλὰ φράσας τῷ σοφῷ Σοφοκλεῖ Demosthenes *On the Fraudulent Embassy* 248). Demosthenes expected his audience to approve of Creon's statements, and so probably did Sophocles a century before.[7] The image of the ship of state imparts to Creon a conservative political stance.[8] Who could gainsay his belief that the safety of all depends upon the salvation of the city? Nor would anyone dispute his contention that the fatherland must be preferred to a friend. Pericles alludes to the image of the upright city with a verbal form of Creon's adjective to bring Athenians together after suffering the plague and the second Peloponnesian invasion: "I consider that the whole city, when it is upright, helps individuals more than when it prospers in individuals' interests but is faltering on the whole" (ἐγὼ γὰρ ἡγοῦμαι πόλιν πλείω ξύμπασαν ὀρθουμένην ὠφελεῖν τοὺς ἰδιώτας ἢ καθ' ἕκαστον τῶν πολιτῶν εὐπραγοῦσαν, ἀθρόαν δὲ σφαλλομένην Thucydides 2.60.2).[9] So far, because he is generalizing, Creon appears in a favorable light and seems to be expressing principles that are without fault. His words, however, open the way for him to deny the status of *philos* to Polyneices.

From Antigone's account of Creon's treatment of Eteocles:

Ἐτεοκλέα μέν, ὡς λέγουσι, †σὺν δίκῃ
χρησθείς† δικαίᾳ καὶ νόμῳ, κατὰ χθονὸς
ἔκρυψε τοῖς ἔνερθεν ἔντιμον νεκροῖς.[10]

Sophocles *Antigone* 23-25

Eteocles, so they say, with just
use of justice and custom, [Creon] hid
beneath the earth, honored among the dead below,

it is clear that Creon could not have conducted a proper burial, since Eteocles' sisters, the women of his family, were not present. Her "so they say" (23) leaves no doubt that Antigone has learned about the burial from rumors in the city. Neither sister tended the body or mourned it. They were dispossessed by Creon of their rights and duties toward Eteocles. Without Eteocles' kinswomen present, "the just and customary" were not carried out, and Eteocles received a silent death. In this event, Creon did not hide the body to place it among the honored dead but to conceal it as when Sophocles' Ajax declares: "I will dig up the earth and hide my sword, most hateful of weapons, where no one will see it" (κρύψω τόδ' ἔγχος τοὐμόν, ἔχθιστον βελῶν, / γαίας ὀρύξας ἔνθα μή τις ὄψεται *Ajax* 658-659). During the night, Creon, without informing the women, slipped Eteocles' body into the ground. Even for the nephew he thinks worthy of burial, Theban Creon cannot

---

7. Sourvinou-Inwood, "Assumptions," 142.

8. Goheen, *Imagery*, 46-47.

9. Bernard M. W. Knox (Introduction to *Sophocles: The Three Theban Plays*, trans. Robert Fagles [New York: Viking Press, 1982], 37) observes of this well-known echoing of Thucydides' version of Pericles' funeral oration that "these phrases come from the common stock of democratic patriotic oratory."

10. The Greek σὺν δίκῃ / χρησθείς is uncertain.

perform the ritual properly, nor could Sophocles, working in anti-Athens mythmaking, have him do otherwise.

The elders arrive, believing they were summoned to discuss a "stratagem" (μῆτιν Sophocles *Antigone* 158) that Creon has been plying like an oarsman. Creon announces that he welcomes advice but, instead of listening, he dominates speech, and they listen to his decree (192) and are told to observe his orders (215).[11] Before Athenians of the audience, a people accustomed to being praised for its collective wisdom and laws that provide for the common prosperity, Creon expends no effort to avoid the appearance of "knowing it all." Demosthenes avers that he would not have come before the Athenians if they were in agreement about a policy, even one he thought wrongheaded, since "I would have considered myself, being one person, less likely to perceive the best measures than all of you" (μᾶλλον γὰρ ἂν ἡγησάμην ἕν' ὄντ' ἐμαυτὸν ἀγνοεῖν τὰ κράτιστ' ἢ πάντας ὑμᾶς *Exordium* 44). In *Suppliant Women*, Euripides exaggerates the commonplace in having Theseus require the whole city to make the decision to retrieve the bodies of the Seven for burial (349). Henry J. Walker explains: "Theseus may be a strong leader like Pericles, but his confidence that the Athenians will heed his advice is based on the justice of his request and not on any power he holds over them."[12] "Athens," Theseus informs the Theban herald, "is not ruled by one man but is a free *polis*" (οὐ γὰρ ἄρχεται / ἑνὸς πρὸς ἀνδρός, ἀλλ' ἐλευθέρα πόλις 404-405). Creon runs amok when his behavior belies his principles, while his treatment of his nephews undercuts his claim to nearness of kin. A pattern is established. Creon knows what is right but does not follow his knowledge with right actions:

καὶ νῦν ἀδελφὰ τῶνδε κηρύξας ἔχω
ἀστοῖσι παίδων τῶν ἀπ' Οἰδίπου πέρι·
Ἐτεοκλέα μέν, ὅς πόλεως ὑπερμαχῶν
ὄλωλε τῆσδε, πάντ' ἀριστεύσας δορί,
τάφῳ τε κρύψαι καὶ τὰ πάντ' ἐφαγνίσαι
ἃ τοῖς ἀρίστοις ἔρχεται κάτω νεκροῖς·
τὸν δ' αὖ ξύναιμον τοῦδε, Πολυνείκη λέγω,
ὅς γῆν πατρῴαν καὶ θεοὺς τοὺς ἐγγενεῖς
φυγὰς κατελθὼν ἠθέλησε μὲν πυρὶ
πρῆσαι κατ' ἄκρας, ἠθέλησε δ' αἵματος
κοινοῦ πάσασθαι, τοὺς δὲ δουλώσας ἄγειν,
τοῦτον πόλει τῇδ' ἐκκεκήρυκται τάφῳ
μήτε κτερίζειν μήτε κωκῦσαί τινα,

---

11. Jebb (*Antigone*, 39-40) observes that λέσχην (*leskhēn* Sophocles *Antigone* 161), which he translates as "conference," is "not the meeting, but the discussion which is to take place there."

12. Henry J. Walker, *Theseus and Athens* (New York and Oxford: Oxford University Press, 1995), 154.

ἐᾶν δ' ἄθαπτον καὶ πρὸς οἰωνῶν δέμας
καὶ πρὸς κυνῶν ἐδεστὸν αἰκισθέν τ' ἰδεῖν.
τοιόνδ' ἐμὸν φρόνημα.

Sophocles *Antigone* 192-207

And now I have issued proclamations, brothers to these laws
for the citizens concerning the children of Oedipus.
Eteocles, who perished fighting for this city,
fully proving his bravery in the spear battle,
let them conceal him with a tomb and perform all the rites
that go to the bravest dead below.
The kindred blood of this man, Polyneices I mean,
the exile who, on returning home, wanted to burn his fatherland
and the temples of his family's gods from top to bottom
with flames, and wanted to taste common blood, and lead
the rest into slavery, this person, it has been proclaimed to the city,
that no one honor with a tomb or lament with cries,
but let him lie unburied, his body devoured by birds
and by dogs and mangled for the seeing.
Such is my thought.

The adjective ἀδελφά (*adelpha*), a common figure in expressing a close relationship, evokes not only the consanguinity of Eteocles and Polyneices but also Creon's relationship to them. He once saw them as the same in being polluted murderers and dead kinsmen. *Adelpha* seems to imply that his metaphorical brothers (decrees) are not going to differentiate either. Instead, his decrees erect differences between his nephews that repudiate his professed knowledge. Creon regards Eteocles a patriot because he died inside the city in its defense and Polyneices a traitor for attacking it from without. But the brothers are *ekhthroi philoi*, an oxymoron that can no more be split into two separate entities than the oxymoron, sophomoric. The latter does not mean now wise, now foolish but denotes a synergetic third, the quality of being simultaneously wise/foolish. Eteocles/Polyneices cannot be distinguished, for they are simultaneously *philoi* and *ekhthroi* (enemies). They comprise a coupling or unity created by one person in two bodies. Eteocles no less than Polyneices brought the ruin of the Argive army upon the citizens of Thebes.[13] By differentiating between them, Creon is blinded to the more compelling reality of their sameness as corpses.

---

13. That both Eteocles and Polyneices endanger the city in their lust for power and wealth, unsaid in the *Antigone*, is expressed in Euripides' *Phoenician Women*. Polyneices is willing to remove the army from Thebes "once I have received what is mine" (τἀμαυτοῦ λαβὼν 484). Eteocles counters with the same lust for power: "I would go to where the sun rises among stars and below the earth, could I do that, so as to hold the greatest of gods, Absolute Rule" (ἄστρων ἂν ἔλθοιμ' ἡλίου πρὸς ἀντολὰς / καὶ γῆς ἔνερθεν, δυνατὸς ὢν δρᾶσαι τάδε, / τὴν θεῶν μεγίστην ὥστε ἔχειν Τυραννίδα 504-506). Each, bent on his own course, forges his own way to the same end: rule and wealth. Jocasta foresees another but still identical end to both her sons'

Funeral orators regularly lauded Athenians for their intelligence.[14] Demosthenes declares, for example, that "Intelligence is the beginning of all bravery" (ἔστιν ἀπάσης ἀρετῆς ἀρχὴ . . . σύνεσις Demosthenes *Funeral Oration* 17). In terms of the Theban myth, intelligence is displayed by the recognition that the dead are dead and that not to bury them is an outrage against gods and men. Theseus delivers a lecture along these lines to the herald of the Euripidean Creon that easily reduces the latter's denial of burial to an absurdity (*Suppliant Women* 543-548), and the Antigone of Euripides' *Phoenician Women* realizes the senselessness (*aphrona*) of Eteocles' orders to expose Polyneices and calls Creon "foolish" (*môros*) for obeying (1645-1649). Sophocles' Creon asserts the presence of differences between his living nephews but fails to acknowledge the absence of differences between his dead nephews.

Scholars have been of two minds about Creon, some accepting him as a democrat and devoted leader with good intentions, and others seeing in him the tyrant made or in the making.[15] The former emphasize his guiding principles; the latter, his behavior. For Sophocles' original audience, however, there could be no doubt. Creon is the stereotypical Theban leader. His exposure of Polyneices and the others is the action of the Theban leaders in the myth of the Theban Dead. Creon's lack of intelligence toward the dead follows from his being a Theban in anti-Athens mythmaking.

---

purposes—the destruction of Thebes (559-565, 568-572). The victory or defeat of one entails the same loss of a ruler for the city and of a son for the household.

14. The topos is found in all the extant funeral orations: "Stopping the senselessness of brawn by the intelligence of their judgment . . ." (τῷ φρονίμῳ τῆς γνώμης παύοντες τὸ ἄφρον τῆς ῥώμης . . . Gorgias fragment B, 6 [Diels-Kranz]); "Who of the other Greeks could have rivaled them in judgment?" (τίνες ἂν τούτοις τῶν ἄλλων Ἑλλήνων ἤρισαν γνώμῃ; Lysias *Funeral Oration* 42); "The strongest in courage would be rightly judged to be those who know dread and joy very clearly and do not, for that reason, turn away from danger" (κράτιστοι δ' ἂν τὴν ψυχὴν δικαίως κριθεῖεν οἱ τά τε δεινὰ καὶ ἡδέα σαφέστατα γιγνώσκοντες καὶ διὰ ταῦτα μὴ ἀποτρεπόμενοι ἐκ τῶν κινδύνων Thucydides 2.40.3); "One standard prevails: the man reputed to be wise or brave has the power of office" (εἷς ὅρος, ὁ δόξας σοφὸς ἢ ἀγαθὸς εἶναι κρατεῖ καὶ ἄρχει Plato *Menexenos* 238 D); "This man so far rose above them in manliness and wisdom" (ὧν οὗτος τοσοῦτον ὑπερέσχεν ἀνδρείᾳ καὶ φρονήσει Hyperides *Funeral Oration* 38).

15. For Creon as tyrant, see Cecil Bowra, *Sophoclean Tragedy* (Oxford: The Clarendon Press, 1944), 72-78; Müller, *Sophokles: Antigone,* 19; Cedric Whitman, *Sophocles: A Study of Heroic Humanism* (Cambridge: Harvard University Press, 1951), 90; Ehrenburg, *Sophocles and Pericles* (Oxford: Basil Blackwell, 1954), 55-58; Anthony J. Podlecki, "Creon and Herodotus," *Transactions and Proceedings of the American Philological Association* 97 (1966), 359-364 who contends that "the poet captures his character in the very act of *becoming* a tyrant" (359); Vickers, *Towards Greek Tragedy*, 529-530; R. P. Willington-Ingram, *Sophocles: An Interpretation* (Cambridge: Cambridge University Press, 1980), 122-127. For a defense of Creon, see Calder, "Sophokles' Political Tragedy, *Antigone*," 391-404; Jordan, *Servants of the Gods*, 85-91, who regards Creon as "a patriot in the best sense of the word" (87).

What extends beyond the stereotype is Creon's treatment of his *philoi*. Early on, he claims the royal house and throne on the basis of kinship (Sophocles *Antigone* 174) and allows that both Eteocles and Polyneices are dead kinsmen. He shows all signs of knowing what is customary, but he fails in his obligation to bury the corpses of both nephews. It soon is known that he considers himself engaged in a contest against those in the city who, he believes, have "long" (289) refused "to love and submit to me " (στέργειν ἐμέ 292). He sets watchers over the body to flush them out. The contest he seeks is the "zero-sum game" that preoccupied most men of the audience and permitted only one winner, leaving everyone else a loser.[16] But Creon stubbornly pursues victory in a contest waged within the family that cannot be won, since, by defeating *philoi*, he injures *philoi*.

Creon proclaims among his principles an apparent readiness to seize "the best counsels," yet his openness to advice is qualified by the word "best." Since, as becomes increasingly clear, the "best" advice is always and uniquely his own, he effectively discharges himself from responsibility for listening to and heeding any other. In his estimation, he is ruler, thinker, and the one to be watched. Others are watchers. Thus, he sets watchers over Polyneices' corpse to see to his orders, he tells the elders to be "watchers of his orders" (σκοποί . . . τῶν εἰρημένων Sophocles *Antigone* 215), and he audaciously calls upon Zeus, "who always sees all" (ὁ πάνθ᾽ ὁρῶν ἀεί 184) to watch and learn from him. As it turns out, his watchers do more than watch as one of them comes to inform him of what they have seen. In this encounter, Sophocles reenacts an interchange for evaluating a course of action familiar from epic, the repository of panhellenic values and beliefs, and from the daily life of democratic Athens.

A prominent lesson to be drawn from the *Iliad* is that it is good sense to accept advice. The disasters that overtake Agamemnon and Achilles and send many ghosts hurling to Hades ensue after Agamemnon spurns the counsel of all the Achaeans to respect Apollo's priest and take the ransom (Homer *Iliad* 1.22-23). At the same time, the poem does not hide the fact that extending advice, especially to someone more powerful, can be dangerous. Calchas speaks to Agamemnon only after he has gained assurances from Achilles. In the *Iliad*, Nestor most notably offers advice and even Achilles counsels Priam, but Poulydamas seems to exist solely to advise Hector in the fighting at the Greek ditch.[17] Their exchanges illustrate the dynamics

---

16. For the contest system, see Alvin W. Gouldner, *Enter Plato: Classical Greece and the Origins of Social Theory* (New York: Basic Books, 1965), 49-55. Iamblichus comments: "It is not agreeable for men to honor someone else (for they consider that they are being deprived of something), but taken in hand by necessity itself and impelled little by little over a long period of time, they become praisers, although unwilling ones" (οὐ γὰρ ἡδὺ τοῖς ἀνθρώποις ἄλλον τινὰ τιμᾶν (αὐτοὶ γὰρ στερίσκεσθαί τινος ἡγοῦνται), χειρωθέντες δὲ ὑπὸ τῆς ἀνάγκης αὐτῆς καὶ κατὰ σμικρὸν ἐκ πολλοῦ ἐπαχθέντες ἐπαινέται [*sic*] καὶ ἄκοντες ὅμως γίγνονται Diels-Kranz fragment 89.2.3).

17. James Redfield, *Nature and Culture in the "Iliad": The Tragedy of Hector* (Chicago and London: The University of Chicago, 1975), 143.

of the adviser scene. Hector has fixed his mind upon a purpose, triumph over the Greeks with Zeus's favor. He accepts Poulydamas' advice when it serves his objective (*Iliad* 12.75-80, 13.740-748). Otherwise, he rejects it and charges Poulydamas with cowardice (12.215-250). The advisee is intent on a worthy action, and to him, his adviser's talk of caution or retreat appears adverse and cowardly. The adviser offers no plan of his own, and his counsel is not infallible.[18] Retreat from the Greek ships will not secure the victory that Hector's attack could bring. Inherent in action, however, is failure, and failure has the effect of turning negative advice into prescience and prophecy. Hector's error in discarding Poulydamas' interpretation of the bird omen (12.211-229) keeps him from seeking the safety of the city walls, an error he later regrets: "Poulydamas will be the first to lay censure on me . . . I would not obey him, but that would have been by far better" (Πουλυδάμας μοι πρῶτος ἐλεγχείην ἀναθήσει . . . ἀλλ' ἐγὼ οὐ πιθόμην· ἦ τ' ἂν πολὺ κέρδιον ἦεν 22.100,103).

A doer undertakes an action; an adviser comes forth to counsel him. There follows an exchange through which the doer's reasons and the worth of his action are evaluated in narrative form. This same dynamic informs the "pattern of advice" Henry R. Immerwahr discovers in Herodotus: "gnomic sayings embodying a view of the world, a general warning often of a negative kind ('don't act rashly,' or the like), and specific advice dealing with a practical problem and usually embodying a positive plan."[19] Elements of the pattern appear in combination throughout the *Histories* but in their entirety only in Artabanus' advice to Xerxes at the Hellespont. Artabanus calls attention to the shortness of human life (Herodotus 7.46.3), warns Xerxes about the dangers posed by land and sea (7.49), and admonishes him not to take the Ionians into Greece (7.50). The gnome hints that Xerxes will lose his armament, and the advice indicates how it will happen. Xerxes dismisses Artabanus' caution: "If you wish to ponder every detail equally in a matter coming before us, you would never do anything at all" (εἰ γὰρ δὴ βούλοιο ἐπὶ τῷ αἰεὶ ἐπεσφερομένῳ πρήγματι τὸ πᾶν ὁμοίως ἐπιλέγεσθαι, ποιήσειας ἂν οὐδαμὰ οὐδέν 7.50.1). The dynamics of advice—initiative/caution, action/deliberation, and folly/futility—favor the doer who, nonetheless, cannot escape the consequences of his actions.

Through its ideology of *ho boulomenos*, the *dêmos* defined its *politeia* (form of government) as one permitting even the lowliest citizen to proffer counsel:

ἐπειδὰν δέ τι περὶ τῶν τῆς πόλεως διοικήσεως δέῃ βουλεύσασθαι, συμβουλεύει αὐτοῖς ἀνιστάμενος περὶ τούτων ὁμοίως μὲν τέκτων,

---

18. Redfield, *Nature and Culture*, 146.

19. Henry R. Immerwahr, *Form and Thought in Herodotus* (Cleveland: Press of Western Reserve University, 1966), 74. See also Richmond Lattimore, "The Wise Adviser in Herodotus," *Classical Philology* 34 (1939), 24-35; Mabel Lang, *Herodotean Narrative and Discourse* (Cambridge, MA, and London: Harvard University Press for Oberlin College, 1984), 34-35.

ὁμοίως δὲ χαλκεὺς σκυτοτόμος, ἔμπορος ναύκληρος, πλούσιος πένης, γενναῖος ἀγεννής.

Plato *Protagoras* 319 C-D

Whenever it behooves them to make resolutions concerning the management of the city, standing up before them, the carpenter equally advises concerning the issue as well as the bronze smith and shoemaker, sea merchant and captain, rich and poor, well and base born.

At its most fundamental, the democracy functioned through giving and accepting or rejecting advice. In reality, because of the dangers in proposing policy on controversial issues, only a few citizens, distinguished as *rhêtores* (speakers/ politicians), approached the bema. The majority listened to their advice and expressed its opinion in both the assembly and law courts by voting. Blame and wrath directed at *rhêtores* preserved the *dêmos'* ideology and the illusion of its wisdom. After news of the Sicilian debacle was received at Athens, for instance, Thucydides tersely comments: "they were angry at those of the politicians who promoted the expedition as if they themselves had not voted" (χαλεποὶ . . . ἦσαν τοῖς ξυμπροθυμηθεῖσι τῶν ῥητόρων τὸν ἔκπλουν, ὥσπερ οὐκ αὐτοὶ ψηφισάμενοι 8.1.1).

Athenians of anti-Athens mythmaking welcome advice:

καὶ οἱ αὐτοὶ ἤτοι κρίνομέν γε ἢ ἐνθυμούμεθα ὀρθῶς τὰ πράγματα, οὐ τοὺς λόγους τοῖς ἔργοις βλάβην ἡγούμενοι, ἀλλὰ μὴ προδιδαχθῆναι μᾶλλον λόγῳ πρότερον ἢ ἐπὶ ἃ δεῖ ἔργῳ ἐλθεῖν. διαφερόντως γὰρ δὴ καὶ τόδε ἔχομεν ὥστε τολμᾶν τε οἱ αὐτοὶ μάλιστα καὶ περὶ ὧν ἐπιχειρήσομεν ἐκλογίζεσθαι.

Thucydides 2.40.2-3

We ourselves judge or deliberate affairs properly, believing that speeches are not a harm to action but, rather, not being instructed by words before entering upon what must be done by action is harmful. In this respect, we are also different [from the others] so that the same people [we Athenians] are especially daring and especially reflective about what we will attempt.

Theseus accepts the advice of his mother, Aethra, despite the social norms that hold "it useless for women to speak for the common good" (ἀχρεῖον τὰς γυναῖκας εὖ λέγειν Euripides *Suppliant Women* 299). "I, too, see these things which you are advising me," he concedes (ὁρῶ δὲ κἀγὼ ταῦθ' ἅπερ με νουθετεῖς 337). Oedipus disdains the advice of a prophet on Theban soil (Sophocles *Oedipus Tyrannus* 429-430), but on Attic soil, he adopts his daughter Antigone's counsel: "Child, you win me over in this, a grievous pleasure" (τέκνον, βαρεῖαν ἡδονὴν νικᾶτέ με Sophocles *Oedipus at Colonus* 1204). When Theban Creon invites others to observe his "spirit, thinking, and judgments" (ψυχήν τε καὶ φρόνημα καὶ γνώμην *Antigone*

176), he unintentionally opens himself to receiving advice, lest they believe that he is not adhering to "the best counsels." However, set on his own course like Hector, he rebukes his advisers and brings ruin upon himself.

A man enters from the direction of the country. He stops often and turns around, only to resume his movement toward Creon's house. Before he speaks, his halting steps announce his reluctance to arrive (223-226). Modern stage directions usually designate him a guard; the manuscripts have him a messenger. He proves to be one of Creon's watchmen who unwittingly brings advice from the gods in the form of events he has watched. His report is certain to displease his lord. Condemned by lot to bear it, he endeavors to defend himself:

> τὸ γὰρ
> πρᾶγμ' οὔτ' ἔδρασ' οὔτ' εἶδον ὅστις ἦν ὁ δρῶν,
> οὐδ' ἂν δικαίως ἐς κακὸν πέσοιμί τι.

Sophocles Antigone 238-240

The deed
I neither did, nor did I see who was the doer.
I would not justly fall into some evil.

His gait and his words manifest fear over what he will suffer from Creon as well as perplexity over what he has seen.[20] The Watchman is the ordinary man reacting to "dreadful things" that cause "much hesitation" (τὰ δεινὰ . . . ὄκνον πολὺν *Antigone* 243). The prophet Poulydamas, "who knows clearly in his mind omens, and [whom] the people obeyed " (ὃς σάφα θυμῷ / εἰδείη τεράων καί οἱ πειθοίατο λαοί Homer *Iliad* 12.228-229) foresees the death of Trojans at the ships in the eagle's loss of its prey (215-227). But the Watchman is not Poulydamas. He does not understand what he reports and is terrified of the ruler to whom he must report it. A man with something to say to the city, who does not lock his tongue from fear, the Watchman is Creon's ideal citizen (*Antigone* 180). Pressed by Creon's direct order, he blurts out:

> καὶ δὴ λέγω σοι. τὸν νεκρόν τις ἀρτίως
> θάψας βέβηκε κἀπὶ χρωτὶ διψίαν
> κόνιν παλύνας κἀφαγιστεύσας ἃ χρή.

Sophocles Antigone 245-247

---

20. The Watchman has been viewed diversely by commentators. G. M. Kirkwood in *A Study of Sophoclean Drama* (Ithaca, NY: Cornell University Press, 1958), 123 sees him as "a solemn fool"; Albin Lesky, *Greek Tragedy*, translated H. A. Frankfort (New York: Barnes and Noble; London: Ernst Benn, 1965), 104, as a "sly, garrulous old man of low birth and mean intelligence"; Joseph S. Margon, "The First Burial of Polyneices," *The Classical Journal* 64 (1969), 293, as sly and humorous; Martha C. Nussbaum, *The Fragility of Goodness: Luck and Ethics in Greek Tragedy* (Cambridge: Cambridge University Press, 1986), 53, as "basely cowardly, crudely egoistic."

Well then, I am telling you. The corpse—someone just now
has performed funeral rites for it and is gone, having scattered
thirsty dust upon its flesh and completed the necessary purifications.

Burial has been completed, he says, and the appropriate rites performed. Some in
Sophocles' audience might reasonably have assumed Antigone had succeeded in
her plan. But as they learned more about the Watchman, they might think back on
this scene, having realized that he tends to change his mind after reflection.[21] He
leaves, vowing never to return to Creon's presence (Sophocles *Antigone* 329), but
he comes back shortly with the explanation: "for mortals nothing is forsworn.
Afterthought belies judgment" (βροτοῖσιν οὐδέν ἐστ' ἀπώμοτον. / ψεύδει γὰρ
ἡ 'πίνοια τὴν γνώμην 388-389). The aphorisms are Sophocles' clues for assessing
how the Watchman conveys information. The audience should not stop on what he
first says but listen to everything. Reacting to his initial pronouncement, Creon
asks: "What are you saying? What man dared do this?" (τί φής; τίς ἀνδρῶν ἦν ὁ
τολμήσας τάδε; 248). His second question the Watchman answers tersely: οὐκ
οἶδ' (I don't know). To the first, he responds with further details that muddy the
certainty he has just expressed:

>   ἐκεῖ γὰρ οὔτε του γενῆδος ἦν
>   πλῆγμ', οὐ δικέλλης ἐκβολή· στύφλος δὲ γῆ
>   καὶ χέρσος, ἀρρὼξ οὐδ' ἐπημαξευμένη
>   τροχοῖσιν, ἀλλ' ἄσημος οὑργάτης τις ἦν.
>   ὅπως δ' ὁ πρῶτος ἡμὶν ἡμεροσκόπος
>   δείκνυσι, πᾶσι θαῦμα δυσχερὲς παρῆν.
>   ὁ μὲν γὰρ ἠφάνιστο, τυμβήρης μὲν οὔ,
>   λεπτὴ δ' ἄγος φεύγοντος ὡς ἐπῆν κόνις.
>   σημεῖα δ' οὔτε θηρὸς οὔτε του κυνῶν
>   ἐλθόντος, οὐ σπάσαντος ἐξεφαίνετο.

Sophocles *Antigone* 249-258

There was no blow of any pickax.
No dirt was dug up by a hoe. The ground
was hard and dry, undisturbed and unscored
by wagon wheels. The doer left no marks.
When the first watchman of the day showed us,
a wonder hard to grasp came over all.
You see, he had disappeared. He was not covered with a tomb,
but a light dust was upon him as if from someone

---

21. Those in Sophocles' theater of the mind also undergo this process or something close to
it. Such spectators see and hear the play as a synchronic whole that can be reviewed any number
of times. Sophocles' original audience received his play diachronically, with reflection depending
on memory of first impressions.

avoiding pollution. No marks appeared
of beast or dog that had come and torn him.

The Watchman's description excludes animal interference, as the body is untouched by scavengers, and denies human activities customarily carried out at a grave. The ground is unbroken by digging tools, unmoistened by liquid offerings and tears, and unscored by the tracks of a wagon.[22] No tomb has been constructed, but the body has been covered with dust—"as if from someone avoiding pollution." The Watchman is aware that an exposed corpse causes pollution and interprets what he saw in those terms. Nothing now indicates to him that someone has performed burial rites; to the contrary, he suggests that the dust was thrown in awe of custom.[23] Action gives way to description, sureness to supposition. The Watchman filters what he has seen through the common knowledge of the ordinary man when he warns Creon there is danger of pollution in the land. Implicit in that warning is advice from the gods. Furthermore, with the sounds of his language, Sophocles hints at what should be done. Creon distinguished Eteocles from his brother by extending all rites (*ta pant' ephagnisai* 196) to Eteocles for proving to be bravest in all ways (*pant' aristeusas* 195). The Watchman's word *k'aphagisteusas* (*Antigone* 247) combines the sounds *aphagnis-* or *ephagnis-* and *-isteusas* heard in Creon's justification of burial for Eteocles.[24] By having the Watchman utter the word *k'aphagisteusas* for what has been done for Polyneices, Sophocles has him unknowingly intimate that Creon should grant to Polyneices what he has granted to his brother.

The events at Polyneices' body are mysterious, and Sophocles surely meant for his audience to ponder what happens there. Much controversy has arisen regarding the dust, because its presence defines what Antigone does or does not do and opposes Creon's exposure of a corpse with an action that may have been carried out by the heroic Antigone or by the gods themselves. The interpretations of modern audiences have been for the most part developed in response to Richard

---

22. The Myrmidons weep for Patroclus until the sands become wet (Homer *Iliad* 23.15).

23. The Scholiast on *Antigone* 255 refers the Watchman's inference that the dust was placed upon the body by "someone avoiding pollution" to a curse imposed by the Athenian culture hero Bouzygos on "those who neglect an unburied body τοῖς περιορῶσιν ἄταφον σῶμα." See also Aelian (*Miscellaneous Stories* 5.14) who records "an Attic law" requiring that earth be thrown upon an unburied corpse (ἐπιβάλλειν αὐτῷ γῆν). The spreading of dust resembles a burial rite but does not achieve a burial. Creon's minions bury Polyneices' remains (Sophocles *Antigone* 1197-1203).

24. Linforth ("Antigone and Creon," 194) points out that *k'aphagisteusai* (*Antigone* 247) "echoes in meaning the word used by Creon for the full ceremonies he has ordained for Eteocles." Linforth (194 n.15) accepts ἀφαγνίσαι, the reading of most manuscripts for Creon's word in 196; ἐφαγνίσαι is preferred by Jebb, *Antigone*, 46 and H. Lloyd-Jones and N. G. Wilson, *Sophoclis Fabulae* (Oxford: Oxford University Press, 1990), 191. Since Sophocles blends *k'aphagisteusai* with *kai* (and), it is not certain whether its first syllable is an alpha or epsilon.

Jebb's suggestion of a "symbolical rite" conducted by Antigone.[25] Symbolic burial, however, as J. E. G. Whitehorne contends, cannot be substantiated since spreading dust to avoid pollution is an actual, not a symbolic, act and, in any case, does not effect a burial which requires a series of rituals celebrated over a period of days and weeks.[26] A second, less popular view holds that a god or gods spread the dust *in a burial*.[27] First proposed by S. M. Adams, it is unsatisfactory because Olympian gods would not bury a body themselves, since they eschew death and its miasma. Apollo, for instance, leaves Admetus' "most beloved chamber of this roof in order that no pollution befall me in the house (μὴ μίασμά μ' ἐν δόμοις κίχῃ, / λείπω μελάθρων τῶνδε φιλτάτην στέγην Euripides *Alcestis* 22-23). But the gods do intervene, particularly in Homer's *Iliad*, to protect exposed corpses until they can be buried by humans. Sophocles' actual audience was familiar with these episodes and could respond to the similarities and differences between them and the play they were watching.[28] As the *Antigone* unfolded, they might have tried to normalize Sophocles' dust as a new version of a commonplace derived from epic. Their knowledge of epic would compel them to respond to the play's intertextual links with it. Indeed, such are the ties between these genres that Tecmessa's plea to Ajax

---

25. Jebb's comment and question (*Antigone*, 86): "The essence of the symbolical rite was the sprinkling of dust. She had done that (245). Was it not, then, done once for all?" inspired a vigorous effort to explain why Antigone returned to Polyneices' corpse when she had given it a "symbolical burial." See above, Introduction, note 54, for scholars who have addressed this question.

26. J. E. G. Whitehorne ("The Background to Polyneices' Disinterment and Reburial," *Greece and Rome* 30 [1983], 129) maintains that "this distinction between a symbolic and a real burial is a modern illusion."

27. See Adams, "Antigone," 51-54, and *Sophocles the Playwright*, 47-50; Kirkwood, *A Study of Sophoclean Drama*, 70-72; McCall, "Divine and Human Action," 109-112; Jordan, *Servants of the Gods*, 91-92; Winnington-Ingram, *Sophocles: An Interpretation*, 125 n. 31; Segal, *Tragedy and Civilization*, 159-160 with note 25; Richard M. Minadeo, "Characterization and Theme in the *Antigone*," *Arethusa* 18 (1985), 143.

28. Homer's *Iliad* and perhaps his *Odyssey* had been performed at the Greater Panathenaia by rhapsodes since the time of Hipparchus, the tyrant Pisistratus' younger son. Hipparchus, who was slain in 514 B.C., is said to have "first brought the epics of Homer to this land" (τὰ 'Ομήρου ἔπη πρῶτος ἐκόμισεν εἰς τὴν γῆν ταυτηνί Plato *Hipparchus* 228 в). In 332 B.C., the politician Lykourgus can claim before a jury of Athenians that their fathers required that only Homer's epics be performed by the rhapsodes (*Against Leocrates* 102). This so-called rule (*nomos*) even if not a legislated rule, could have been easily contradicted if Homer's poems were not exclusively recited. The Athenians must have not only known the incidents of the story, especially such important ones as those of *Iliad* 24, but perhaps were even able to notice deviations from the "text" used as the standard. For the rhapsodes at the Panathenaia, see Shapiro, *Iconography*, 72-75. Scenes from the *Iliad* on black figure (after 530 B.C.) and red figure (in the first quarter of the fifth century) vases, scenes from the Trojan War on the Stoa Poikile and the Parthenon rising above the theater as *Antigone* was being performed, as well as references in Herodotus and Thucydides, and verbal and metrical allusions to Homer in comedy assure that Athenians were aware of the scenes in question.

in Sophocles' *Ajax* (485-524), produced shortly before *Antigone*, cannot be fully understood without reference to that of Andromache in *Iliad* 6.[29] More particularly, as Richard Garner demostrates, the fourth stasimon of *Antigone* interacts with Dione's consolation of Aphrodite in *Iliad* 5 (382-415).[30] By interpreting the dust through Homer's myth of the exposed corpse, a modern audience gains a context and critical tool for understanding what happens at Polyneices' corpse. Instead of the questions "When and how did Antigone spread the dust unseen?"[31] Sophocles may be provoking the inference that, once animals and humans have been ruled out, the gods, the remaining agent in the universe, have intervened.

Homer's myth unfolds in three acts: protection of an unburied body, the gods' anger over its prolonged exposure, the gods' appeal to humans to bury it. Act one begins with the slaying of Sarpedon and the gods' rescue of his body (Homer *Iliad* 16.667-675).[32] Homer interrupts the fighting and shifts the scene from Troy to Olympus where the squabbling Hera and Zeus nevertheless concur on burial as "the honorary portion of the dead" (τὸ . . . γέρας . . . θανόντων 16.457). The scenes on Olympus, while marking the importance of Sarpedon, confer the sanction of the gods, preeminently Zeus, upon the act of burial. The gods remove Sarpedon's body from the fighting and convey it to his kinsmen who bury him with a tomb and gravestone. "For that," repeats Zeus, "is the honorary portion of the dead" (τὸ γὰρ γέρας ἐστὶ θανόντων 16.675).

The treatment of Sarpedon's corpse by gods and men provides a foil for their treatment of the bodies of Patroclus and Hector. When, out of love for Patroclus and fury toward Hector, Achilles denies their bodies burial rites, the gods intervene. At Achilles' request, Thetis forestalls the effects of the flies upon Patroclus' corpse (Homer *Iliad* 19.29-39). Aphrodite keeps the dogs from Hector's body and, with ambrosial oil, prevents it from being mangled by Achilles (23.184-187). Apollo checks the withering power of the sun by casting a dark cloud over Hector's body and, later, a golden aegis (23.188-191, 24.18-21). When Priam asks about his son: "Did Achilles chop him into pieces and set him forth for the dogs?" (ἦέ μιν ἤδη / ᾗσι κυσὶν μελεϊστὶ ταμὼν προύθηκεν Ἀχιλλεύς; 24.408-409), Hermes describes what the gods have done for Hector.

> θηοῖό κεν αὐτὸς ἐπελθὼν
> οἷον ἐερσήεις κεῖται, περὶ δ' αἷμα νένιπται,

---

29. See W. B. Stanford, *Sophocles: "Ajax,"* (London: Macmillan, 1963), 122-125.

30. Garner, *From Homer to Tragedy*, 85-89.

31. These questions have taxed proponents of Antigone's involvement in a "first burial." See, for example, Bradshaw, "Watchman Scenes," 202-204.

32. The myth of the exposed corpse belongs to the wider theme of the mutilation of the corpse, for which, see Charles Segal, *The Theme of the Mutilation of the Corpse in the "Iliad"* (Leiden: E. J. Brill, 1971). The gods are, in part, the conveyors of the "repugnance and even some measure of moral outrage" that Segal (13) finds in Homer's attitude toward the exposure and mutilation of a corpse.

οὐδέ ποθι μιαρός· σὺν δ᾽ ἕλκεα πάντα μέμυκεν,
ὅσσ᾽ ἐτύπη· πολέες γὰρ ἐν αὐτῷ χαλκὸν ἔλασσαν.
ὡς τοι κήδονται μάκαρες θεοὶ υἷος ἑῆος
καὶ νέκυός περ ἐόντος, ἐπεί σφι φίλος περὶ κῆρι.

Homer Iliad 24.418-423

Going there, you could see for yourself
how he lies fresh as dew. The blood is washed away,
and nowhere is he defiled. All his wounds are closed
every one he was struck, for many drove bronze into him.
In this way do the blessed gods care for your son,
though a corpse, since he is *philos* to them in their hearts.

Priam later observes of Hector: "You were *philos* to the gods when alive, and they care for you even in the lot of death" (ἦ μέν μοι ζωός περ ἐὼν φίλος ἦσθα θεοῖσιν / οἱ δ᾽ ἄρα σεῦ κήδοντο καὶ ἐν θανάτοιό περ αἴσῃ *Iliad* 24.749). The gods do not bury bodies; this is the task of mortals consigned to death. Rather, as Jean-Pierre Vernant points out, "the gods perform the human rituals of cleansing and beautification but use divine unguents: these elixirs of immortality preserve 'intact,' despite all the abuse, that youth and beauty, which can only fade on the body of a living man, but which death in battle fixes forever on the hero's form."[33] The gods care for a corpse deprived of its due, protecting it from the ravages of its mortal frailty and from its enemies who would deprive it of its "beautiful death."[34] In the first act of Homer's myth, the gods protect the corpse by creating a liminal zone where sacred and profane overlap, and the limitations of the latter are suspended by the powers of the former.

In accord with the first act of the Homeric model, the dust over Polyneices' corpse is spread by a god or gods to safeguard it from its mortality.[35] The night is the time for "supernatural and miraculous" events.[36] The watchmen see nothing. "Everything could be possible," Sophocles has Ajax say, "when a god is devising" (γένοιτο μέντἂν πᾶν θεοῦ τεχνωμένου *Ajax* 86). When the first watcher of the day comes on duty, he notices that the body cannot be seen for the dust. The watchmen are dumbfounded, genuinely ignorant of what has happened, and left

---

33. Jean-Pierre Vernant, *Mortals and Immortals: Collected Essays*, ed. Froma I. Zeitlin (Princeton, NJ: Princeton University Press, 1991), 74.

34. Vernant, *Mortals and Immortals*, 67-74.

35. McCall ("Divine and Human Action," 112) notes that the dust protects Polyneices. See also Bernard M. W. Knox *(The Heroic Temper: Studies in Sophoclean Tragedy* [Berkeley and Los Angeles: University of California Press, 1964], 68-69) who observes: "The chorus is impressed by the mysterious details of the burial: the absence of any trace of human activity (249-252), the fact that no bird or beast had come near the body—a sign perhaps of that divine protection which kept untouched the bodies of Sarpedon (*Il.* 16.667) and Hector (*Il.* 24.18 ff.)."

36. Jordan, *Servants of the Gods*, 97.

only to mutual recriminations (Sophocles *Antigone* 259-267). Sophocles emphasizes that the body is not under a mound, that is to say, the type of burial specified by Antigone (80-81) has not been performed. The absence of signs of humans prompts the conclusion—which the Coryphaeus soon offers—that no human has intervened. The dust conveys the gods' advice for Creon to tend to the corpse, undoing his thought (207) point by point. Creon offers the corpse to birds and dogs, but no devouring beasts have touched it. He wants to dishonor the corpse by setting it forth mangled before men's eyes in a mock *prothesis* (wake). Instead, it is hidden from view and from his watchmen's eyes. These antitheses underline the protection offered by the gods' dust. By repudiating the advice borne by the dust, Creon turns it into a warning against his thinking that he can control the corpse by dispensing burial rites at his discretion.

Creon's next adviser embodies another of his ideal citizens, the man who holds the fatherland above a *philos* (Sophocles *Antigone* 182-183). The Coryphaeus has already demonstrated his desire to please Creon. This time, after due consideration, he offers advice. In the absence of animal or human activity, he accepts the only other agent possible—the gods: "Lord, my thoughts have long been counseling, might not the deed have been somehow driven by the gods?" (ἄναξ, ἐμοί τοι μή τι καὶ θεήλατον / τοὔργον τόδ' ἡ ξύννοια βουλεύει πάλαι 278-279). His tentativeness, understandable in the face of an already menacing Creon, is ironically belied by *theêlaton* (θεήλατον driven by the gods), a strong word which, as Bernard M.W. Knox suggests, clearly implies "the divine will shown in the apparently miraculous burial (*pace*) of Polynices."[37] Creon, whose assigning of watchmen demonstrates his awareness of contravening custom, explodes: "Stop, before your words fill me with rage, so you will not be discovered senseless and old at once" (παῦσαι, πρὶν ὀργῆς καί με μεστῶσαι λέγων, / μὴ 'φευρεθῇς ἄνους τε καὶ γέρων ἅμα 280-281). The intensity of his anger goes far to argue that he agrees with the Coryphaeus. His very defensiveness makes clear that "Creon takes [what the Coryphaeus says] seriously, and so must we."[38] Moreover, his denial, "You are saying what is unendurable when you say that divinities have forethought for this corpse" (λέγεις γὰρ οὐκ ἀνεκτὰ δαίμονας λέγων / πρόνοιαν ἴσχειν τοῦδε τοῦ νεκροῦ πέρι 282-283), does not dispute the premise that gods care for bodies. Rather, Creon decides on his own precepts (284-289) that they are not looking out for *this* body: οὐκ ἔστι (it is not possible 289).[39] He silences discussion—*Pausai*

---

37. Knox, *Heroic Temper*, 69. For Calder ("Sophokles' Political Tragedy, *Antigone*," 395), "No audience would expect a god and everything depends on a single word, θεήλατον (278), spoken in rapid dialogue."

38. H. D. F. Kitto, *Form and Meaning in Drama* (London: Methuen, 1956), 156.

39. As Linforth ("Antigone and Creon," 195) states: "He does not scoff at divine intervention as such, but it is intolerable to him to suppose that the gods would show special care for a man who had behaved as outrageously as Polyneices."

(Stop!)—and maligns the Coryphaeus for being old and foolish. Creon's implicit concurrence with the Coryphaeus further guides the audience in reacting to the dust on Polyneices' body, while his resistance stamps him as a Theban leader of their own mythmaking.

To identify a culprit, Creon resorts to bribed men (Sophocles *Antigone* 294). Bribery was pernicious for the democracy of the city producing the *Antigone*. It imperiled the *politeia* which, to function, depended upon politicians and generals honorably formulating policy and implementing decisions for the *dêmos*. Yet the belief that every man could enrich himself at public expense was widespread, and suspicions of bribery were easily aroused and readily believed.[40] Creon might thus have struck a cord in the Athenian audience, were it not a commonplace of funeral oratory that the Athenians never act from motives of money and profit. Men impelled by these venalities do not bury the Theban Dead. Athenians do not act for profit. "We alone extend someone aid fearlessly not with the calculation of our advantage but in confidence of our freedom" says the orator (μόνοι οὐ τοῦ ξυμφέροντος μᾶλλον λογισμῷ ἢ τῆς ἐλευθερίας τῷ πιστῷ ἀδεῶς τινὰ ὠφελοῦμεν Thucydides 2.40.5). Athenians oppose those who are motivated by profit: "they [Athenians] erected a trophy on behalf of Hellas over the foreigners who left their own land and invaded another's for money" (ἔστησαν μὲν τρόπαιον ὑπὲρ τῆς Ἑλλάδος τῶν βαρβάρων, ἐκ τῆς αὑτων ὑπὲρ χρημάτων εἰς τὴν ἀλλοτρίαν ἐμβαλόντων Lysias *Funeral Oration* 25). Athenians move against the Thebans, "considering it right that those killed in war receive the customary rites" (τοὺς τεθνεῶτας ἐν τῷ πολέμῳ ἀξιοῦντες τῶν νομιζομένων τυγχάνειν), and intercede militarily so that the Thebans may stop outraging the gods by transgressing against the dead and that the slain Argives may receive what is their due and right (Lysias *Funeral Oration* 9). In the dramatic version of the myth, Thebes lies open after Theseus has crushed their army, but "Theseus held up. He said he did not come to ravage the city but to ask for the corpses back" (Θησεὺς ἐπέσχεν· οὐ γὰρ ὡς πέρσων πόλιν / μολεῖν ἔφασκεν, ἀλλ' ἀπαιτήσων νεκρούς Euripides *Suppliant Women* 724-725). Similarly, the men of the funeral orator "did not lust for greater retribution from the Cadmeians" (καὶ οὐχ . . . μείζονος παρὰ Καδμείων τιμωρίας ἐπεθύμησαν Lysias *Funeral Oration* 10). It is other Greeks who yield to Xerxes because of "the persuasive forces of profit and fear" (τὰ πείθοντα, κέρδος καὶ δέος *Funeral Oration* 29). There are no bribed men, but Creon's conviction that such men are at work both contrasts his understanding of human motivation with that of the Athenians of the subtext and reveals him as a man who, with his ascension to power, instantly suspects disloyalty.

Indeed, he affirms that men have been resisting his authority:

> ἀλλὰ ταῦτα καὶ πάλαι πόλεως
> ἄνδρες μόλις φέροντες ἐρρόθουν ἐμοὶ

---

40. Ober, *Mass and Elite*, 236-238.

κρυφῇ, κάρα σείοντες, οὐδ᾽ ὑπὸ ζυγῷ
λόφον δικαίως εἶχον, ὡς στέργειν ἐμέ.

Sophocles Antigone 289-292

From the first, men of the city, bearing
these things with difficulty, have been howling at me
in secret, shaking their heads and not keeping their necks
rightly beneath the yoke so as to love and submit to me.

Whether such a movement exists is moot, since it remains in Creon's imagination. But that he imagines it betrays his suspicion that there is something wrong with his edict. Thebans are howling (290: *errhothoun*) with the same howling (*rhothos*) as Hesiod's Dike (Justice) when she is dragged by bribe-devouring men of crooked judgments (*Works and Days* 220-221). Creon has imposed his rule like a yoke upon men, reducing them to recalcitrant beasts and shrewish women. But, as Sophocles' language (*errhothoun*) intimates, they are just in chafing against that yoke.

Creon often speaks of the city, but his city is not the Athens of Theseus and the orators but the Thebes of mythmaking. The Euripidean Creon's herald declares: "The city that I have come here from is under the power of one man, not of a mob" (πόλις γὰρ ἧς ἐγὼ πάρειμ᾽ ἄπο / ἑνὸς πρὸς ἀνδρός, οὐκ ὄχλῳ κρατύνεται *Suppliant Women* 410-411). Theseus counters that nothing is worse than a tyrant, because the laws are not held in common: "One man, possessing the law, holds the power at his side" (κρατεῖ δ᾽ εἷς τὸν νόμον κεκτημένος / αὐτὸς παρ᾽ αὑτῷ 431-432). Athens is the city of laws; therefore, Thebes is the city of the tyrant's caprice. Creon of Sophocles' *Oedipus at Colonus* expects to run roughshod over the laws of Attica and have his will by force (911-916).[41] Sophocles' Creon is not a well-meaning, misguided ruler; he is someone who shows himself a tyrant of anti-Athens Thebes. He does not express the belief that the city belongs to the ruler until line 738, but it is predicated by the mythmaking. Like Euripides' Creon, he conforms to the mythic pattern: he is foolish and impious, foolish because he fails to accept advice, impious because he knows gods protect corpses and balks at doing what they call for him to do.

Antigone for the authorial audience is about who is in control of the dead and of mourning for the dead. That Creon is impious and that the gods have protected Polyneices' body momentarily contribute to Sophocles' presentation of fodder for thought about such social issues.

---

41. Sophocles refrains from criticizing the *dêmos*, even the fictional *dêmos* of Thebes, by distinguishing the law-abiding citizens from Creon in *Oedipus at Colonus* (919-923), and in *Antigone*, by portraying (693-695) the Theban city as grieving for Antigone's suffering "because of very glorious deeds" (ἀπ᾽ ἔργων εὐκλεεστάτων).

4. Antigone, *Teras*
First Stasimon and Second Episode (332-581)

The elders begin the first stasimon: "Many things cause terror [or, wonder: *deina*], yet nothing is more terrifying [or wonderful: *deina*] than man" (πολλὰ τὰ δεινὰ κοὐδὲν ἀν- / θρώπου δεινότερον πέλει (Sophocles *Antigone* 332-333).[1] The ensuing ode has been anthologized so often that it has acquired a name, *Hymn to Man*. Excised from its context, it praises man, his accomplishments and advances over nature, with death alone escaping his power. The ode reproduces the self-congratulatory tone of the funeral orator's commonplace that praised Attica as the birthplace of civilization, intelligence, and justice, and the favorite of the gods.[2] But, as Charles Segal explains, the very words the elders speak contain dual and even contradictory meanings, and, in the course of the play, the ode's claims to man's domination over nature and himself prove to be false.[3] Moreover, the elders have just learned that someone has flouted Creon's edict. They and the Watchman rightly suspect the wrath of a defied Creon. In its immediate context, then, the ode must be heard and understood as a complex, uneasy mix of praise for the innovative daring and wide-sweeping ingenuity that prompts men to great deeds, and trepidation that these same qualities endow men with a lack of prudence, the potential for

---

1. For the various meanings of *deinos*, see Goheen, *Imagery*, 53, 141 n. 1; Segal, *Tragedy and Civilization*, 441 n. 4.

2. Examples are: "The beginning of [our ancestors'] life was just (for unlike the majority) . . . being born of the earth, they possessed it as both their mother and fatherland" (ἥ τε γὰρ ἀρχὴ τοῦ βίου δικαία . . . αὐτόχθονες ὄντες τὴν αὐτὴν ἐκέκτηντο καὶ μητέρα καὶ πατρίδα Lysias *Funeral Oration* 17); "It seems to me that the fact that the fruits by which men live first appeared among us, apart from its being a very great benefit for all . . ." (δοκεῖ δέ μοι καὶ τὸ τοὺς καρπούς, οἷς ζῶσιν ἄνθρωποι παρ' ἡμῖν πρώτοις φανῆναι, χωρὶς τοῦ μέγιστον εὐεργέτημ' εἰς πάντας γενέσθαι . . . Demosthenes *Funeral Oration* 5); "The land is worthy of being praised by all men, not only by us, but everywhere else, and first and foremost because it is a land beloved by gods (Ἐστι δὲ ἀξία ἡ χώρα καὶ ὑπὸ πάντων ἀνθρώπων ἐπαινεῖσθαι, οὐ μόνον ὑφ' ἡμῶν, πολλαχῇ μὲν καὶ ἄλλῃ, πρῶτον δὲ καὶ μέγιστον ὅτι τυγχάνει οὖσα θεοφιλής Plato *Menexenos* 237 c).

3. Segal, *Tragedy and Civilization*, 137-161.

unrestrained violence, and the means to their own ruin. And any man may slip into such daring. The elders seem again to speak in general terms of apparently universal truths, but the specifics confronting them challenge the validity of their praise.

The Watchman returns, leading Antigone and accompanied by one or more watchmen (Sophocles *Antigone* 382). All in the theater see them enter, but the Coryphaeus adds to the sight the quality of its being a *daimonion teras* (divine portent): "As to this divine portent, I am of two minds" (ἐς δαιμόνιον τέρας ἀμφινοῶ / τόδε 376-377). He knows it is Antigone who stands before him but cannot, or does not want to, believe what he sees. That he expresses his thought in a series of rhetorical questions reflects his bewilderment and ambivalence:

> πῶς εἰδὼς ἀντιλογήσω
> τήνδ' οὐκ εἶναι παῖδ' 'Αντιγόνην;
> ὦ δύστηνος καὶ δυστήνου
> πατρὸς Οἰδιπόδα,
> τί ποτ'; οὐ δή που σέ γ' ἀπιστοῦσαν
> τοῖς βασιλείοις ἀπάγουσι νόμοις
> καὶ ἐν ἀφροσύνῃ καθελόντες;

Sophocles Antigone 377-383

> How, when I know her, will I deny
> that this is the girl Antigone?
> O unhappy one,
> child of unhappy father Oedipus,
> what does this mean? Surely they are not bringing
> you who are in disobedience of royal laws
> after they caught you in folly?

David Seale reads in his comment "awe as though god himself has come,"[4] and certainly *daimonion teras* is too charged for an embellishment and too consistent with the Coryphaeus' previous observation (*theêlaton* 278) to be otiose. Sophocles is spinning a thread for the audience to follow as it listens to what is said about Antigone's arrest. The audience must regard Antigone as something besides a *pais* (child 378). She is a portent, enveloped in a divine whirlwind, whom the gods have sent as the vehicle for their advice to Creon concerning the unburied corpse of Polyneices.

When the Watchman returns to his post, he and his fellows remove the dust. The body, damp from Polyneices' blood, begins to smell (Sophocles *Antigone* 410-412). Their action, as if extracting Thetis' ambrosia and nectar from Patroclus' body, breaks the liminal zone created in profane space by divine-sent dust. The first dust appeared at night, unseen by Creon's watchmen, and, despite its thinness (256), lay upon Polyneices' corpse, mysteriously protecting it. When it appears again, all is

---

4. Seale, *Vision*, 90.

reversed: in the daylight of high noon, with a stinging force, it fills the watchmen's eyes, preventing them from watching. This dust is not a passive covering but "a thunderbolt raised by a whirlwind" that constitutes "a pain from heaven" (τυφὼς ἀγείρας σκηπτόν, οὐράνιον ἄχος 418) and "a divine sickness" (θείαν νόσον 421). It mangles (*aikizôn* 419) trees on the plain, preempting the mangling (*aikisthen* 206) Creon desired for Polyneices' corpse. It leaves the body uninjured and bare (*psilon* 426).[5] That the body amid such a storm should be left bare contradicts empirical reality but may delimit another reality. Antigone sought out Ismene in order to avoid a silent death for Polyneices. A silent death among Maniat women is "a naked death," where nakedness evokes "the cold, the damp, and winter" and "the bare tree."[6] Such images educe the body bereft of kin to care for it. Bareness, then, contrary to what has often been thought, may say less about Antigone's placing of dust upon her brother's corpse and more about the corpse left naked of caretakers and thus abandoned to savagery as opposed to the civilized realm of burial rites.

Through evocative language that calls forth the heavenly and divine (*ouranion achos* [Sophocles *Antigone* 418]; *theian noson* [421]), Sophocles obliquely associates the dust with the gods.[7] This dust unleashes anger analogous to that vented by the gods in the second act of Homer's myth of the exposed corpse. On one side, Apollo is enraged at Achilles for prolonged exposure of Hector's body and threatens that all the gods will become so (Homer *Iliad* 24.52-54). On the other, Hera, Poseidon, and Athena oppose burial of Hector because he is a Trojan like Paris who long ago insulted the goddesses in his delusion (24.56-64). Hera overlooks "the honorary portion of the dead" (τὸ . . . γέρας . . . θανόντων 16.457, 675) and dishonors the dead Hector because of something true of the living Hector. Zeus dismisses her argument in favor of his obligations to Hector "most *philos*" (24.67) in return for the latter's piety toward the gods and, especially, toward himself (24.66-70). Sophocles' Creon has distinguished between his nephews on the basis of their deeds when alive. The gods have become angry over Creon's continued exposure of the corpse and have sent dust as a warning. Enclosed within is their *teras,* Antigone.

The watchmen's eyes stay closed for a long time as the storm continues. When it lets up, Antigone is sighted. Some have judged the storm to be a dramatic device to allow Antigone to reach the body unseen.[8] It is that, but it is also much more than that. The storm is comparable to Zeus's "beautiful golden cloud" (νεφέλην ...

---

5. *Psilos* denotes both "uncovered" after being covered and "not covered" as never covered (Liddell, Scott, and Jones, *Lexicon*, 2024 s.v. ψιλός).

6. Seremetakis, *Last Word*, 76.

7. Adams ("*Antigone*," 54; *Sophocles the Playwright*, 49) remarks that these phrases "are just such sign-posts as a dramatist might erect to point the way."

8. See, for instance, Jebb, *Antigone*, 84: "The incident of the storm was a dramatic necessity, to account for Antigone reaching the corpse unobserved"; Brown, *Antigone,* 158: "The vividly

καλὴν χρυσείην Homer *Iliad* 14.350-351) that wards off prying eyes, or to Athena's *aêr* that shields Odysseus from xenophobic eyes (Homer *Ody*sseus 7.139-143),[9] or to the *aêr* encompassing Zeus's guardians who attend a city suffering from one man's recklessness (Hesiod *Works and Days* 252-255). Against this background, Sophocles' audience would understand that the gods, unbeknownst to Antigone, are helping her reach the body. She set out to do what she could for Polyneices, and the gods have joined in sending her. They have become for her what they have been from the outset, *metaitioi*, "sharers in the responsibility" toward the corpse.[10]

With the gods' aid, Antigone eludes Creon's watchmen and reaches the body. At this moment, the storm abating, she is seen. At the same time, "she wails a bitter bird's shrill sound (κἀνακωκύει πικρᾶς / ὄρνιθος ὀξὺν φθόγγον Sophocles *Antigone* 423-424). Less than three minutes of speaking time after the identification of Antigone as a *teras*, she utters a bird's cry.[11] The metaphor transforms her into a bird. Throughout Greek culture, birds serve the gods as vehicles for revealing their will (Euripides *Ion* 179-181) and for sending signs to those who lack them (Euripides *Suppliant Women* 211-213). Not every bird is ominous, but the coincidence of a portent that arouses wonder and fear with the sudden presence of a bird lends to the bird—to Antigone—movements and sounds both prophetic and threatening. A corpse purposefully exposed, where the differences between human dead and animal carrion have broken down, only amplifies the situation. Sophocles leads the audience to ponder in what ways or why Antigone may be a bird of omen. The adjective *pikros* expresses foreboding of disaster.[12] In epic and tragedy, the disaster is frequently directed toward a marriage: Athena prays that Penelope's suitors prove to be "bitter of marriage" (*pikrogamoi* Homer *Odyssey* 1.266), and, in fact,

---

described dust-storm is dramatically convenient, as it enables Antigone to reach the body unobserved." See also Adams, "*Antigone*," 53, and *Sophocles the Playwright*, 49; Bradshaw, "Watchman Scenes," 206.

9. Ruth Scodel, "Epic Doublets," 54.

10. Fraenkel (*Agamemnon*, 2.373) recalls that: "The confidence that the god will take his share in fighting or working alongside man is deeply rooted in Greek religious feeling"—a belief well illustrated by the metope of Atlas on the temple of Zeus at Olympia. For a discussion of gods as *metaitoi*, see Fraenkel 2.371-274. For an illustration of "Heracles and Atlas with the Apples of the Hesperides," which provides a graphic representation of this notion, see J. R. Charbonneaux and F. Villard, *Classical Greek Art, 480-330 B.C.* (London: Thames and Hudson, 1972), figure 136.

11. The elapsed time is based on a rate of three hundred syllables spoken per minute (W. B. Stanford, *The Sound of Greek: Studies in the Greek Theory and Practice of Euphony* [Berkeley and Los Angeles: University of California Press, 1967], 37).

12. Collard, *Supplices*, 317. According to C. G. Cobet, *Variae Lectiones* (Leiden 1873), 573, quoted in Fraenkel 1950.2.301 n. 1: "saepe solet πικρός in iracundi et minaci oratione poni de ea re quae magnum aliquod malum et infortunium alicui allatura esse dicatur" (*pikros* is often used in resentful and threatening speech concerning that matter which is said to bring some evil and misfortune to someone).

their desire to marry Penelope brings about their deaths; Adrastus lives to see the marriages he arranged for his daughters turn out bitter in the defeat (*pikrous*) before Thebes (Euripides *Suppliant Women* 832); Medea intends to make Jason's marriage to Creon's daughter *pikrous* (Euripides *Medea* 399). The bitter bird Antigone is an omen auguring disasters hanging over Creon and his household, disasters somehow related to marriage. Sophocles expands the metaphorical bird's shrill sound with a simile whose words have anthropomorphic connotations:

ὡς ὅταν κενῆς
εὐνῆς νεοσσῶν ὀρφανὸν βλέψῃ λέχος

Sophocles *Antigone* 424-425

as when she [bird] sees
a bed of empty bedding orphaned of nestlings.

As long as the words are limited by *neossôn* (nestlings), used mainly of animal young, they cannot escape their immediate referent, a bird and her chicks. But by foregrounding things human, the Watchman's language spills over its referent with the polyvalence evoked by ominous birds elsewhere in tragedy.[13] εὐνή (*eunê*) denotes a bird's nest, bedding, especially that of a field soldier, an animal lair, a grave, and a marriage bed; λέχος (*lekhos*), a bird's nest, a bier, a marriage bed, and marriage generally.[14] "She," the unexpressed subject of the verb βλέψῃ (*blepsêi*, beholds), alludes simultaneously to the actual and the metaphorical bird; ὀρφανὸν (*orphanon*) to the nest barren of nestlings and, by implication, of the children that might have been born to Antigone; and νεοσσῶν (*neossôn*), owing to this language, to any young animal, bestial or human.[15] Such plasticity combined with open syntax allows a multiplicity of readings, all of which are relevant to the action of *Antigone* and none of which may justifiably take precedence over any other. Thus, the empty nest, bed, or bier may recall the grave empty of Polyneices' body as a result of both his battle actions and his marriage with Adrastus' daughter, but it also anticipates the deprivation of the marriage-bed for Antigone and Haemon, the

---

13. Precedents available for both Sophocles' original and modern audiences are Homer, *Odyssey* 2.146-159, the simile in the anapests (49-59) of Aeschylus' *Agamemnon* that compares the Atreidae to bereaved vultures, and the omen that follows in the lyrics (*Agamemnon* 109-155) that identifies the Atreidae with avenging eagles. Simile and omen are interlinked in that "both simile and omen explore the causes of Agamemnon's ruin, the latter directly, the former indirectly" (Anne Lebeck, *The "Oresteia": A Study in Language and Structure* [Washington, DC: The Center for Hellenic Studies: 1971], 8). Sophocles telescopes the omen of Antigone *teras* and the simile into one incident.

14. Liddell, Scott, and Jones, *Lexicon*, 1043 s.v. λέχομαι and λέχος; 1257 s.v. ὀρφανός; 723 s.v. εὐνή.

15. Similarly, in the vulture simile of Aeschylus' *Agamemnon* (49-59), the animal young of the vulture become confounded with the human Helen and the young of Agamemnon and Clytemnestra, Iphigenia.

human nest emptied of children—Creon's as well as theirs—and the bitter disaster that comes to Creon's marriage with the deaths of his son and wife. Reinforcing all this is the notable repetition of *eunê* (*Antigone* 1224) and *lekhos* (1225) in the *exodos* in connection with Eurydice's suicide. For the moment, what is essential is that the simile foretells the warning for Creon that gods have sent the *teras* to convey. Without due rites given the dead, the body left exposed harbingers bitterness for marriage and infertility for Creon's house.

Seeing her brother's body bare, Antigone hurls evil curses at those—whoever they may be—who did the deed (Sophocles *Antigone* 428). Then she displays the proper way to treat a corpse: she undertakes burial rites. She brings "thirsty dust" and pours three offerings from a bronze pitcher. She is arrested and questioned "about the previous and the present actions" (τὰς τε πρόσθεν τάς τε νῦν . . . / πράξεις 434-435). When Creon learned of the dust, he demanded of the Watchman: "What man dared this?" (248). "[H]e does not think of women," Richard Jebb correctly remarks.[16] Indeed, Creon has no reason to suppose a woman has done the deed. Daring is a quality of men, properly directed by men against men.[17] Women do not swear an oath of allegiance or assume a place in the hoplite ranks. The person being led in under the watchmen's arrest is not even a woman but a *pais*. Antigone, surrounded by men, taller and stronger, and confronted by lord Creon resplendent in the robes of his station, is an improper adversary for any man.[18] The spectacle undercuts what Creon expected, namely, someone to test his mettle. The Watchman leaves no way out: "I saw this one burying the corpse that you forbade. Do I speak clearly and plainly?" (ταύτην γ᾽ ἰδὼν θάπτουσαν ὃν σὺ τὸν νεκρὸν / ἀπεῖπας. ἆρ᾽ ἔνδηλα καὶ σαφῆ λέγω; 404-405). "She did not try to deny anything" (ἄπαρνος δ᾽ οὐδενὸς καθίστατο 435), he informs Creon. Antigone herself excludes room for doubt: "I say I did these things, and I do not deny them" (καὶ φημὶ δρᾶσαι κοὐκ ἀπαρνοῦμαι τὸ μή 443). Although "I do not deny them" is not logically equivalent to "I admit everything," the fact remains that Antigone unequivocally assumes responsibility for "the past and the present

---

16. Jebb, *Antigone*, 56.

17. Thucydides (7.21.3-4) highlights the maleness of daring in a speech of the Syracusan Hermocrates who is encouraging his men to face the Athenians: "For daring men such as the Athenians, those who are daring in return would seem the most difficult to handle" (καὶ πρὸς ἄνδρας τολμηρούς, οἵους καὶ Ἀθηναίους, τοὺς ἀντιτολμῶντας χαλεπωτάτους ἂν [αὐτοῖς] φαίνεσθαι (7.21.3). The Syracusans, Hermocrates said, could equally confront the Athenians with the very daring used by them to attack and terrify neighbors often not much weaker than themselves. He knew well that the Syracusans, by daring to resist the fleet of the Athenians against their expectations, would come out ahead.

18. The Dolon Painter heightens the physical disparity between Creon and Antigone by placing Creon on a throne to the left of Antigone before whom and behind whom stands a watchman. The vase is kept in the British Museum (BMF F 155). A photograph may be found as the frontispiece of Ehrenberg, *Sophocles and Pericles* and as plate 1 of Steiner, *Antigones*.

doings." In our view, Antigone acts unwittingly as the gods' portent and performs burial rites only once. She does not elude the watchmen to perform a first burial or return to the corpse but appears for the only time out of the whirlwind. She has no part in, or even knowledge of, the dust spread over Polyneices' corpse during the night until informed by the watchmen. To assume otherwise, that is, to infer that there is a double burial, alters the focus from a play about the ramifications of not burying a corpse to a play about burial.[19] Why, then, does she adamantly affirm responsibility for both actions? R. G. A. Buxton has rightly cautioned against asking such a question,[20] and a revision of the question seems appropriate: if Antigone did not spread the dust, what does Sophocles gain by having her aver that she did? Most obviously, he strengthens Antigone's convictions and resolve (450-458) and her claims for renown (502) by having her admit to twice disobeying Creon's edict. Her affirmation also further irritates the almost petulant Creon who, with reference to Ismene, declares: "I really hate it when someone, caught in ugliness afterwards wants to make it look pretty" (μισῶ γε μέντοι χὤταν ἐν κακοῖσί τις / ἁλοὺς ἔπειτα τοῦτο καλλύνειν θέλῃ 495-496). Finally, and perhaps most significantly, she becomes in Creon's eyes doubly daring, and provoked by her *hubris*, he freely vents his spleen on the recalcitrant young woman.[21]

The Watchman's assertion that Antigone was caught "burying the body" (Sophocles *Antigone* θάπτουσαν 404), like his first report about a completed burial (245-247), is refined until the comprehensive term is narrowed to laments, dust, and libations, that is, to funeral rites. But Creon has prohibited all burial activities and must go on with it: "Did you know that it was decreed not to do that?" (ᾔδησθα κηρυχθέντα μὴ πράσσειν τάδε; 447). "I knew. How was I likely not to? It was public" (ᾔδη· τί δ' οὐκ ἔμελλον; ἐμφανῆ γὰρ ἦν 448). Astonished by a girl caught challenging his authority, he asks, "And still you dared to transgress these *nomoi* (laws)?" (καὶ δῆτ' ἐτόλμας τούσδ' ὑπερβαίνειν νόμους; 449). Antigone denies any moral imperative in Creon's burial proscription by calling it a *kerugma* (decree 8) instead of *nomoi* and by appealing to a related word, *nomima* (traditions 455), to express her sense of what is right. Upon her response and justification of her actions rests much of the admiration she has aroused in readers for her courage

---

19. The argument of Winnington-Ingram (*Sophocles: An Interpretation*, 125 note 31) and others that Antigone eluded the watchmen at 245ff., spread dust as a burial act, and now returns at 423ff., seems to be based primarily, if not solely, on inference. It depends in large part on analysis of Antigone's character and the invention of actions (she said she would heap a mound, so—despite the specific denial of a mound—she must have done so) for which there is at best no convincing textual support. On the other hand, there is, as we have seen, both textual and metatextual support for the gods sending the dust.

20. See Buxton, *Sophocles*, 13, quoted above, Introduction, n. 45.

21. Since this effect is achieved whether or not Antigone spread the dust at 245ff., Creon's acceptance of her defiance in the "previous actions" renders the issue of her responsibility moot.

against oppression, loyalty to her family, and steadfast duty toward what she—and most others—hold to be right and sacred. Her lines, or at least the idea they express, are famous, and like all famous or overly familiar texts, they tend to inhibit rethinking which may result in a possible departure from accepted understandings. The risk, however, in examining them afresh may prove fruitful:

οὐ γάρ τί μοι Ζεὺς ἦν ὁ κηρύξας τάδε,
οὐδ' ἡ ξύνοικος τῶν κάτω θεῶν Δίκη
τοιούσδ' ἐν ἀνθρώποισιν ὥρισεν νόμους,
οὐδὲ σθένειν τοσοῦτον ᾠόμην τὰ σὰ
κηρύγμαθ' ὥστ' ἄγραπτα κἀσφαλῆ θεῶν
νόμιμα δύνασθαι θνητά γ' ὄνθ' ὑπερδραμεῖν.
οὐ γάρ τι νῦν κἀχθές, ἀλλ' ἀεί ποτε
ζῇ ταῦτα, κοὐδεὶς οἶδεν ἐξ ὅτου 'φάνη.
τούτων ἐγὼ οὐκ ἔμελλον, ἀνδρὸς οὐδενὸς
φρόνημα δείσασ', ἐν θεοῖσι τὴν δίκην
δώσειν.

Sophocles Antigone 450-460

Zeus was not the one who decreed this for me,
nor did Justice, who dwells with the gods below,
define such laws among mankind.
I did not think your decrees so strong
that you, a mortal, could overstep
gods' unwritten and unshakable traditions.
Not today and yesterday but always
they live, and no one knows when they appeared.
I was not about to pay the penalty before gods
for neglecting them out of fear of any man's
thought.

The lines evoke two commonplaces of funeral oratory. Antigone's refusal to cower before Creon aligns her with the Athenians who, unlike other Greeks, do not fear Eurystheus' might (Lysias *Funeral Oration* 11-12), who put an end to Greek fears of the Persian king's ships and men (Plato *Menexenos* 241 B), and who face dangers of all sorts (*kindunoi*).[22] Secondly, her *nomima* are like the *nomoi* Pericles' Athenians especially obey because "they are laid down to assist those who are wronged and, being unwritten, bear acknowledged shame" to those who disobey them (ὅσοι τε ἐπ' ὠφελίᾳ τῶν ἀδικουμένων κεῖνται καὶ ὅσοι ἄγραφοι ὄντες αἰσχύνην ὁμολογουμένην φέρουσιν Thucydides 2.37.3). Sophocles' audience might therefore have seen Athenians, in the person of Antigone, confronting an impious Theban. The Coryphaeus' censure of her for not yielding to evils (Sophocles

---

22. For references to these *kindunoi*, see Chapter 2 n. 33.

Antigone 472) is thus tantamount to praise, since the evils she does not tolerate are those that leave exposed one of the Theban Dead.

Some in the audience may have heard Antigone's following references to profit as snide irony, as a reproach against Creon's way of talking: "This [to die] is truly the wage. But profit with its hopes often destroys men" (καὶ μὴν ὁ μισθός γ' οὗτος. ἀλλ' ὑπ' ἐλπίδων / ἄνδρας τὸ κέρδος πολλάκις διώλεσεν Sophocles *Antigone* 221-222), but the careful observer would remember that she did not hear him speak these words. Rather, she has her own notions of profit; death represents to her a personal gain "because she will then be with those she loves"[23] and avoid the pain that besets her life (463). Surrounded by evils originating from Oedipus (2), she prefers to die. This is the profit to be realized from serving "one born from my mother" (τὸν ἐξ ἐμῆς / μητρὸς 466-467). Clearly, Antigone not only acts on behalf of *nomima*; she also uses them to justify her actions with an eye to her own interests:

> θανουμένη γὰρ ἐξῄδη, τί δ' οὔ;
> κεἰ μὴ σὺ προύκήρυξας. εἰ δὲ τοῦ χρόνου
> πρόσθεν θανοῦμαι, κέρδος αὔτ' ἐγὼ λέγω.

Sophocles Antigone 460-462

I knew very well that I would die (why not?),
even if you had not decreed this. But if
I shall die before my time, I declare it a profit.

In seeking profit, she departs from the Athenians of the subtext who undertake dangers altruistically and selflessly—"These men, undergoing toil after toil, and in dangers every day while assuming the eternal terrors of citizens and Greeks, paid out their lives so that others may live nobly" (οὗτοι πόνους πόνων διαδόχους ποιούμενοι καὶ τοῖς καθ' ἡμέραν κινδύνοις τοὺς‹ς› εἰς τὸν ἅπαντα χρόνον φόβους τῶν πολιτῶν καὶ τῶν Ἑλλήνων παραιρούμενοι τὸ ζῆν ἀνήλωσαν εἰς τὸ τοὺς ἄλλους καλῶς ζῆν Hyperides *Funeral Oration* 26)—and veers toward other Greeks who, faced with the invading Xerxes, submitted to "persuasive forces of profit and fear" (τὰ πείθοντα, κέρδος καὶ δέος Lysias *Funeral Oration* 29). However different the profits Antigone hopes to reap—and their difference is incontrovertible—the fact that Sophocles allows her to hope for profit of any sort and that her actions have been tainted by the crassness of profit distances her from the Athenians. Simply stated, there is "something in it" for Antigone beyond the piety of burial itself. Burying of kin will earn her renown (*Antigone* 502). As Seth Bernardete says, "The holy thus turns into a means for making herself dear."[24]

---

23. Bernardete, "Reading of Sophocles' *Antigone*," 5 (1975), 10.

24. Bernardete ("Reading of Sophocles' *Antigone*," 4 [1975], 159) continues: "but it [the holy] can only be such a means through Creon's decree. Creon is essential to Antigone's obtaining something for herself in nobly devoting herself to another."

Antigone cannot conceive that her reasoning could be folly, but the Coryphaeus implies its wrongheadedness by attributing her nature to the savagery derived from the socially dominant reckoning of kinship through the father: "Clearly the offspring is savage from the girl's savage father" (δηλοῖ τὸ γέννημ' ὠμὸν ἐξ ὠμοῦ πατρὸς / τῆς παιδός Sophocles *Antigone* 471-472). *Ômos* (raw, savage) is a value-laden word "reserved for the worst crimes and especially for the strong taboos pertaining to the sanctions of the family."[25] Closely associated with *ômos* are the notions of animals' eating meat raw and of men, at least in mythmaking, stripped of their humanness and reduced to cannibalism. These meanings impart to the word the power to denote the loss of civilization into primal savagery. The rawness of Oedipus, the incestuous parricide, consists of his transgression of the incest taboos and the curbs upon violence that make the family possible.[26] Antigone's *gennêma* (471: birth, person) reincarnates the bestiality innate in a family whose immediate founder, Laïus, Apollo warned against begetting a son (Euripides *Phoenician Women* 17-20). In having the Coryphaeus call her back from mother to father as the true parent of her savagery, Sophocles hints at "Antigone's secret," namely, her desire for "consanguinity without generation."[27] Antigone is true to her Cadmeian descent as well as to her name, *anti-* (against) + -*gone* (generation).

By virtue of her sex, Antigone frightens Creon. He fears that she will assume his sexual role and oust him from the throne. Although he never speaks the word Amazon, his terror leads him to cast Antigone in the role of an Amazon, the warrior woman who rivaled men for supremacy in fighting (Sophocles *Antigone* 678), rule (485), and renown (502). As his rival for power, she becomes the Amazon familiar to Athenians from their myths and monuments and funeral orators.[28] Indeed, even modern readers have felt intimidated by Antigone's forcefulness. Cedric Whitman, for example, confessed to be so abused by "such a challenging piece of ungentle womanhood" that he thought Antigone's nature "has tended to throw some sympathy on Creon's side and raise the presumption that the king had a right to decree what he would regarding the burial of traitors."[29] No man had that right, as *Antigone* shows. But Antigone's excess may have been softened somewhat for some in Sophocles' original audience because it was motivated by obligations to a wombmate. For others, it may have been easier to frame the conflict over the corpse as an Amazonomachy rather than to face the trampling that the public funeral practiced upon what was due peaceful and dutiful women at home.

Despite Creon's assessment of her actions, Antigone is not primarily defying him. She is pursuing her own purpose with focused determination that Bernard M.

---

25. Segal, *Tragedy and Civilization*, 34.

26. Segal, *Tragedy and Civilization*, 224-226.

27. Bernardete, "Reading of Sophocles' *Antigone*," 5 (1975), 13.

28. Tyrrell, *Amazons*, 13-21; Castriota, *Myth*, 43-58, 76-89, 143-151.

29. Whitman, *Sophocles,* 85.

W. Knox has identified as the essence of Sophocles' "tragic hero."[30] Knox's model is chiefly a masculine one and thereby fails to encompass all aspects of a woman in this role. Antigone's motives for intruding upon men's public space derive from being her mother's daughter and a woman herself. Apart from her birth, Sophocles needs his audience to regard Antigone as an ordinary product of Greek society. Within the house, the women of her family would have taught her her place as a woman and prepared her for the grim business of readying a *philos*' body for burial. Women and men in the theater would realize the authority and influence women wielded by conducting religious rituals of such critical magnitude as burial and would recognize this power in any woman of Antigone's years. Antigone's quest, then, for a reputation acquired "from trying to place one from the same womb in a mound" (τὸν αὐτάδελφον ἐν τάφῳ / τιθεῖσα Sophocles *Antigone* 503-504) alludes to the pride Athenian women have in managing the dead. The certainty in her position not to allow "one born from my mother, dead and a corpse, to be unburied" (τὸν ἐξ ἐμῆς / μητρὸς θανόντ' ἄθαπτον ... νέκυν 466-467) accords with qualities of Knox's male Sophoclean hero, but in a woman these qualities are doubly terrifying for Creon.

Through Creon, Sophocles voices the negative aspects that emerge by viewing Antigone through the outer frame. Acting outside her place makes Antigone, as we have seen, a woman at war with her city. At first, Creon does not accept that Antigone knowingly discounted his *nomoi*. Once convinced of her daring, he is outraged by her "thoughts" (*phronêmata* Sophocles *Antigone* 473) about the corpses. By a series of images that move from inanimate to animate nature and then from slave to woman, he intimates that he will crush this woman's thoughts, thoughts too rigid and prone to fall (473-474).[31] Creon charges that Antigone has treated him hubristically by ignoring his laws and by boasting and exulting in her deed (480-483). He sexualizes her transgression of his edict by attributing to her the motives he harbors of men (248). To him, Antigone is an opponent in a contest for power, victory, and sovereignty, all dimensions of *kratê* (485). Defeat for Creon confers more than shame. A victorious Antigone will take everything from him, including his masculinity: "In this circumstance, I am not the man but this one is the man, if *kratê* will be hers with impunity" (ἦ νῦν ἐγὼ μὲν οὐκ ἀνήρ, αὕτη δ' ἀνήρ, / εἰ

---

30. For Knox (*Heroic Temper*, 5), a Sophoclean hero is "one who, unsupported by the gods and in the face of human opposition, makes a decision which springs from the deepest layer of his individual nature, his *physis*, and then blindly, ferociously, heroically maintains that decision even to the point of self-destruction."

31. Sophocles leaves unsaid the association of women with slaves. Vidal-Naquet explains (*Black Hunter*, 206): "The justification for examining the place of slaves together with that of women is this. The Greek city in its classical form was marked by a double exclusion: the exclusion of women, which made it a 'men's club'; and the exclusion of slaves, which made it a 'citizens' club'."

ταῦτ' ἀνατεὶ τῇδε κείσεται κράτη 484-485).[32] His fear comes from the same terror among Greek men that created Heracles, the archetypal male whose most indomitable foes are women.[33] "Better," he concedes, "if it is bound to happen, to be displaced by a man. We could not be called 'defeated by a woman' " (κρεῖσσον γάρ, εἴπερ δεῖ, πρὸς ἀνδρὸς ἐκπεσεῖν, / κοὐκ ἂν γυναικῶν ἥσσονες καλοίμεθ' ἂν 679-680).

Seething over her *hubris,* behavior he would expect of a man, he becomes paroxysmal over the treachery from within his own household. He calls upon Zeus Herkeios, Zeus in his capacity as protector of his courtyard and possessions and guardian of his *kyrieia* (mastery), to witness how the females inside are "devising crooked schemes in the dark" (τῶν μηδὲν ὀρθῶς ἐν σκότῳ τεχνωμένων 494). He saw Ismene raving and out of her mind (492) and now charges her with planning this burial. His accusation reveals that he recognizes the obligations of *philotês* and the insufficiency of one woman to mourn the dead. He concludes that Ismene must have acted in concert with Antigone and condemns them both to "a most direful doom" (μόρου κακίστου 489). Again, Creon shows that he knows what is right, namely, how a corpse should be treated, and fails to act upon his knowledge.

Throughout Creon's explosion of indignation, Antigone has waited calmly to ask: "Do you want something more than to take and kill me?" (θέλεις τι μεῖζον ἢ κατακτεῖναί μ' ἑλών; Sophocles *Antigone* 497). Nothing he has to say does she consent to hear. Creon replies, "With that I have all," but, as it turns out, he wants something more from her. He wants her acquiescence. To get this, he has to rule her, defeat her commitment to "uterine kin" (τοὺς ὁμοσπλάγχνους 511), and prove himself the man. He must win the contest. He goads her into a stichomythic "battle" between his *phronêma* and her *phronêmata* that evaluates Antigone's action toward the corpse and disobedience of Creon's *nomoi* through the inner framework of the obligations of *philotês*. It is a battle he cannot win as long as he thinks about corpses in a way that is invalidated both by Homer's Zeus and by the sameness of Eteocles and Polyneices not only as corpses but also as living enemy brothers.

As in his first words, Creon admits that Polyneices and Eteocles were of the same blood:

Κρ.   οὔκουν ὅμαιμος χὠ καταντίον θανών;
Αν.   ὅμαιμος ἐκ μιᾶς τε καὶ ταὐτοῦ πατρός.
Κρ.   πῶς δῆτ' ἐκείνῳ δυσσεβῆ τιμᾷς χάριν;
Αν.   οὐ μαρτυρήσει ταῦθ' ὁ κατθανὼν νέκυς.

---

32. As Gouldner (*Enter Plato,* 49) makes clear, the principle that someone can win only if someone else loses is the heart of the zero-sum game practiced by Greek men in the contest system.

33. Nicole Loraux, "Herakles: The Super-Male and the Feminine," in *Before Sexuality: The Construction of Erotic Experience in the Ancient Greek World,* ed. David M. Halperin, John J. Winkler, and Froma I. Zeitlin (Princeton, NJ: Princeton University Press, 1990), 21-52.

Sophocles Antigone 512-515

Cr. Was not the one who perished opposing him of the same blood?
An. Same blood from one mother and the same father.
Cr. How, when it is impious in his judgment, do you grant this kindness?
An. The dead corpse will not bear witness to that.

Antigone responds, underlining their consanguinity with a hyperbole that stresses their unity as offspring of the same parents and anticipates her later emphasis on parents (*Antigone* 911). She is indifferent to any criterion other than *philotês,* but that criterion is such that her obligation to the corpse would be the same were the body that of Oedipus, Jocasta, or Eteocles. With the expulsion of Ismene, all members of her family are dead, and the excessive inclusiveness of her perspective confounds individual identities. Creon, however, aware of the strife among the living, maintains that Eteocles would never abide equal honors with the impious Polyneices (516). That seems certain, but Antigone's reply: "He was not a slave but a brother who died" (οὐ γάρ τι δοῦλος, ἀλλ᾽ ἀδελφὸς ὤλετο 517), reveals her belief that her brothers held the same *philotês* toward one another that she feels toward both. Creon argues the atrocities of past behavior, and Antigone counters with reflection on the afterlife (518-519). No middle ground for agreement may be found, for they are not even on the same plane.

Desperate, Creon advances his fundamental thought: Polyneices *ekhthros* (enemy; Sophocles *Antigone* 522) cannot be a *philos* even in death. Antigone rejoins with one of those lines crucial to modern interpretations of her character: *outoi synekhthein, alla symphilein ephun* (523). *Synekhthein,* in proximity to *symphilein,* is usually considered poetically equivalent to *synekhthairein* (to join in hate), yielding the translation, "My nature is to join in love, not hate."[34] Accordingly, the line is usually thought to delineate a "higher" love; for example, Karl Reinhardt maintains: "Not that Antigone is the personification of love, but her hate and love spring from a different level from that which produces Creon's friendships and enmities."[35] Albin Lesky, arguing against the mainstream, concludes that "[Antigone] is announcing a trait of her nature that is crucial for her nature and fate and inalienable from her whole being."[36] Lesky justifiably points out how intensely she speaks of herself. In context, her declaration, perhaps more effectively translated "not of the nature to side with an enemy but with a *philos,*" corresponds

---

34. See, for example, Grene, *Antigone,* 181. For *synekhthein* as a poetic equivalent of *synekhthairein,* see Liddell, Scott, and Jones, *Lexicon,* 1714 s.v. συνεχθαίρω.

35. Karl Reinhardt, *Sophocles,* trans. Hazel Harvey and David Harvey (New York: Barnes and Noble, 1979), 79. Müller (*Sophokles: "Antigone,"* 107) affirms that "this relationship is of the kind that pleads for and defends a realm beyond and above all the differences which, as if legitimate, always have decisive power among men. For this, a great soul and its peculiar self-confidence are required."

36. Albin Lesky, "Zwei Sophokles-Interpretationen," *Hermes* 89 (1952), 98.

to Creon's "Never is an enemy even when dead a *philos*" (οὔτοι ποθ' οὐχθρός, οὐδ' ὅταν θάνῃ, φίλος 522). Instead of utterly rejecting Creon's political world for a higher love, she concurs with him that an enemy is always an enemy even when he is dead. But the enemy are the Argives, the fate of whose bodies never concerns her. Her *synekhthein*, "to side with an enemy," is not synonymous with *synekhthairein* but rather verbalizes Creon's *ekhthros*. Similarly, her infinitive *symphilein*, "to side with a *philos*," verbalizes Creon's *philos*. It is her nature (*ephun*), then, to stand against enemies and with *philoi*. No matter how Eteocles and Polyneices treated each other when alive, she is on the side of both in death because both are *philoi* and, as such, can never be *ekhthroi* to her.[37] Creon and Antigone both pursue narrow thinking. His unwillingness to discriminate between corpses vis-à-vis burial is as bankrupt as Antigone's inability to discriminate between *philoi* vis-à-vis the public welfare.

While inside the house, Creon saw Ismene raving senselessly (Sophocles *Antigone* 491-492). He now commands his slaves to summon her (491). With the sounds of his self-declared victory over Antigone: "While I am alive, no woman will rule me" (ἐμοῦ δὲ ζῶντος οὐκ ἄρξει γυνή 525) still ringing in the ears of the spectators, Ismene enters from the house. The Coryphaeus describes her appearance: "Here is Ismene before the gates, shedding *philadelpha* tears" (καὶ μὴν πρὸ πυλῶν ἥδ' Ἰσμήνη, / φιλάδελφα κάτω δάκρυ' εἰβομένη 526-527). Her tears are far more than "sisterly"; they are tears of *philotês*, the obligation that she feels for one born of the "self-same womb" (*adelph-*). Antigone accuses Ismene of feeling that obligation in name only (*logois . . . philousan* 543), but it is Antigone who limits the definition of a *philê* by words, indeed, words which are properly reserved for men (*eugenês, esthlôn* 38). Once implicated by Creon (531-533), Ismene is willing to die with her wombmate. Antigone and the audience know that she had no hand in Antigone's deed. Ismene offers her life, now that her *philotês* for Antigone may be shown without opposing the citizens, solely because Antigone is her *philê*, and she cannot face life without her (548). Like Antigone (511) but without her ulterior motives and quest for profit, Ismene is not ashamed to aid uterine kin (540-541).

Although long viewed as a foil for her sister's heroism or a coward for not venturing to aid her brother, Ismene was undoubtedly something else for Sophocles' original audience who would agree with the moral drawn from Clytemnestra's murder of her husband by Aeschylus' chorus of captive Trojan women: "I honor a hearth without heat within the house and a woman's spear without daring" (τίω δ' ἀθέρμαντον ἑστίαν δόμων / γυναικείαν ⟨τ'⟩ ἄτολμον αἰχμάν *Libation Bearers* 629-630). In the imagery of the *Oresteia*, the women prize a woman free of sexual passion and daring in defending her privileges.[38] For an *Antigone* read in

---

37. Brown, *Sophocles: "Antigone,"* 165-166.
38. The hearth warmed by fire acquires sexual connotations from Clytemnestra's boast:

the light of the public funeral, this would be a woman who esteems marriage and surrenders her rights over a kinsman killed in battle to the citizens. She is the model for how an Athenian woman should act. She would be Ismene who refuses to battle men or act violently against citizens (βίᾳ πολιτῶν Sophocles *Antigone* 79) and, as the audience learns shortly, supports the marriage bond. Creon has infringed upon the privileges of women in his household, and, to his ruin, reaps an Antigone. Ismene is a foil not so much for Antigone's rebellion (which, however admirable its motivation, was always dangerous in a woman) but a model for the compliance and submission expected of women. Ismene grants the men of Athens what they require for their public funeral. As if confirming Ismene as the paradigm, Sophocles brings Antigone to the same resolve in not acting βίᾳ πολιτῶν (in violence of the citizens 907) regarding a husband or son.

Ismene tells Creon that she has done the deed—she is a doer—if Antigone "rows at my side" (ὁμορροθεῖ Sophocles *Antigone* 536).[39] Her nautical imagery returns the sisters to their separation in the prologue when Antigone admonished her to "Set straight the course of your own fate" (τὸν σὸν ἐξόρθου πότμον 83). Antigone will not accept Ismene, despite the latter's willingness to offer herself as an accomplice, as "a fellow voyager of her suffering" (ξύμπλουν . . . τοῦ πάθους 541). She makes Ismene realize that her death, like her deed, is not Ismene's for the offering: "I will satisfy this rite by dying—I myself" (ἀρκέσω θνῄσκουσ' ἐγώ 547). The line is a pronouncement of what Antigone is going to do, and the nominative *egô*, postponed to the end of the sentence, draws attention to the fact that it is she alone who is going to do it. Ismene, it seems, receives the message, because she turns from death to the future without Antigone, wondering "what life will be *philos* without you?" (καὶ τίς βίος μοι σοῦ λελειμμένῃ φίλος;) to which Antigone replies: "Ask Creon, your kinship caring goes to him" (Κρέοντ' ἐρώτα· τοῦδε γὰρ σὺ κηδεμών 549). Her gibe cuts them both, taunting Ismene with her submission to Creon and Antigone herself with the consequences of that loyalty. But it stirs Ismene to an offer of a different kind: "I could still help you now—I myself" (νῦν σ' ἔτ' ὠφελοῖμ' ἐγώ 552). The line may be her statement of intention, with the postponed *egô* implying that her determination is comparable to Antigone's. The latter refuses any help. The sisters set out on separate voyages, and they have arrived at different destinations: "You chose to live, I chose to die" (σὺ μὲν γὰρ εἵλου ζῆν, ἐγὼ δὲ κατθανεῖν 555). Ismene insists that she argued for another, equally valid course of action. And Antigone seems to concur: "Nobly you seemed to some, and I to others, to think" (καλῶς σὺ μὲν τοῖς, τοῖς δ' ἐγὼ 'δόκουν

"The expectation of Terror will not tread the halls for me as long as Aegisthus lights the fire in my hearth" (οὔ μοι φόβου μέλαθρον ἐλπὶς ἐμπατεῖ / ἕως ἂν αἴθῃ πῦρ ἐφ' ἑστίας ἐμῆς / Αἴγισθος Aeschylus *Agamemnon* 1434-1436).

39. For imagery of the sea, see Goheen, *Imagery*, 45-49.

φρονεῖν 557). Antigone's first and last words here suggest an acceptance of their difference. "Nobly" (*kalôs*) is Antigone's word for how she wants to die (97), and now she uses that same word which confers upon Ismene's decision to live a similar nobility.

They are alike, the two of them, Ismene observes, in their "error," their "missing the mark" ('ξαμαρτία 558). She reasserts their lost unity with a dual (*nôin*), "the two of us." Antigone does not respond in kind but does seem to recall their life together before Creon's edict, that life beset on all sides by the evils from Oedipus (2-3). Thus Antigone's encouragement, *Tharsei. Su men zêis* (θάρσει. σὺ μὲν ζῇς 559), is far grimmer than "Take heart. You live" or "Be happy. You are living."[40] Ismene will need all her courage to survive. "Gather your strength," Antigone admonishes her, "You are still living." In the life they received from Oedipus, Antigone concedes their likeness. Her next words, however, pronounce the abyss that lies between them: "My life has perished."

Creon has been standing by, listening to the sisters, and now intrudes in his usual fashion. He picks up Ismene's unrequited dual to declare them a pair, a senseless pair (Sophocles *Antigone* 561-562). Having erected differences between Oedipus' sons when Eteocles and Polyneices were alike in being dead, he is now deaf to the differences between the living Ismene and the "dead" Antigone. True to her offer, Ismene tries to help Antigone. To Creon's charge that both are senseless, she answers: "The sense that grows within, lord, does not abide with those doing badly, but it departs" (οὐ γάρ ποτ', ὦναξ, οὐδ' ὃς ἂν βλάστῃ μένει / νοῦς τοῖς κακῶς πράσσουσιν, ἀλλ' ἐξίσταται 563-564). Creon again throws her words in her teeth. "For you, I am sure, when you chose to do bad things with bad people" (σοὶ γοῦν, ὅθ' εἵλου σὺν κακοῖς πράσσειν κακά 565). Their exchange serves to shift the focus from Antigone to Ismene.

Ismene has already espoused the woman's place vis-à-vis the city. She does so now vis-à-vis Creon's house. She asks him whether he is going to kill his son's *nympheia*, a word meaning both "bride" and "nuptial rites."[41] In essence, it is the same question that Antigone asked her: Will you fulfill your obligations to your *philos*? Unlike Antigone's, however, Ismene's question does not encompass disobedience to public authority; it is also proper since Ismene and Creon should both be concerned for the future of their house. Creon retorts with a common metaphor for sexual intercourse, "the fields of others are fit for plowing" (ἀρώσιμοι γὰρ χἀτέρων εἰσὶν γύαι Sophocles *Antigone* 569), an expression Sophocles' original audience would normally not have found offensive but which might have sounded obscene even to them, given Creon's lack of regard for the people

---

40. For "heart," see Elizabeth Wyckoff, trans., *Antigone* in *The Complete Greek Tragedies: Sophocles I*, ed. David Grene and Richmond Lattimore (Chicago and London: The University of Chicago, 1954) 178. For "happy," see Braun, *Sophocles: "Antigone,"* 43.

41. Liddell, Scott, and Jones, *Lexicon*, 1184 s.v. νυμφεῖος.

involved.[42] When Ismene pleads on behalf of the special harmony Haemon and Antigone share, Creon avoids mention of his son and talks generally about hating evil wives for sons. Ismene does not let the specific escape: "O most *philos* Haemon, how your father dishonors you" (ὦ φίλταθ' Αἷμον, ὡς σ' ἀτιμάζει πατήρ 572).[43] Ismene's attribution of *philos* to Haemon suggests her obligations to defend him as a member of her household and as her sister's betrothed. Creon's exasperation with this conversation spills over in his rejoinder: "You and your bed cause too much pain" (ἄγαν γε λυπεῖς καὶ σὺ καὶ τὸ σὸν λέχος 573). Believing the reply, "Will you really deprive your own son of this one?" (ἦ γὰρ στερήσεις τῆσδε τὸν σαυτοῦ γόνον; 574) could not be Ismene's, some commentators shift the line to the Coryphaeus. But Ismene has been speaking of Haemon and Antigone all along as flesh and blood members of her household. The bed belongs to Haemon and Antigone in marriage, but Creon's sarcasm makes it Ismene's in this stichomythic exchange.

Throughout, Creon has emptied his son's *nympheia* of all affection and obligations by characterizing both Haemon's bride and his nuptials in the crudest terms. He ends by declaring that Hades will put a stop to these "couplings" (γάμους Sophocles *Antigone* 575) for him. It is the same kind of remark that he hurled at Antigone: "Go below, and if you must be *philê*, be *philê* to them" (κάτω νυν ἐλθοῦσ', εἰ φιλητέον, φίλει / κείνους 524-525). In his mind, the contest is concluded. The primary manuscript gives the next line, "So it is settled, it seems, this one will die" (δεδογμέν', ὡς ἔοικε, τήνδε κατθανεῖν 576), to the Coryphaeus, but, coming from the orchestra, the words appear sudden and unexpected. It may be argued that the line has more to offer as Ismene's, as a concession of final defeat, particularly since she does not appear again in the play. Her failure in defending the marriage bed of her *philoi* parallels Antigone's failure in defending the funeral bed, the grave, of her *philos*. Creon's reply, καὶ σοί γε κἀμοί (Yes, for you and for me 577) is the cry of triumph that he could not achieve over Ismene's sister. Unlike Antigone, however, Ismene has spoken on behalf of the future and its promise of new *philoi*, the wish of Demeter *Orêphoros Aglaodôros*, Bringer of Seasons and Giver of Wondrous Gifts, for all women. Antigone aborted all this for ties laid down in the past, ties that are unalterable, savage, and barren. Ismene has thought for her family

---

42. For the metaphor of the woman's body as a field and furrow for plowing, see Page DuBois, *Sowing the Body: Psychoanalysis and Ancient Representations of Women* (Chicago and London: The University of Chicago Press, 1988), 39-85.

43. The manuscripts attribute line 572 to Ismene, but scholars have often given it to Antigone on the assumption that Antigone should be allowed to voice her love for Haemon and that the line sounds too intimate for Ismene to say. Although manuscripts are not infallible in distinguishing speakers, expectations of romantic love do not outweigh Antigone's concern for her mother's womb. Sophocles cannot compromise her position as a virgin defending her *philos* on the basis of kin blood to have her assert *philotês* founded on marriage. See Jebb, *Antigone*, 110; Lloyd-Jones and Wilson, *Sophoclea*, 127-28.

in the context of the city and the future, first, to relinquish its dead to public law and, secondly, to replace its dead with new *philoi*. Antigone values death, her sister values life, and, consequently, Ismene's defeat is as costly for the household as Antigone's suicide in the cave.

5. Haemon, Son and Citizen
Second Stasimon and Third Episode (582-780)

Because *Antigone*, like all Greek tragedy, used only three actors, the reader may have the impression that the spectacle was sparse. But in the scene just concluded, Creon is attended by at least two servants (Sophocles *Antigone* 491), Antigone stands before him, the Watchman having been dismissed, and Ismene is accompanied by female servants who, since they escort her back into the house (578), must have entered with her. Now, all have disappeared save for Creon who remains visible before the house. The contrast could hardly have failed to strike Sophocles' original audience and bears noting by his modern audiences. The spectacle foreshadows Creon's fate, and the elders' song reinforces what they see.

The elders begin their song with an adynaton about the fortunate, a one-line generalization that contains its own untruth, for what life has "no taste of troubles" (κακῶν ἄγευστος αἰών Sophocles *Antigone* 583)?[1] Not surprisingly, they quickly turn their attention to those whose house is incessantly afflicted with recklessness, ruin, and delusion, that is, with *atê* from the gods that creeps over the house like a wave driven by storm winds of Thrace (584-592).[2] Behind them stands such a house whose succeeding generations bring no release from pain. They speak of the doom awaiting its final progeny:

νῦν γὰρ ἐσχάτας ὑπὲρ
ῥίζας ἐτέτατο φάος ἐν Οἰδίπου δόμοις·
κατ' αὖ νιν φοινία

---

1. For discussions of the second stasimon, see Linforth, "Antigone and Creon," 212-215; Burton, *The Chorus in Sophocles' Tragedies*, 105-112; P. E. Easterling, "The Second Stasimon of *Antigone*," in *Dionysiaca: Nine Studies in Greek Poetry by Former Pupils Presented to Sir Denys Page on his Seventieth Birthday*," ed. R. D. Dawe, J. Diggle, and P. E. Easterling (Cambridge: The Editors, 1978), 141-158.

2. For *atê*, see E. R. Dodds, *The Greeks and the Irrational* (Berkeley and Los Angeles: University of California Press, 1951), 37-41; R. D. Dawe, "Some Reflections on Ate and Hamartia," *Harvard Studies in Classical Philology* 72 (1967), 89-123.

θεῶν τῶν νερτέρων ἁμᾷ κόνις,
λόγου τ' ἄνοια καὶ φρενῶν 'Ερινύς.

Sophocles Antigone 599-603

Now, above the last
root a light had been stretched over Oedipus' house.
Again the bloody dust[3]
of nether gods mows it down,
folly of word and Erinys of mind.

The promise of continuity is broken. Underworld gods, because of foolish words spoken by a deluded mind, are preparing to destroy "the last root" of the house. The gist of the elders' message is clear, yet its structure and imagery have elicited much controversy and therefore warrant elaboration.

After a clear reference to the continual suffering of "the house of Labdacus' sons" (Sophocles *Antigone* 594), the elders regard the fate of the present generation, the "Now" that rests in Antigone. The pluperfect tense of the verb indicates that the hope that had been vested in Antigone is lost. The "bloody dust," reminiscent of that which covered the "oozing" body of Polyneices (μυδῶν 410), is now the instrument of revenge of the nether gods.[4] The image of dust mowing down a root must have been palpable to an audience living in a land where dust or sand was ubiquitous and dust storms plagued its dry season,[5] particularly since they had just heard such a storm vividly described, a storm that injured men and "all the foliage of the trees on the plains" (πᾶσαν . . . φόβην / ὕλης πεδιάδος 419-420). The dust belongs to the nether gods who are concerned with both the unburied dead and the honors due themselves. Though a root is more likely to be "mowed down," in the world of metaphor, the "it" (*nin*) of line 601 could refer to either root or light and has been read as both.[6] Its very ambiguity seems to secure the bond

---

3. *Konis* (dust: Sophocles *Antigone* 602), found in the manuscripts, came under the emendator's knife when Jortin, Reiske, and Askew independently conjectured *kopis*. See Jebb, *Antigone*, 114-115, 253-254; H. Lloyd-Jones, "Notes on Sophocles' *Antigone*," *Classical Quarterly* 7 (1957), 17. Jebb describes the *kopis* as "a large curved knife, known to the Greeks chiefly as (a) a butcher's or cook's implement, (b) an oriental military weapon" (115). It provides a cutting tool as the subject of a verb for reaping but at the cost of an incongruous image—that of nether gods mowing down a root with an instrument from a kitchen or a barbarian army. *Konis,* consistent with the nature imagery of root and light (Linforth, "Antigone and Creon," 212-213), far more enriches lines 602 and 603 by building upon and continuing the motif of dust from the actions at Polyneices' corpse. See Segal, *Tragedy and Civilization*, 172 n. 62. But if *konis* was not the word in 602, the actual word used has been lost. Since *kopis* has been so widely accepted, the legitimacy of *konis* may always be doubted, and the problem with line 602 never resolved.

4. This is to say, *phoinia* (bloody) can be both an attributive and an predicate adjective. In the latter sense, it prefigures the blood that will flow from mowing down the root.

5. Linforth, "Antigone and Creon," 212.

6. For *nin* (Sophocles *Antigone* 601) referring to *phaos* (light), see Kamerbeek, *Antigone*, 120; referring to *rhizas* (root), see Easterling, "The Second Stasimon of *Antigone*," 147.

that ties both words to Antigone. Since *anoia* (folly) and Erinys are in the nominative, they can only stand in apposition to the dust. Foolishness and fury will destroy the root (and the light). The connection between folly of word, fury of mind, and the dust has perplexed Sophocles' modern readers, but it may have been less difficult for his original audience who were guided in their understanding of the gods by the Homeric poems. "Erinys" and "mind" (*phrenôn*) as well as *atê* are all part of Agamemnon's famous apology for the quarrel with Achilles: "I am not responsible, but Zeus and Destiny and an Erinys walking in mist who in assembly put savage *atê* in my mind" (ἐγὼ δ' οὐκ αἴτιός εἰμι, / ἀλλὰ Ζεὺς καὶ Μοῖρα καὶ ἠεροφοῖτις Ἐρινύς, / οἵ τέ μοι εἰν ἀγορῇ φρεσὶν ἔμβαλον ἄγριον ἄτην Homer *Iliad* 19.86-88). Deluded by *atê* sent by a supernatural power unknown to him, Agamemnon speaks and acts against his own interests toward the men and toward his best fighter.

The second strophic pair develop the implications of the appositives, referring ultimate responsibility to Zeus, another of Agamemnon's agents. Zeus, enthroned on Olympus, is master throughout all time, and throughout time this law pertains: nothing "enormous" (πάμπολυς Sophocles *Antigone* 614) comes to men free of ruin (*atê*). Other men (in the grip of the enormous), led astray by hope, are destroyed before they see disaster coming, for the god deceives the mind of the one whom he intends to bring to ruin.

The elders watched Antigone and Ismene being led into the house under sentence of death. They begin the second stasimon by reflecting generally on houses doomed to destruction. They are trying to comprehend what has happened to Antigone and attribute her ruin to her folly and lineage (Sophocles *Antigone* 594-603). They have said as much before (379-380, 471-472). Yet there are serious problems in agreeing with the elders. Although Antigone's opposition to Creon's edict has been judged foolhardy, her attempt to bury the exposed corpse cannot be foolishness, since its rectitude is validated by the nether gods. Antigone gives them their due rights by honoring Polyneices' body. Ismene is still living, but there is no doubt that, for the elders, Antigone is the last root.[7] It is her marriage to Haemon that would continue the line not only of the house of Labdacus but of her uncle, Creon. But Oedipus' house is already mingled with Creon's.[8] Indeed, for all purposes, it is the same house, and Haemon its last male root. The elders' image thus harbors a hidden— even unintended (by them)—allusion to Haemon. In addition, dust, as we have seen, has been independent of Antigone and the medium of *theoi metaitioi* for expressing their will. It protects Polyneices' body until humans can care for it. After

---

7. Seaford (*Reciprocity and Ritual*, 347) points out that as a consequence of "the tragic pattern of familial self-destruction and salvation for the polis," Sophocles ignores Ismene, and Antigone goes to her death as the last of the royal line.

8. Creon's wife, Eurydice, lives in the house as do his nieces and son, so that it does not serve the play to distinguish too closely whose house it is, Oedipus' or Creon's.

the watchmen sweep it away, it inflicts pain on them while bringing a *teras* to Creon. Each time, Creon rejects these warnings. Dust, no longer anonymous but attributed to nether gods, comes to destroy the last root of the house. The spectators are prepared for Creon to ignore this. Truly, his self-deception is folly.

Creon stands before the house alone for all in the theater to see as they listen to the elders' song. Sophocles' chorus may well be speaking and thinking of Antigone, but his authorial audience, steeped in anti-Athens mythmaking, surely could not dismiss Creon's foolishness nor, more importantly, consider Antigone's folly in opposing Creon's edict tantamount to Creon's folly in promulgating it. The elders' words spill over their intended meaning for Antigone to encompass Creon.[9] The fertility of Creon's house will be destroyed by the foolishness of what he will say to his son under the delusion caused by the Erinys in his mind. The elders do not knowingly point to Creon or predict Creon's fate with their lyrics. Instead, their song places the quarrel that ensues between Creon and Haemon in the context of divine retribution for Creon at the cost of his house (*oikos*) and kin (*oiketai*). It directs the audience to watch as Creon mows down his son, the last root of his house, unwittingly and unintentionally:

τὸ κακὸν δοκεῖν ποτ᾽ ἐσθλὸν
τῷδ᾽ ἔμμεν ὅτῳ φρένας
θεὸς ἄγει πρὸς ἄταν.

Sophocles Antigone 622-624

Evil seemeth[10] at some time a good
to one whose mind the god
is leading to ruin.

Haemon enters from the city where he has heard things in the dark (Sophocles *Antigone* 692). The Coryphaeus identifies him and glosses his name with "the last born" or "youngest" (νέατον 627) of Creon's sons. The actor wears the beardless mask of a youth of some eighteen years, the season of a young man's prime when his beard is first blooming along with his strength and vigor. Creon wears the bearded mask of the mature man. Differences in their ages must be visible in their appearances as a way of visualizing the other conflicts that erupt between them. Sophocles had the option of having the actor who played either Antigone or Ismene play Haemon with different effects.[11] The Antigone actor, with his voice suitably modified, would convey audibly the harmony that Ismene says Haemon shares

---

9. Müller, *Sophokles: "Antigone,"* 135-36; Easterling, "The Second Stasimon of *Antigone,*" 156-157.

10. The archaism imitates Sophocles' ἔμμεν (to be *Antigone* 623), an epicism that does not appear elsewhere in extant tragedy.

11. Distribution of acting parts depends upon Aristotle's evidence in the *Poetics* that tragedies were staged with three actors (1449 A 15-19) and upon the assumption that the audience could

with her sister. At the same time, this vocal continuity would play against Antigone's silence about Haemon and their relationship. If the actor impersonating Ismene played Haemon, the overlapping of parts and voice would join characters who know their social station, Ismene's as woman and Haemon's as ephebe, and who are incapable of acting against the citizenry for motives of personal profit.

The Coryphaeus, aware that Haemon may be troubled, asks Creon whether he is tormented over the fate of his betrothed Antigone and in pain at being cheated of his marriage bed (Sophocles *Antigone* 627-630). His is a reasonable question, but it also brings to the fore the marriage insinuated in the second stasimon by light. Creon follows the Coryphaeus' lead:

ὦ παῖ, τελείαν ψῆφον ἆρα μὴ κλυὼν
τῆς μελλονύμφου πατρὶ λυσσαίνων πάρει;
ἢ σοὶ μὲν ἡμεῖς πανταχῇ δρῶντες φίλοι;

Sophocles Antigone 632-634

My boy, you're not here, are you, after hearing
my fixed decree about your intended bride, in a rage at your father?
Or as far as you are concerned are we, whatever we do, *philoi*?

Creon's "we" doubtless refers only to himself. Haemon proves not to be lost in love but concerned for the city and his father's welfare. He gives his father the answer Creon wants: "Father, I am yours" (πάτερ, σός εἰμι 635) but with a condition Creon misses: "If you have sound judgments that I will follow, you would guide me aright (*aporthoîs*)" (καὶ σύ μοι γνώμας ἔχων / χρηστὰς ἀπορθοῖς, αἷς ἔγωγ' ἐφέψομαι 635-636). Haemon speaks his verb *aporthoîs* as an optative in a conditional sentence.[12] Creon hears *aporthoîs* as an indicative, the more common mood for the inflection: "Since you have sound judgments that I will follow, you guide me aright." Creon's misapprehension betrays what he expects of a son: obedience, support in avenging an injury, and no grief or embarrassment (641-647). All in Creon's house must remain orderly (659-660), by which is meant submission to Creon's judgments in every respect. Pleased by his son's declaration of loyalty, Creon enters upon a lengthy diatribe insisting on the rightness of his action and denouncing Antigone: "Therefore, spit the girl out like an enemy" (ἀποπτύσας οὖν ὥστε δυσμενῆ 653);

---

perceive the same voice, more or less changed, in two or more roles. An instance of an actor's mistake in pronunciation suggests how keen was the audience's hearing. At the first performance of Euripides' *Orestes*, Hegelochus missed the rising inflection of *galén* (γαλήν') and pronounced it with a rising-falling inflection to produce *galên* (γαλῆν), which altered the meaning from "I see calm weather" to "I see a skunk" (Aristophanes *Frogs* 303 and scholia). The audience roared at his mistake in sounding the pitch accent (Stanford, *Sound of Greek*, 31).

12. Kamerbeek (*Antigone*, 126) remarks: "I should say that the word [*aporthoîs*] conveys an ambiguity which Haemon is supposed to intend and which is lost upon Creon. (The words are at any rate ambiguous because of the double meaning of ἔχων [*echôn*] ('if you have'— 'since you have')."

"I shall kill her" (κτενῶ 658). Despite the Coryphaeus' acquiescence to Creon, Haemon, in the name of the city, comes to Antigone's defense with a compassion and understanding of her "deeds most glorious" (695) that is totally lacking in Creon's tirade:

ἐμοὶ δ' ἀκούειν ἔσθ' ὑπὸ σκότου τάδε,
τὴν παῖδα ταύτην οἷ' ὀδύρεται πόλις,
πασῶν γυναικῶν ὡς ἀναξιωτάτη
κάκιστ' ἀπ' ἔργων εὐκλεεστάτων φθίνει·
ἥτις τὸν αὑτῆς αὐτάδελφον ἐν φοναῖς
πεπτῶτ' ἄθαπτον μήθ' ὑπ' ὠμηστῶν κυνῶν
εἴασ' ὀλέσθαι μήθ' ὑπ' οἰωνῶν τινος·
οὐχ ἥδε χρυσῆς ἀξία τιμῆς λαχεῖν;

Sophocles Antigone 692-699

It is possible for me to hear things in the shadows,
how the city grieves for this girl,
that the most undeserving of all women
is perishing in the foulest way for deeds most glorious.
She did not allow one of the same womb, lying
without rites amid the carnage, to be ravaged
by raw-eating dogs or some one of the birds.
Is she not worthy of receiving a golden meed of honor?

Haemon's appeal could not have fallen on deaf ears in Sophocles' original audience. The only deaf ears he encounters are Creon's.

Such exchanges do not afford much sympathy to Creon. Through the perspective of the outer frame, he emerges as a stick figure drawn by the impiety and foolishness revealed by Theban leaders of Athenian mythmaking. Seen as master of the household (*kyrios*) through the inner frame, he fails his obligations so monstrously that feeling for him is overwhelmed by commiseration with the *philoi* he has wronged. Yet the audience may have been moved as they watched him slip into a wrenching quarrel with his son and then deeper into a bitter and irremediable split. Haemon is a youth, suspended between the house of his birth and childhood, on the one hand, and the city of his manhood as a citizen, hoplite, and father, on the other. He has absorbed the values of this city—his words reveal as much, as they do his love for his father. He comes, intending to advise his father on a public matter, although he has spent most of his years in a house dominated by his mother and occupied mainly by women. Typically, the Greek father's strength resided outside the household, and Creon resents his son's effort as an intrusion into the realm of older, wiser men. Creon convinces himself, refusing to be dissuaded, that Haemon is doing Antigone's bidding. Nothing can redeem the ruler Creon for his foolishness and indifference toward *themis* (what is right) regarding the dead. But Creon the father makes the kind of mistakes any parent can make, and even as he or she is making them, cannot hold off or stop. Creon has reared his son to respect and love him (Sophocles *Antigone* 635, 703-704) but also to be loyal to his city. When Haemon tries to sway his father with values that he learned at home and in his city, Creon cannot listen to him. When Creon demands Haemon's loyalty in the face of his own betrayal of the values in which his son was reared, he thwarts his son's transition from family to city, and Haemon is left in limbo.[13] Neither adolescent nor adult male, he flees to Antigone's cave, back to the realm of women. And Creon, in repudiating Haemon's advice, repudiates himself.

Haemon sees ruin approaching the city, something Creon said he would act against (Sophocles *Antigone* 185-186), and comes to its leader. Creon, however, rejects such a notion out-of-hand and will not let his son function as a citizen in giving advice. Rather, he appeals to Haemon as a *philos* to betray the city. Every male citizen on becoming of age swore an oath to obey those who were ruling ἐμφρόνως, "reasonably," literally, "in their right minds."[14] Creon's language rings with the promise of the ephebe's oath:

ἀλλ᾽ ὃν πόλις στήσειε, τοῦδε χρὴ κλύειν
καὶ σμικρὰ καὶ δίκαια καὶ τἀναντία.
καὶ τοῦτον ἂν τὸν ἄνδρα θαρσοίην ἐγὼ
καλῶς μὲν ἄρχειν, εὖ δ᾽ ἂν ἄρχεσθαι θέλειν,
δορός τ᾽ ἂν ἐν χειμῶνι προστεταγμένον
μένειν δίκαιον κἀγαθὸν παραστάτην.
ἀναρχίας δὲ μεῖζον οὐκ ἔστιν κακόν.
αὕτη πόλεις ὄλλυσιν, ἥδ᾽ ἀναστάτους
οἴκους τίθησιν, ἥδε συμμάχου δορὸς
τροπὰς καταρρήγνυσι.

Sophocles *Antigone* 666-675

Whomever the city may appoint, one should
obey in things small and just, as well as in their opposites.
For my part, I would encourage this man
to rule nobly and consent to be well ruled,
and when assigned a post amid the spear storm, to remain,

---

13. Louise J. Kaplan (*Adolesence: The Farewell to Childhood* [New York: Simon and Schuster, 1984], 13) states: Adolescence is the time when "the individual passes from family life into cultural existence."

14. Inscription 204, line 12 in Marcus N. Tod, *A Selection of Greek Historical Inscriptions*, vol. 2: *From 403 to 323 B.C.* (Oxford: Oxford University Press, 1948), 303. For a text and discussion of the oath and allusions to it in Sophocles' *Antigone*, see Siewert 1977, especially 106-107. Jebb (Sophocles, 127) noticed Creon's allusion in "to remain a just and brave *parastatês*" (μένειν δίκαιον κἀγαθὸν παραστάτην Sophocles *Antigone* 671) to the oath's declaration, οὐδὲ λείψω τὸν πραρστάτην ὅπου ἂν στ⟨ο⟩ιχήσω (I will not desert the *parastatês* wherever I shall be stationed). A *parastatês* had to remain next to the man on his left so as to protect his neighbor with the left half of his shield and help maintain the cohesion of the phalanx.

there, a just and brave comrade beside his comrades.
There is no greater evil than lack of rule.
This destroys cities, this renders
houses desolate, this in the spear battle
causes routs to break out.

Creon does not exaggerate the consequences of deserting one's *parastatês* (Sophocles *Antigone* 671: he who stands at one's side). When the hoplite ranks were penetrated and the formation collapsed, rout brought rampant slaughter and ignominious defeat.[15] All this, members of Sophocles' actual audience knew, many from experience. But Creon prefaces his plea for Haemon's allegiance in language that mitigates its outrageousness by avoiding the words "great" and "unjust" (667). He expects his son to obey him even when he is acting unjustly in some great matter. Further, he speaks of remaining at the assigned place in the phalanx and amid the maelstrom of spears shattered by the armor and flesh of colliding hoplites. His military language is aimed at enlisting Haemon in the defense against an enemy (677-678). Convinced his son favors Antigone, he wants Haemon at his side. The issue for him is filial allegiance claimed above Haemon's standing as a citizen and as a betrothed. He uses language appropriate to his own status as a hoplite. Haemon continues his father's idiom but modifies it to his status as an ephebe:

σοῦ δ' οὖν πέφυκα πάντα προσκοπεῖν ὅσα
λέγει τις ἢ πράσσει τις ἢ ψέγειν ἔχει.
. . . .
ἐμοὶ δ' ἀκούειν ἔσθ' ὑπὸ σκότου τάδε.

Sophocles Antigone 688-689, 692

It is my nature to scout out for you
everything someone says or someone does or has to blame
. . . .
It is possible for me to hear things in the shadows.

When Haemon refers to himself as a "younger" man and "young," he acknowledges his status as an ephebe or "pre-hoplite."[16] The latter, a youth of

---

15. For "the push and collapse" of hoplite phalanx, see Victor Davis Hanson, *The Western Way of War* (New York and Oxford: Oxford University Press, 1989), 171-84.

16. The expression "pre-hoplite" is that of Vidal-Naquet, *Black Hunter*, 120. *Neôterou* (younger 719) and especially *neos* (young 728) denote youth but connote the young Athenian who, like Aeschines, upon leaving childhood, joined his fellow ephebes in roaming as a *peripolos* (a goer-around) (Aeschines *On the Embassy* 167). That Aeschines and the others fought beside mercenary troops also testifies to their marginality from the hoplite who fights beside citizens. For the institution of the ephebeia, see O. W. Reinmuch, "The Genesis of the Athenian Ephebia," *Transactions and Proceedings of the American Philological Association* 83 (1952), 34-50; Chrysis Pélékidis, *Histoire de l'éphébie attique des origines à 31 avant Jésus-Christ* (Paris: E. de Boccard, 1962), 71-79; Vidal-Naquet, *Black Hunter*, 106-128.

eighteen to twenty years, once roamed the frontiers with his age-mates patrolling and reconnoitering. In Attica of the 430s, ephebes probably served one year on guard duty at the Piraeus and another in forts on the frontiers. Before beginning the second year, they were paraded before the community and given a shield and spear. At this time, they swore the oath of citizenship in the shrine of Aglaurus on the Acropolis. Sophocles imbues Haemon's encounter with Creon with the respect not only of the son for the father but also of the young for the elder, more experienced warrior. Implied is the impropriety of conflict between a stripling and an adult normally averted by their different spheres of military service. At the same time, Sophocles phrases their encounter in terms of the scout reporting what he has learned to his superior. *Hêmeroskopoi* (day-watchers) regularly observed the enemy and reported what they saw. The messenger scout of Aeschylus' *Seven Against Thebes* assures Eteocles: "As for the rest, I will keep an eye faithfully watching by day, and when you know the situation outside the gates from the clarity of my report, you will be unharmed" (κἀγὼ τὰ λοιπὰ πιστὸν ἡμεροσκόπον / ὀφθαλμὸν ἔξω, καὶ σαφηνείᾳ λόγου / εἰδὼς τὰ τῶν θύραθεν ἀβλαβὴς ἔσῃ 66-68). But like Creon's day-watcher (Sophocles *Antigone* 253), the eye of Eteocles' scout can see only in the daylight. The ephebe Haemon scouts out things in the dark and brings information.

In the relationship of the scout with his officer, differences of age are subsumed beneath the cooperation of keener eyes and wiser minds. It is a relationship based also on trust and acceptance as well as the possibility of disaster should the officer reject the news conveyed by the ephebe and scout. Haemon appeals to such trust and mutual success:

ἐμοὶ δὲ σοῦ πράσσοντος εὐτυχῶς, πάτερ,
οὐκ ἔστιν οὐδὲν κτῆμα τιμιώτερον.
τί γὰρ πατρὸς θάλλοντος εὐκλείᾳ τέκνοις
ἄγαλμα μεῖζον, ἢ τί πρὸς παίδων πατρί;

Sophocles Antigone 701-704

As far as I am concerned, there is no possession more valuable,
father, than a father who is prospering in good fortune.
What greater pride and joy is there for children than
a father flourishing in fame, or what for a father in children?

Haemon tries to bring his father to realize that when one prospers, they both prosper, and that age matters not at all in comparison with judgment rightly spoken (*Antigone* 719-723). That he devotes almost half of his speech to soothing Creon's feelings indicates that he fears his father's ability to yield.

Haemon couches his plea in the language of the contest, but he fails to persuade Creon, because honor and renown are won by action and lost by yielding to one's opponent. Alvin W. Gouldner remarks: "Since [contestants in the Greek contest system] seek to increase their superiority vis-à-vis all others, they cannot, in consequence, always be wholeheartedly committed to a victory of their own team when it enters into a contest with others."[17] Creon undermines his own rule by acting like a competitor in a contest with Antigone, a contest played out for honor and renown before the Theban people. He cannot yield and preserve the honor and renown of his household without forfeiting to Antigone the approval he wants from the citizens (Sophocles *Antigone* 292) and granting her the honor that he wants for himself. To maintain the contest, he attacks his adviser for his youth, the ephebe's most treasured quality. In the ensuing stichomythic battle, however, Creon's claim to an elder's wisdom (726) proves to be invalid. Reminded of the people's approval of Antigone (733), he rebuts: "Will the city tell me what I should order?" (πόλις γὰρ ἡμῖν ἁμὲ χρὴ τάσσειν ἐρεῖ; 734). The question strikes Haemon as a juvenile remark. But Creon means it, as his next words reveal: "Should I rule the land for anyone else but myself?" (ἄλλῳ γὰρ ἢ 'μοὶ χρή με τῆσδ' ἄρχειν χθονός 736). "Isn't the city considered to belong to the man in power?" (οὐ τοῦ κρατοῦντος ἡ πόλις νομίζεται 738). His son tells him: "There is no city that belongs to one man" (πόλις γὰρ οὐκ ἔσθ' ἥτις ἀνδρός ἐσθ' ἑνός 737), and "Nobly would you rule a desert alone" (καλῶς ἐρήμης γ' ἂν σὺ γῆς ἄρχοις μόνος 739). Creon places himself above the city. He is the man of the first stasimon who dares the ignoble and thus renders himself *apolis* (without a city). Haemon knows that what Creon is doing he is doing for himself, not for Thebans, who approve of Antigone.

Creon's behavior epitomizes K. J. Dover's definition of *hubris* as "a term applied to any kind of behaviour in which one treats other people just as one pleases, with an arrogant confidence that one will escape paying any penalty for violating their rights and disobeying any law or moral rule accepted by society, whether or not such a law or moral rule is regarded as resting ultimately on divine sanctions."[18] By discounting the city, Creon treats its citizens and Antigone as he chooses and intervenes in matters that concern the gods. Haemon perseveres, advising his father against erring by trampling upon the honors of the gods (Sophocles *Antigone* 743, 745), and only gives up when Creon seems to him to be without good sense (755) and no longer listening (757). Creon fails to meet the conditions of Haemon's *aporthoîs*, and Haemon no longer follows him. For Creon, Haemon's refusal to accept his judgments aligns his son as Antigone's ally in his "battle" against her. "This one, it seems, battles as an ally for the woman (ὅδ', ὡς ἔοικε, τῇ γυναικὶ συμμαχεῖ 740).[19] Haemon has spoken with the best of filial motives, but, to his father, he comes on the side of an enemy and therefore is an enemy. Creon never grasps the sincerity of Haemon's concern for him.

---

17. Gouldner, *Enter Plato*, 52.

18. K. J. Dover, *Greek Homosexuality* (Cambridge: Harvard University Press, 1978), 34.

19. The prefix *sym-* of *symmachei* (Sophocles *Antigone* 740) designates Haemon as someone fighting "with" Antigone as her ally (*symmachos*).

Haemon is comparable to the Athenian heralds of the Theban Dead myth in that both offer an opportunity for a peaceful removal of the corpses. He also comes as a messenger scout with the news for his leader and as a son concerned for his father. But when he does not concede absolute obedience, Creon accuses him of being "inferior to a woman" (γυναικὸς ὕστερον Sophocles *Antigone* 746), a vulgarity that may play on the assonance of *hysteron* (inferior) with *hystera* (ὑστέρα womb). Under no circumstances does it have a place on a father's lips. A father injures himself and his household by impugning his son's social standing as a man. Haemon feels some such sting: "You would not catch this person succumbing to disgrace" (οὔ τἂν ἕλοις ἥσσω γε τῶν αἰσχρῶν ἐμέ 747). "This person," translating an emphatic *eme* (me), implies that it is Creon who is guilty of a disgrace: he has convicted himself from his own mouth of fearing submission to a woman (678, 680). Haemon does not deny concern for Antigone, but with his reply to Creon's "And yet, your every word now is for her" (ὁ γοῦν λόγος σοι πᾶς ὑπὲρ κείνης ὅδε 748), he insists that he speaks "also for you and me and the gods below" (καὶ σοῦ γε κἀμοῦ, καὶ θεῶν τῶν νερτέρων 749). His purpose is to keep his father from transgressing against the gods and the citizens—to no avail.

Creon cannot escape Antigone's hold on his mind: "There is no way you will ever marry her while she lives" (ταύτην ποτ' οὐκ ἔσθ' ὡς ἔτι ζῶσαν γαμεῖς Sophocles *Antigone* 750). "Then she'll die," his son replies, "and in dying, she will destroy someone" (ἥδ' οὖν θανεῖται καὶ θανοῦσ' ὀλεῖ τινα 751). The Scholiast understands that Haemon may be proposing his own death but also suggests that Creon thinks Haemon will kill him.[20] "Do you go so far as to be brazenly threatening?" Creon asks (752). To whom the threat is directed, Sophocles leaves uncertain to good dramatic effect, but there is no doubt that Creon perceives a threat to himself in Haemon's words and takes it seriously. Haemon denies that he is threatening him (753). H. Lloyd-Jones and N. G. Wilson offer an attractive suggestion for emending line 753 that strengthens Haemon's denial: "What manner of threat is it to acquaint you with my resolutions?" (τίς δ' ἔστ' ἀπειλὴ πρός σ' ἐμὰς γνώμας λέγειν;)[21] Haemon does not, then, proffer a threat or ploy of any sort but his judgment that

---

20. Scholiast on Sophocles *Antigone* 751: δι' ἑαυτὸν ἔφη· ὁ δὲ Κρέων ᾤετο δι' αὐτὸν λέγειν (He spoke about himself, but Creon thought he was speaking about him).

21. Lloyd-Jones and Wilson (*Sophoclis Fabulae*, 213) emend πρὸς κενὰς γνώμας (against empty judgments Sophocles *Antigone* 753) το πρός σ' ἐμὰς γνώμας (you with my resolutions). H. Lloyd-Jones ("Sophoclea," *Classical Quarterly* 4 [1954], 93) explains: "Haemon is using the word γνώμας to mean 'intentions, purposes, resolves' (see sense III.5 in LSJ) [that is, Liddell, Scott, and Jones, *Lexicon*, 354 s.v. γνώμη]. But Creon thinks he is using it to mean 'judgments, opinions' (sense III.1 in LSJ). That is why he complains that Haemon is trying to lecture him: a complaint that might, it is true, have been provoked by the words the manuscripts assign to Haemon at 753. But it is more likely that this retort was stimulated by a sentence which Creon could misinterpret to mean 'to tell you my judgement or opinions'." See also Lloyd-Jones and Wilson, *Sophoclea*, 135.

someone will die. Still, Creon understands Haemon to be threatening him, and he and his son end on the same note as they began—using the same words but speaking different languages.

Creon, whose ruling principles condemned putting a *philos* above the city, demands his son's loyalty before all else. He who invited citizens to come forward and speak now tries to silence his son: "Empty of good sense, you will instruct me to your sorrow" (κλαίων φρενώσεις, ὧν φρενῶν αὐτὸς κενός Sophocles *Antigone* 754). Unless Haemon stops talking—unless he shuts up—Creon will hurt him. Still reluctant to point out his father's folly in not accepting good advice, Haemon responds indirectly: "If you were not my father, I would say you are the one without good sense" (εἰ μὴ πατὴρ ἦσθ', εἶπον ἄν σ' οὐκ εὖ φρονεῖν 755). After threatening his son with pain, it is no wonder Creon thinks Haemon is trying to flatter him with talk of father in order to wheedle Antigone free. He cannot comprehend that his son is loyal to him as well as to the city. Clinging to the idea of Haemon as Antigone's ally, he reviles him: "You woman's slave thing, do not try to play up to me" (γυναικὸς ὢν δούλευμα, μὴ κώτιλλέ με 756). With that, Creon banishes his son from his statuses as son, free man, and citizen.

Haemon asks: "Do you wish to speak and, while speaking, hear nothing?" (βούλῃ λέγειν τι καὶ λέγων μηδὲν κλύειν Sophocles *Antigone* 757). His words are unthreatening and without violence. They ask whether his father gets to do all the talking, but they recognize the futility of talking to him. Haemon comes to inform Creon for Creon's own good and, once silenced, he ceases to be an adviser. Creon's next word quickens the wrath that Haemon vents in his exit and next meeting with his father: "*Alêthes!*"[22] There is nothing playful or ironic about Creon's response. He does not intend, even in pretense, to listen to his son. *Alêthes* is blunt: "Right!" Creon will end the contest by eliminating what he perceives to be its cause— Antigone: "Bring that hated thing so this instant before his eyes she may die next to her bridegroom" (ἄγετε τὸ μῖσος, ὡς κατ' ὄμματ' αὐτίκα / παρόντι θνῄσκῃ πλησία τῷ νυμφίῳ 760-761). Aristotle, in formulating his culture's prejudices as a philosophical system, states that "the older, more dignified and powerful, more mature" man is more fit to rule than "the younger and immature" (πρεσβύτερον καὶ τέλειον τοῦ νεωτέρου καὶ ἀτελοῦς *Politics* 1259 B 3-4). Creon fails to benefit from the prejudices of Sophocles' audience, and his use of "bridegroom" in relinquishing Haemon to Antigone betrays the fears that also peer forth from Aristotle's prescriptions on male leadership in the body politic of the family.[23] Creon dreads that Antigone will defeat him through her control of Haemon. In the

---

22. Liddell, Scott, and Jones (*Lexicon*, 64 s.v. ἀληθής) find ἄληθες (Sophocles *Antigone* 758) to be spoken "ironically."

23. John H. Winkler (*The Constraints of Desire* [New York and London: Routledge, 1990], 7) observes: "The relation of husband to wife, says Aristotle, is like a democracy. In a democracy all citizens are equal in rights and are equally eligible for office. Those elected to office are

cosmogony of the audience, the mighty father Ouranos and King Cronus, his son, were both vanquished by the collusion of a female and a young male (Hesiod *Theogony* 164-182, 467-491).

Throughout the episode, Creon becomes ever more insistent upon the deference due him because of his age and position as father and absolute ruler. Haemon moves from being cautious with his touchy father to astonished bewilderment over Creon's views on leadership to being hurt by his father's refusal to recognize his son's love for him. Later, the audience may rethink Creon's love for his son (Sophocles *Antigone* 1214, 1226-1230), but for now they cannot overlook the folly of his words or the madness of mind that threatens to slay Antigone before Haemon's eyes. The Coryphaeus realizes how deeply Haemon has been wounded, but Creon dismisses his son with the promise that he will not release Antigone and Ismene from death (769). Nevertheless, with but a slight urging from the Coryphaeus, he suddenly releases Ismene, illustrating a propensity for snap judgments that he stubbornly defends but abruptly abandons when he pauses to admit what he knows is right. It is a tendency that will again show itself after Creon's encounter with Tiresias.

μόρῳ δὲ ποίῳ καί σφε βουλεύῃ κτανεῖν, the Coryphaeus asks ("By what death are you planning to kill her?" Sophocles *Antigone* 772). Creon announces his plans for Antigone's funeral:

ἄγων ἐρῆμος ἔνθ' ἂν ἦ βροτῶν στίβος
κρύψω πετρώδει ζῶσαν ἐν κατώρυχι,
φορβῆς τοσοῦτον ὅσον ἄγος φεύγειν προθείς
ὅπως μίασμα πᾶσ' ὑπεκφύγῃ πόλις.

Sophocles Antigone 773-776

By leading her where the path is deserted of people
I will hide her alive in a rocky cave,
setting forth enough food to escape pollution
so that the whole city may escape miasma.

Creon's food invokes the funeral feast for the daughter who died before marriage, while his language, "setting forth" (προθείς), evokes the *prothesis* (wake). Following custom, her mother dressed the body in wedding clothes and left as a marker for a

---

invested with insignia marking their temporary and purely conventional difference from the rest of the citizens. When the period of office is over, they take off those insignia and return to a state of equality. The only difference, says Aristotle, is that in the case of husband and wife the distinction is permanent. This is mind-boggling. Given Aristotle's other conceptions of the inherent, definitional inferiority of the female, there was no need for him to compare the relation of husband and wife to democratic equality, no need to raise the thought that wives might, if elected, govern the household in turn with their husbands, and no need to conjure up the paradoxical image of a democratic system in which the same citizens always hold office."

virgin's grave a *loutophoros*, an urn for holding water for the nuptial bath, or its representation in stone.[24] But food also recalls the wedding feast for a departing daughter. Hades seizes Persephone from the "meadow of her virginity" and, speeding her to his nether realm, consummates their union with a pomegranate seed.[25] The death of the virgin daughter necessarily precedes her birth as a mother, a necessity evoking the sense of loss and finality found in wedding hymns and funeral dirges alike.[26] But when, in reality, death intervenes before marriage, aborting and reifying this symbolic death, then grief is twofold—for the dead and for the loss of all that should have been. To suggest the depths of Achilles' grief for Patroclus, Homer draws upon "a father who laments as he burns the bones of his son, just now married, who died and brought grief to his wretched parents" (πατὴρ οὗ παιδὸς ὀδύρεται ὀστέα καίων, / νυμφίου, ὅς τε θανὼν δειλοὺς ἀκάχησε τοκῆας *Iliad* 23.222-223). The *Palatine Anthology* provides another example: "Hades came first and took Crocale's virginity. The Hymenaios [Wedding Song] ended in cries of grief. It was not the bed chamber lulled her parents' hopes but the tomb" ("Αιδης τὴν Κροκάλης ἔφθασε παρθενίην· εἰς δὲ γόους Ὑμέναιος ἐπαύσατο· τὰς δὲ γαμούντων ἐλπίδας οὐ θάλαμος κοίμισεν, ἀλλὰ τάφος *Palatine Anthology* 7.183). Athenians called the woman who died before marriage "a bride of Hades," a paradox that expresses this profound anomaly by blending the transitions of marriage and funeral.[27]

Creon is focused on avoiding pollution, but as a Theban in anti-Athens mythmaking, "he has only the most limited notion of what constitutes pollution and

---

24. On wedding clothes, see Alexiou, *Ritual Lament*, 120. Hecuba speaks of robes she uses in dressing Astyanax's body for burial: "These fineries from Phrygia that you should have worn at your wedding to a high-born woman of Asia, I now am placing on your body" (ἃ δ' ἐν γάμοισι χρῆν σε προσθέσθαι χροΐ / Ἀσιατίδων γήμαντα τὴν ὑπερτάτην, / Φρύγια πέπλων ἀγάλματ' ἐξάπτω χροός Euripides *Trojan Women* 1218-1220). For *loutrophoros*, see H. J. Rose, "The Bride of Hades," *Classical Philology* 20 (1925), 238; Eva Keuls, *The Reign of the Phallus* (New York: Harper and Row, 1985), 131 and Illustration 113; John H. Oakley and Rebecca H. Sinos, *The Wedding in Ancient Athens* (Madison: The University of Wisconsin Press, 1993), 5-7 and figures 92-95, 122.

25. For Antigone as Kore, see Segal, *Tragedy and Civilization*, 179-181. For the meadow as symbol of virginity, see Marylin B. Arthur, "Politics and Pomegranates: An Interpretation of the Homeric *Hymn to Demeter*," in *"Homeric 'Hymn to Demeter',"* ed. Helene P. Foley, 219-221.

26. Alexiou, *Ritual and Lament*, 120.

27. Richard Seaford ("The Tragic Wedding," *Journal of Hellenic Studies* 107 [1987], 106) notes: "A transition effected by nature (death) is enclosed by the imagination with a similar transition effected by culture (marriage)." The bride of Hades is common in funerary epigrams. See *Palatine Anthology* 7.13, 182, 183, 185, 492, 507b, 508, 547. For the bride of Hades, see Rose, "The Bride of Hades," 238-242; Schmid-Stählin, *Die griechische Literatur*, 354 n. 4; Ian Jenkins, "Is There Life After Marriage? A Study of the Abduction Motif in Vase Paintings of the Athenian Wedding Ceremony," *Bulletin of the Institute of Classical Studies of the University of*

what constitutes purity."[28] The sickness that has afflicted the *polis* manifests the loss of differences between the living and dead resulting from his thinking (Sophocles *Antigone* 1015, 1052). Creon, however, imputes the sickness to Antigone (732, 776) and, after sending her away, declares: "The fact is, we are pure in the matter of this maiden" (ἡμεῖς γὰρ ἁγνοὶ τοὐπὶ τήνδε τὴν κόρην 889). Yet the attempt to make a *pharmakos* (human drug) of Antigone cannot succeed. The *pharmakos* assumes the community's pollution for murder (Photius *Library* 534 A), for example, or for the desecration of a temple (Harpocration *Lexicon of the Ten Orators* s.v. *pharmakos*), and, with his expulsion, removes the pollution from the community. Antigone is not guilty of impiety and therefore does not bear the miasma and cannot remove it.[29] Moreover, the citizens do not agree with Creon's assessment of her guilt (733). It is he who introduced the pollution into the community by exposing Polyneices' corpse and those of the Argives. What is more, his expulsion of Antigone spreads the pollution by depriving his house of fertility when he prevents her transition from girl to wife and mother of children. Loss of fertility, foretold by Antigone *teras* and refined by the chorus' image of the mowing down of the last root, has already occurred.

The Antigone who enters the house after line 581 is a *pais*, as her hair, long and flowing, as we imagine it, and her freedom of movement indicate.[30] Her roaming the city on the dreadful night of the Argives, which seems so unrealistic, and her quitting the house and Ismene for the country, send the same cultural message as Iasos' virgin daughter, Atalanta, hunting in the wilderness and running too swiftly for any suitor to catch.[31] Sexually "ripe," Atalanta spurns marital consummation (*gamos*), flees Hippomenes and her father's house, and "goes into the mountains' lofty peaks" (ᾤχετο δ' ὑψηλὰς ἐς κορυφὰς ὀρέων Theognis 1292). There the watchmen catch her like an animal in the hunt,[32] an encoding of her virginity. The

---

28. Segal, *Tragedy and Civilization*, 174.

29. For Antigone as *pharmakos*, see Richmond Y. Hathorn, "Sophocles' *Antigone*: Eros in Politics," *The Classical Journal* 54 (1958-1959), 113; Segal, *Tragedy and Civilization*, 175. For the *pharmakos*, see Jane Ellen Harrison, *Prolegomena to the Study of Greek Religion*, 3d ed. (Cambridge: Cambridge University Press, 1922), 95-114; Vernant, *Myth and Tragedy*, 128-135; Girard, *Violence and the Sacred*, 101-110; J. Bremmer, "Scapegoat Rituals in Ancient Greece," *Harvard Studies in Classical Philology* 87 (1983), 299-320.

30. The text gives no clues beyond Antigone's status as a *pais* to the appearance of her hair, but masks were probably realistic and appropriate for the role (Pickard-Cambridge, *The Dramatic Festivals of Athens*, 192). In wedding scenes, the binding up of a bride's long hair, emblem of her virginity, is part of her preparations for the wedding. See the Attic red-figure *lebes* by the Washing Painter in Oakley and Sinos, *The Wedding in Ancient Athens*, 14-17, and figure 23.

31. Apollodorus *The Library* 3.9.2; Marcel Detienne, *Dionysus Slain*, trans. Mireille Muellner and Leonard Muellner (Baltimore and London: The Johns Hopkins University Press, 1979), 27-34.

32. Liddell, Scott, and Jones, *Lexicon*, 799 s.v. θηράω.

woman before marriage is a wild animal. Thus, Ischomachus' wife had to be "gentled to the hand" before he could converse with her (χειροήθης Xenophon *Oeconomicus* 7.10). The savagery that the elders see (Sophocles *Antigone* 471) betrays Antigone's virginity as well as her lineage. Creon asserts that she is a "field to be plowed," an *arôsimos* (569), ready for the work of the sexual act.[33] Without sowing and work, the soil reverts to a wild state, and, without being sown, Antigone remains in a wild state. This is the Antigone Creon has enclosed in a rocky cavern.

---

33. DuBois, *Sowing the Body*, 72.

6. Antigone, Bride of Hades
Third Stasimon and Fourth Episode (781-943)

Having built an atmosphere of wedding and funeral, Sophocles has his chorus of elders pass over the political and moral concerns of the argument between father and son for a hymn of praise to Eros, god of sexual passion. Shown in vase paintings as a winged boy, Eros was present throughout the wedding ceremony, hovering before the *loutophoros* and assisting in dressing and veiling the bride.[1] He embodies the physical force that transforms the bride to a wife and bearer of children and so is involved with the accoutrements of change in the ceremony. The elders have found Eros "in the soft cheeks of a young girl" (ἐν μαλακαῖς παρειαῖς / νεάνιδος Sophocles *Antigone* 783-784), attributing Haemon's quarrel with his father to Antigone's influence. They sing of the gods of erotic passion and the game that Aphrodite and Eros have been playing with the men and recognize:

νικᾷ δ' ἐναργὴς βλεφάρων
ἵμερος εὐλέκτρου
νύμφας, τῶν μεγάλων πάρεδρος ἐν ἀρχαῖς
θεσμῶν.

Sophocles *Antigone* 795-799

Desire radiant from the eyelids
of a well-bedded bride prevails,
companion in rule with the great
ordinances.

But it is Creon, not Antigone, who initiates this game when he keeps Haemon from marrying her and shutting her away in the women's quarters and master bedroom of the house. Now things are passing beyond Creon's control. Aphrodite is playing a

---

1. See Max Collignon, "Cérémonies du marriage," in *Dictionnaire des antiquités grecques et romaines*, vol. 3, ed. Ch. Daremberg and Edm. Saglio (Paris: Librairie Hachette, 1918), 1649-1650 and figures 4861, 4865, 4866, 4870; Oakley and Sinos, *The Wedding in Ancient Athens*, 14-21 and figures 14, 15, 20, 21, 23, 24, 29, 30, 31.

different game with Creon and Haemon, the deadly kind she plays with those like Atalanta and Hippolytus who flee marriage.[2] The Eros of the third stasimon is "an *eros* reaching for death, not life."[3] Energies that should be spent on living are going to be squandered on Haemon's dying, since Eros' power to create life and quicken the root of the house ranges outside the civilized bonds of marriage. The force of Eros, free of the civilizing restraints of marriage, has been unleashed to wreak havoc over Creon's household. The audience now are spectators at the game the goddess will play with Haemon through the "radiant desire" he has been denied.

Among Athenians, intimations of death pervaded marriage's joyous promise of the child, while beside the laments and mourning of burial were practiced fertility rituals. Underlying each celebration was the spirit of the other, because both marriage and funeral effected an irreversible transition. Associations between marriage and funeral in Athenian culture had deep roots in these transitions.[4] The dead entered Hades' house, never to return. The bride left her father's house, never to return as the same person, to enter another man's house where she perished as a virgin. This contiguity between life and death was concretized by common rituals for both the corpse and the bride.[5] Marriage and death mainly concerned women; they dressed and perfumed the corpse and the bride, adorning both with special clothes and garlanding the heads; they joined in the appropriate hymns and cries. In both ceremonies, a mule cart enacted the transition in a procession that took place on the margins of the day. The bride was escorted by her groom, her *nympheutria* (she who adorns the bride) and his *parochos* (he who rides beside in a chariot), the girl's parents, children crowned with myrtle, and friends, through an evening lighted by torches and resounding with hymns sung to the lyre and flute. A similarly elaborate procession conducted the body to the cemetery in the darkness of early dawn. Feasts, torches, and sacrifices, strictly controlled by legislation, accompanied both ceremonies. These associations, ordinary and familiar from countless enactments, helped form Athenians as Athenians. Sophocles could depend upon his audience to respond to his clues to them.

Antigone is a character in the play and has no existence apart from its dialogue, song, and actions. At the same time, she represents a very real phenomenon,

2. For Atalanta, see Detienne, *Dionysus Slain*, 40-45; Vernant, *Mortals and Immortals: Collected Essays*, 198-200.

3. Segal, *Tragedy and Civilization*, 198.

4. For rituals of marriage, see Collignon, "Cérémonies du marriage," 1647-1654; James Redfield, "Notes on the Greek Wedding," *Arethusa* 15 (1982), 181-201; Robert Garland, *The Greek Way of Life* (Ithaca, NY: Cornell University Press, 1990), 217-225; Oakley and Sinos, *The Wedding in Ancient Athens*, 22-37. For rituals of the funeral, see Monceaux, "Funus," 1370-1381; Kurtz and Boardman, *Greek Burial Customs*, 142-161; Robert Garland, *The Greek Way of Death* (London: Duckworth, 1985), 21-37; Shapiro, "Iconography," 631-644.

5. Alexiou, *Ritual Lament*, 120; Redfield, "Notes on the Greek Wedding," 188-189; Seaford, "The Tragic Wedding," 106-107.

namely, a young nubile woman.[6] In life, immortals and mortals alike envied such a woman during the days of her wedding for her youthful beauty and vibrant potential and perhaps for the slipping of the bonds of the human condition in ritual death and rebirth.[7] She had spent all her life surrounded by household implements (vases, cosmetic boxes, perfume containers) with scenes of weddings. Weddings were among her first memories, and she participated from an early age in the preparations and celebration of weddings for relatives and friends. Even as a child, she felt an excited and fearful anticipation of her own "woman's day" sometime far off, and too soon. With Antigone, Sophocles depicts such a girl and woman deprived by a man of the day that even the iambic poet Hipponax granted in his crabby verse was one of her two happiest days alive–the other being the day her husband carries her dead body to the grave (fr. 68 West).

As Antigone comes out of her *kyrios'* house, escorted by his slaves (Sophocles *Antigone* 885, 931), the Coryphaeus draws attention to her entrance: "I am no longer able to hold streams of tears when I see Antigone here approaching the bridal chambers that give rest to all" (οὐκέτι πηγὰς δύναμαι δακρύων, / τὸν παγκοίταν ὅθ' ὁρῶ θάλαμον / τήνδ' Ἀντιγόνην ἀνύτουσαν 803-805).[8] She stands before the door and cries out: "See me, citizens of my paternal land" (ὁρᾶτέ μ', ὦ γᾶς πατρίας πολῖται 806). Sophocles' elders are already watching Antigone, but she evidently wants something more: she wants them to *look at* her. Nothing is said about the actor's costume except for its "noose of fine linen" (βρόχῳ μιτώδει σινδόνος 1222), variously considered a girdle, headband, or veil.[9] Antigone herself, however, implicitly reveals what she is wearing, a violet-colored dress, instantly

6. It should be remembered that, in supplementing Antigone's words and deeds with general information from the culture, we are not dealing with unavailable details of the character's imaginary life. On the contrary, we agree with Kirkwood (*A Study of Sophoclean Drama*, 68) that "We have no right to construct a picture of Oedipus as a boy and trace his psychological development from that age." But to reconstruct a social experience common to most young Athenian women as background for what is happening to Antigone is not only appropriate but consistent with our approach to recapturing the play through the eyes of Sophocles' original audience. Indeed, it is fair to say that *Antigone* cannot be fully comprehended by any audience without knowledge of this sort.

7. Oakley and Sinos (*The Wedding in Ancient Athens*, 27) suggest that "The custom of pelting the bride and groom with flowers" might provide jealous onlookers with a means of unleashing their aggression. They point to the custom of pelting (*phyllobolia*) victors in the panhellenic games with leaves as an abreaction of aggressive feeling.

8. Creon commands his slaves to lead Antigone off (Sophocles *Antigone* 885) and threatens them (931) for their slowness, so Antigone must be escorted by more than one slave.

9. For the suggestion that the "noose of fine linen" is her girdle, see Scholiast on line 1222: μιτρώδη βρόχον λέγει, ὅστις ἦν ζώνη ἀπὸ σινδόνος (he says "noose of fine linen, which was her girdle from linen"). Kamerbeek (*Antigone* 197) adds "headband" to the Scholiast's suggestion, while Jebb (*Antigone*, 217) states "Antigone used her veil."

recognizable from its color as a wedding dress.[10] She has bound up her hair for her wedding and arranged a veil over her face:

ἀλλά μ' ὁ παγ-
κοίτας "Αιδας ζῶσαν ἄγει
τὰν Ἀχέροντος
ἀκτάν, οὔθ' ὑμεναίων
ἔγκληρον, οὔτ' ἐπὶ νυμ-
φείοις πώ μέ τις ὕμνος ὕ-
μνησεν, ἀλλ' Ἀχέροντι νυμφεύσω.

Sophocles Antigone 810-816

But Hades,
the all-provider of rest, is leading me alive
to Acheron's shore,
without a share of wedding
hymns. No song
at my wedding sang out for me,
but I shall wed Acheron.

The *pais* has been transformed, rather, Antigone has transformed herself from *pais* into bride.

During the wedding feast, relatives and guests dined, segregated by sex. The bride enjoyed little of the food celebrating her giving out. She was hindered by the veil drawn over her face and anxiously awaited the rite that initiated her passage to her groom and procession to his house. The feast was at last over, and time had come to celebrate the *anakaluptêria* (rite of unveiling). She stood, turned toward the men, and removed her veil for the first time among the men.[11] It was her "moment of consent" for which she received from her groom the "gifts of the unveiling" that compensate her for her lost virginity. "This act signified that the marriage was in some way officially sanctified, and that the young girl is henceforth a married woman."[12] Anne Carson elaborates:[13]

---

10. Calder ("Sophokles' Political Tragedy, *Antigone*," 401) observes without comment: "Exit wronged maiden to death in bridal array." See also Seaford, "The Tragic Wedding," 113; Larry J. Bennett and Wm. Blake Tyrrell, "What Is Antigone Wearing?" *The Classical World* 85 (1991), 107-109. For the color, which is speculative, see Sappho (47 Edmonds) who calls the bride "violet-robed" (ἰοκόλπω), and Achilles Tatius (*Leucippe and Cleitophon* 2.11.4) for a wedding dress dyed with purple, the dye for Aphrodite's dress. See also Oakley and Sinos, *The Wedding in Ancient Athens*, 16.

11. For the *anakaluptêria*, see the entries for the term in Harpokration, *Lexicon of the Ten Orators*, Hesychius, *Orator's Lexicon*, Pollux, *Library* (2.59; 3.36) and the *Suda*. See also Collignon, "Cérémonies du marriage," 1650-1651; John H. Oakley, "The Anakalypteria," *Archäologischer Anzeiger* 97 (1982), 113-118.

12. Collingnon, "Cérémonies du marriage," 1651.

13. Anne Carson, "Putting Her in Her Place: Women, Dirt, and Desire," in *Before Sexuality:*

At the moment of unveiling, for the first time, the intact boundary of her person is violated by contact: the contact of vision. Ancient lexical sources leave no doubt that visual exposure was the function and official point of the ritual of the *anakalyptêria*. "In order that she may be seen by the men" is the reason why the bride rises and unveils. Once she has done so, the glance of the bridegroom from across the room penetrates her opened veil. She is no longer *parthenos* ("maiden"). She is touched.

Creon gives Antigone out in marriage without a feast and songs and without a "moment of consent." By his thinking, he is "pure" of her (ἀγνοὶ Sophocles *Antigone* 889); he has banished her permanently beyond the boundaries of his house and city and outside civilized space to the wilds of a cave. He has given her out to Hades to be his bride and ended her "residency up here" (μετοικίας . . . τῆς ἄνω 890), both in his house and in life. In the street, before the doors of the house where wedding processions customarily formed, Antigone calls out to the elders of the chorus, ὁρᾶτέ με (*horate me*, See me!) as she lifts her veil. The old men look at her, and Antigone is touched through her version of the *anakalyptêria*. Spoken by a woman in wedding clothes, *horate me* constitutes a speech act, words with the power to accomplish what they say.[14] In the *anakalyptêria*, the bride did not speak but silently lifted her veil. Passivity marked the bride. But just as Creon's edict forced Antigone to improvise in her rituals for Polyneices, so, too, must she act for herself in this matter. She calls the elders to see her, she lifts her veil, she gives herself to her groom, Hades. She is a woman deprived of marriage in life but a bride in death. The theme of the bride of Hades is reified in the Antigone who stands before the elders commanding them to see her.[15]

In the fourth episode, Sophocles intertwines motifs and rites of funeral and marriage that create a liminal zone or marginal state in time and space in which Antigone is simultaneously daughter of Oedipus' incest with Jocasta and bride of Hades. In the first capacity, she is moving away from her marriage with Haemon to the family of her origin.[16] Creon has corrupted the rituals of the funeral that aggregate the dead into the world of the dead by exposing the dead unwept and unmourned and by escorting the living to the grave. Antigone responds by performing rituals

---

The Construction of Erotic Experience in the Ancient Greek World, ed. David M. Halperin, John J. Winkler, and Froma I. Zeitlin (Princeton, NJ: Princeton University Press, 1990), 163.

14. J. L. Austin, *How to Do Things with Words*, 2d ed., ed. J. O. Urmson and Marina Sbisà (Cambridge: Harvard University Press, 1975), 60. Performance utterances are especially common in the plays of Aeschylus, for which see H. D. Cameron, "The Power of Words in the *Seven Against Thebes*," *Transactions and Proceedings of the American Philological Association* 101 (1970), 95-110; Yopie Prins, "The Power of the Speech Act: Aeschylus' Furies and Their Binding Song," *Arethusa* 24 (1991), 117-195.

15. For sources dealing with the bride of Hades, see Chapter 5, n. 27.

16. Richard Seaford ("The Imprisonment of Women in Greek Tragedy," *Journal of Hellenic Studies* 110 [1990], 76-90; *Reciprocity and Ritual*, 349-351) develops the idea of incest as a ramification of this movement.

of the wedding that are necessarily corrupted by her circumstances and solitary condition and by the fact that her groom is Hades. Creon's funeral is Antigone's wedding since, in the imagination, the one is a reflex of the other. Antigone, the young girl who dies before her wedding, conducts her own wedding rituals in her marriage to Hades and converts Creon's funeral procession to Hades' house into her bridal procession to her husband's wedding chamber (νυμφεῖον Sophocles *Antigone* 891). Thus, Antigone, like the living bride, simultaneously undergoes the transition from life to death and from virginity to motherhood. Like another bride of Hades, Hecuba's daughter Polyxena, she is no longer a bride and virgin.[17] For the living bride, the first transition is symbolic while the second comes through marriage and the intimacies of the wedding night. Both end in death for Antigone, but unlike Creon's transition rite, Antigone's allows her to experience, if only in her imagination, the joys of a husband and child.

During the days of her wedding, from the moment that preparations got under way for the bride's bath until after the *epaulia*, the day of feasting and presenting of gifts following her first night with her husband, the bride was never alone. She was the focus of everyone's attention. Women fussed over her clothes and adornments; men guarded her in public. During her wedding, her relatives and guests sang hymns of praise for her and her groom. Antigone's is a silent wedding—paralleling her silent death—without the torches, music, and songs that accompanied the brides of Athenians and those depicted on Achilles' shield:

νύμφας δ᾽ ἐκ θαλάμων δαΐδων ὕπο λαμπομενάων
ἠγίνεον ἀνὰ ἄστυ, πολὺς δ᾽ ὑμέναιος ὀρώρει·
κοῦροι δ᾽ ὀρχηστῆρες ἐδίνεον, ἐν δ᾽ ἄρα τοῖσιν
αὐλοὶ φόρμιγγές τε βοὴν ἔχον.

Homer Iliad 18.492-495

Brides from their bridal chambers, beneath shining torches,
they were leading up through the town. The loud wedding hymn
was rising. Young men were dancing and whirling about.
Among them, flutes and lyres resounded.

Antigone herself breaks the silence (Sophocles *Antigone* 806) when she begins to sing a wedding hymn for herself that is also a song of grief. She sings antiphonally with the Coryphaeus who responds in stately anapests. For an audience accustomed to song being answered by song, the Coryphaeus' reserved replies must have seemed strange, disrespectful, almost impious.

Creon disappears from the dialogue after line 780, not to be heard again for a hundred lines (Sophocles *Antigone* 883), but he remains before the audience

---

17. Hecuba calls for sea water so she can bathe and lay forth (as in a *prothesis*) her daughter who is "bride no bride and maiden no maiden" (νύμφην τ᾽ ἄνυμφον παρθένον τ᾽ ἀπάρθενον Euripides *Hecuba* 612).

throughout Antigone's scene with the Coryphaeus. It "means something," as H. D. F. Kitto remarks.[18] Earlier, when the Coryphaeus issued the collective opinion of the elders regarding god-sent dust (278-279), Creon brutally silenced him as an old fool. Creon was inside the house when the Coryphaeus expressed the elders' compassion for Antigone (376-383). Now, although Creon does not speak, he remains within earshot of all that is said. Creon's presence not only intimidates the Coryphaeus; it also gives Sophocles the motivation for the doubleness of the Coryphaeus' language in his observations before Antigone. The Coryphaeus in character as a Theban elder admonishes Antigone for her behavior, but he also speaks as the voice of a subtext consisting of the phrases and themes used to laud the Athenian dead at public funerals. For this reason, the Coryphaeus' responses have struck some readers as strange when addressed to a dying young woman.[19] Yet Sophocles' original audience may well have heard them as praise for Antigone who has forfeited her life to reprise a deed of the Athenians. With Creon's prolonged presence, Sophocles accounts for the Coryphaeus' language having one range of meanings for Creon and Antigone and another for an audience steeped in funeral oratory.

Antigone's actions in defying Creon's edict force her into the limbo of the woman who attempts a deed proper only for men. She becomes a woman at war with her city in Creon's estimation, that is, the marginal Amazon of Athenian mythmaking.[20] Creon triumphs over his Amazon by leading her to her death. The Coryphaeus justifies his triumph:

οὔκουν κλεινὴ καὶ ἔπαινον ἔχουσ᾽
ἐς τόδ᾽ ἀπέρχῃ κεῦθος νεκύων
οὔτε φθινάσιν πληγεῖσα νόσοις
οὔτε ξιφέων ἐπίχειρα λαχοῦσ᾽;[21]

---

18. Kitto, *Form and Meaning in Drama*, 147. Editors commonly have Creon exit after line 780 and return at 883, but there is nothing indicating his departure in the text. See Kitto's balanced discussions (146-147, 167-173).

19. For example, Vickers (*Towards Greek Tragedy*, 538) notes: "They weep with her, offering what seem to me to be empty and insincere consolations—we must all die; you will die famous, like a god"; Ronnet (*Sophocle*, 150) comments: "In fact, the chorus does not say a single word of sympathy or pity; to the appeal that Antigone addresses to it ('Look at me, citizens of my fatherland, walking on my last way'), it responds with hostile indifference that the young girl senses perfectly: 'Without being wept for, without loved ones . . . I undertake this road that waits for me' (v. 876-877)."

20. On the marginality of the *Amazons*, see Tyrrell, *Amazons*, 64-87.

21. Acceptance of J. D. Denniston's emendation of οὔκουν for οὐκοῦν (*The Greek Particles*, 2d ed. [Oxford: Oxford University Press, 1950], 436) raises the need to locate the question mark. Properly, the Greek does not allow one until line 822. The tone of the Coryphaeus' speech is interrogative before ἀλλ᾽ and declarative after ἀλλ᾽. Accordingly, we place the question mark after line 820, but the break, needed in written form, would probably have been a transition effected by the actor's voice.

ἀλλ᾽ αὐτόνομος ζῶσα μόνη δὴ
θνητῶν Ἀΐδην καταβήσῃ.

Sophocles Antigone 817-822

You are not departing, are you, for the recesses of the dead,
renowned and possessing praise,
neither struck by wasting diseases,
nor by the wages of the sword?
Rather, under your own law, alive, alone, and unique
among mortals, you will make your way down to Hades.

The drama of the Coryphaeus' speech derives from the actor's pronunciation of his first lines and the ambiguity that differences in intonation may provoke. For his first word, editors commonly print οὐκοῦν, the reading of the manuscripts, but J. D. Denniston's emendation, οὔκουν, is preferable.[22] Pronounced with a gliding upward pitch of the voice, as indicated by the acute accent, *oúkoun* is interrogative and strongly negative. On the other hand, *oukoûn*, pronounced with a gliding up followed by a gliding down of the pitch of the last syllable, lacks negative connotations and signals a statement.[23] Speaking before Creon, the Coryphaeus cannot preface his thoughts with οὐκοῦν. He implies with αὐτόνομος (*autonomos*) that Antigone has behaved like an independent state with her own law.[24] For Creon, she is a rebellious young woman and treacherous *philê* and cannot be going to the underworld amid renown and praise. Kitto describes the tensions on stage:[25]

> Few will deny that this is one of the most moving passages in lyric poetry. But it was written for the theatre—and what does the theatre show us here? Antigone, singing her young life away like this; the chorus, sympathetic, but gently condemning her—and then there is Creon, standing somewhere at the back, utterly unmoved. For him, it counts for nothing.

The operative word in Kitto's assessment is "gently," for it glosses over the apparent contradiction between the Coryphaeus' tears for Antigone ("sympathetic") and the harshness he now evinces ("condemning"). The Coryphaeus apologized for his tears, as it were, by placing them "outside gods' ordinances" (θεσμῶν / ἔξω

---

22. Denniston, *The Greek Particles*, 436.

23. On the distinctions between οὐκοῦν and οὔκουν, see Herbert Weir Smyth, *Greek Grammar*, rev. Gordon M. Messing (Cambridge: Harvard University Press, 1956; c. 1920), 663-664.

24. For example, see Herodotus 1.96.1: "While all the nations throughout the mainland were under their own laws, they came around into tyrannies in the following way" (ἐόντων δὲ αὐτονόμων πάντων ἀνὰ τὴν ἤπειρον ὧδε αὖτις ἐς τυραννίδας περιῆλθον). The decree marking the establishment of the Second Athenian Confederacy (February or March 377 B.C.) states as the purpose of the confederacy: "that the Lacedaemonians allow the Greeks to live in peace as free men and under their own laws" (ὅπως ἂν Λακεδ[αιμό]νιοι ἐῶσι τοὺς Ἕλληνας ἐλευθέ[ρ]ους [κα]ὶ αὐτονόμους ἡσυχίαν ἄγειν Tod, *Selection of Greek Historical Inscriptions*, 60).

25. Kitto, *Form and Meaning in Drama*, 169-170.

Sophocles *Antigone* 801-802). In his sober reply to Antigone's lament over her lost marriage, he speaks as a Theban elder in the presence of his lord. He is censuring Antigone with a question that is not really a question ("You're not going, are you?"), since he is not truly asking her. Accordingly, Denniston's emendation should be printed. The possibility remains, however, that Antigone may understand the Coryphaeus' words as praise of her womanhood in not dying a man's death and that this prompts her allusion in her next lyrics to Niobe, who is killed for boasting of her motherhood.

But there is more theater at work than meets an eye focused on the written οὔκουν. Sophocles could have his actor pronounce οὔκουν, anticipating a question to follow, but intone the ensuing lines more as a statement than a question. Such a misdirection of the audience's expectations would be facilitated by the fact that the Coryphaeus is not really asking a question. In this way, Sophocles could arouse doubts in the audience whether they had heard οὔκουν or οὐκοῦν. Received as a positive statement, the Coryphaeus' words confer upon Antigone the praise spoken over the dead by funeral orators in the Kerameikos: "Free of sickness of the body and without experience of the anxieties of the spirit that afflict the living, they obtain customary rites in great honor and much envy" (νόσων ἀπαθεῖς τὰ σώματα καὶ λυπῶν ἄπειροι τὰς ψυχάς, ἃς ἐπὶ τοῖς συμβεβηκόσιν οἱ ζῶντες ἔχουσιν, ἐν μεγάλῃ τιμῇ καὶ πολλῷ ζήλῳ τῶν νομιζομένων τυγχάνουσιν Demosthenes *Funeral Oration* 33); "They have ended their lives in this way, not entrusting themselves to chance or awaiting the death that comes of its own law but choosing for themselves the noblest death" (οὕτως τὸν βίον ἐτελεύτησαν, οὐκ ἐπιτρέψαντες περὶ αὑτῶν τῇ τύχῃ, οὐδ' ἀναμείναντες τὸν αὐτόματον θάνατον, ἀλλ' ἐκλεξάμενοι τὸν κάλλιστον Lysias *Funeral Oration* 79). Readers have often been puzzled by the Coryphaeus' wavering toward Antigone and have responded by probing his motives and character.[26] This approach, however, leads to those psychological questions we do better not to ask of a tragic character. More to the point, the confusion in meanings prompts the audience to hear what the Coryphaeus says as praise of Antigone and so of their own dead: "You are departing for the recesses of the dead, renowned and possessing praise."[27] The Coryphaeus' feelings cannot enter into an interchange between Sophocles and his audience because it works on a subtextual level not available to the Coryphaeus as a Theban

26. Winnington-Ingram (*Sophocles: An Interpretation*, 139) reasons that, since the Chorus "can hardly be hostile or sarcastic," "[i]t seems as though they have beaten around for some consolation to offer and hit upon the exceptional mode of her death as a source of fame."

27. The distinction between what Creon and Antigone hear and what the audience hears (given the actor's skill and the dynamics of οὐκοῦν and οὔκουν) resolves the debate over the Coryphaeus' reply. He is disapproving as heard by Creon and Antigone, but to the ears of the audience, he is praising Antigone. Thus Knox's question (*Heroic Temper*, 177 n. 8), namely, "Who is praising her?" receives an answer: the Coryphaeus as the voice of the subtext of funeral oratory.

elder. This doubleness, which depends upon the actor's skill, creates a meaning antithetical to that intended for Creon and Antigone, and one that cannot be printed on the page (with οὐκοῦν) without impoverishing the play's power to communicate with and arouse communication from its audience.

This subtextual interplay, in turn, conveys positive as well as subtextual meanings to αὐτόματος. Reference to Antigone's "own (*aut-*) law or custom (*nom-*) may recall the *agrapta nomima* (unwritten usages; Sophocles *Antigone* 454-455) that she honors above Creon's laws, while, through its subtextual meaning in funeral oratory, it foreshadows Antigone's *nomos* (908, 914) that she obeys at the greatest expense. Athenians also had a *nomos* concerning burial that was unique among Greeks (Demosthenes *Against Leptines* 141), and obedience to the funeral law became a topos of funeral oratory. "Following the law, I, too, must try to attain the wishes and expectations of each of you as far as possible" (χρὴ καὶ ἐμὲ ἑπόμενον τῷ νόμῳ πειρᾶσθαι ὑμῶν τῆς ἑκάστου βουλήσεώς τε καὶ δόξης τυχεῖν ὡς ἐπὶ πλεῖστον Thucydides 2.35.3). "Nevertheless, we must follow our ancient customs and, serving our ancestral law, lament those being buried" (ὅμως δ' ἀνάγκη τοῖς ἀρχαίοις ἔθεσι χρῆσθαι, καὶ θεραπεύοντας τὸν πάτριον νόμον ὀλοφύρεσθαι τοὺς θαπτομένους Lysias *Funeral Oration* 81). So also is Antigone acting under her own (*aut-*) both "in the choice of her enterprise" (πρὸς τὴν προαίρεσιν τοῦ ἐπιχειρήματος Scholiast *ad Antigone* 821) and "by using her own laws" (ἰδίοις αὐτῆς νόμοις χρησαμένη Scholiast *ad* 821). The Scholiast offers these as alternative explanations of her *nomos*, but both are the case in that Antigone dies for an enterprise comparable in many ways to that of the Athenians by obeying her own law (*nomos;* 908, 914).

At the wedding feast, relatives and guests praised the bride and groom by comparing them to gods and heroes. Such hyperbole comprises most of the wedding songs that have been preserved.[28] Without feasters to praise her, Antigone is compelled to find her own comparison:

> ἤκουσα δὴ λυγροτάταν ὀλέσθαι
> τὰν Φρυγίαν ξέναν
> Ταντάλου Σιπύλῳ πρὸς ἄ-
> κρῳ, τὰν κισσὸς ὡς ἀτενὴς
> πετραία βλάστα δάμασεν . . .
> ἅ με δαί-
> μων ὁμοιοτάταν κατευνάζει.

Sophocles Antigone 823-827, 832-833

I heard that she perished most sorrowfully,
the Phrygian guest,

---

28. Oakley and Sinos, *The Wedding in Ancient Athens*, 23-24.

daughter of Tantalus, on the peak
of Mt. Sipylus, whom a rocky
growth like tenacious ivy subdued . . .
    Very like her,
the deity beds me.

Richard Seaford has unveiled the "symbolic meaning" of the enclosure of women—
and both Antigone and Niobe are enclosed in rock—"namely, the retention of a girl
by her natal family at the expense of her sexual union with an outsider or marriage."[29]
After the death of her children in Thebes and the failure of her marriage, Niobe in
Aeschylus' play of this name returns to her father at Mt. Sipylus (Aeschylus fr.
154a Radt). Creon ends Antigone's marriage with Haemon by sending her back to
the family from which she came. She is no longer Haemon's betrothed but the
daughter of Jocasta and Oedipus.

    The Coryphaeus objects to Antigone's comparison: "No, [Niobe] is a god
begotten of god while we are mortals born to die" (ἀλλὰ θεός τοι καὶ θεογεννής,
/ ἡμεῖς δὲ βροτοὶ καὶ θνητογενεῖς Sophocles *Antigone* 834-835). He reproves
Antigone for comparing herself to a god, something others could have done for
Antigone with impunity in the joyous freedom of the wedding. To suit his purposes,
Sophocles makes Niobe a god, but his audience knew—and he knew they knew—
that in other myths she is a mortal, indeed, that her punishment came as a result of
her likening herself to a deity. Such boastfulness went beyond the pale. Nevertheless,
the doubleness of the Coryphaeus' language continues:

καίτοι φθιμένῃ μέγα κἀκοῦσαι
τοῖς ἰσοθέοις ἔγκληρα λαχεῖν
ζῶσαν καὶ ἔπειτα θανοῦσαν.

Sophocles Antigone 836-838

Still, it is a great thing for a dead woman to hear
that she obtains a portion with the godlike
while alive and, afterwards, while dead.

His is a comment that Creon would hear as ironic but which, in the subtext, lacks
irony and may be understood as a softening of the Coryphaeus' reproof and a
consolation promising Antigone future rewards.

    According to Jebb, Antigone wants pity, not recompense in the "hope for
posthumous fame."[30] Knox responds in the opposite vein, that Antigone has her
sight *sub specie aeternitatis*: "the hero, pitting himself alone against man's city and
its demand for submission to time and change, can find consolation only in some
kind of immortality, the quality of the gods."[31] Sophocles leaves Antigone's reason

---

29. Seaford, "Imprisonment of Women," 76.

30. Jebb, *Antigone*, 153.

31. Knox, *Heroic Temper*, 66. Whitman (*Sophocles*, 94) offers: "like Antigone and Electra,

for the comparison to the listener's imagination, and any reason will suffice provided the audience thinks about Antigone in a context of immortality. In this way, he appropriates for Antigone the consolation the funeral orator offers the surviving kin.[32] The aptness of Hyperides' remark cannot go unnoticed:

εἰ δ' ἔστιν αἴσθησις ἐν "Αιδου καὶ ἐμπιμέλεια παρὰ τοῦ δαιμονίου, ὥσπερ ὑπολαμβάνομεν, εἰκὸς τοὺς ταῖς τιμαῖς τῶν θεῶν καταλυομέναις βοηθήσαντας πλείστης ἐπιμελείας καὶ κηδεμονίας ὑπὸ τοῦ δαιμονίου τυγχάνειν.

Hyperides, Funeral Oration 43

If any perception does exist in Hades and any care from the deity, as we suppose, it is likely that those who were destroyed while coming to the aid of the gods' honors obtained care and attention from the deity.[33]

Antigone hears the Coryphaeus in the same way as Creon. To her, the young woman consigned alive to a rocky tomb, the Coryphaeus' comments cut to the quick: "I am mocked" (γελῶμαι Sophocles *Antigone* 838). She sees herself like Niobe only in terms of death and, when the Coryphaeus asserts a similarity between "portions" in life, Antigone revolts: "Why, by the gods of our fathers, do you insult me before I leave, and while I am still here before your eyes?" (τί με, πρὸς θεῶν πατρῴων, / οὐκ οἰχομέναν ὑβρίζεις / ἀλλὰ ἐπίφαντον; 839-841). Niobe boasted that she was more blessed with children than Leto (Νιόβη τῆς Λητοῦς εὐτεκνοτέρα εἶπεν ὑπάρχειν Apollodorus *The Library* 3.5.6). Leto took offense and sent her children, Artemis and Apollo, who killed all of Niobe's children. But Niobe also enjoyed the blessings of husband and childbearing, rightful expectations that Creon denies Antigone. Niobe offended a goddess; Antigone perishes by a man's *nomos*. Niobe mourns her children; Antigone, while comparing herself to Niobe *mater dolorosa*,[34] has no children to mourn.

When Antigone bemoans the fact that "Very like [Niobe], the deity beds me" (Sophocles *Antigone* 883), the verb (*kateunazei*) she uses might have assumed sexual connotations on another bride's lips. But the groom Antigone is thinking of is a *daimon*, "the veiled countenance of divine activity," in Walter Burkert's felicitous

---

Niobe followed a blameless love to excess, and in that excess found ruin but no reason for repentance, and her steadfastness itself—that continued excess—made her in very truth divine."

32. Ziolkowski (*Thucydides and the Tradition*, 127) notes, "Immortality is mentioned in every speech except the *Menexenus*."

33. See also: "[The dead] are mourned as mortals because of their nature, they are celebrated as immortals because of their bravery" (οἳ πενθοῦνται μὲν διὰ φύσιν ὡς θνητοί, ὑμνοῦνται δὲ ὡς ἀθάνατοι διὰ τὴν ἀρετήν Lysias *Funeral Oration* 80); Thucydides 2.43.2; Demosthenes, *Funeral Oration* 34.

34. Segal, *Tragedy and Civilization*, 180-181.

phrase.[35] Hades works his will with her, unseen. Allusions to her wedding give way to those of her funeral. Antigone now laments the manner of her death. She calls the elders to witness "how, unwept by *philoi* and under what laws, to the heaped-up mound of my unheard-of tomb, I am going" (οἵα φίλων ἄκλαυτος οἵοις νόμοις / πρὸς ἕρμα τυμβόχωστον ἔρ- / χομαι τάφου ποται-νίου 847-849). She does not lament her death itself, for that would undermine her allegiance to her *philos*. She laments how she is dying—condemned by Creon's *nomoi*, shut up alive in a tomb, and unwept. But no woman can lament her own death, not only because the dead do not mourn themselves but also because others are needed to mourn them. So painful is it to die without laments and hymns cried out by *philoi* that Sophocles has Antigone grieve that loss again some lines later (876-882). Antigone's is the silent death that Clytemnestra gives the hated Agamemnon.[36]

The Coryphaeus is moved to paternal feelings for Antigone whom he considers little more than a *pais* (Sophocles *Antigone* 378), but the lofty tone of his reply conveys reproach:

προβᾶσ᾽ ἐπ᾽ ἔσχατον θράσους
ὑψηλὸν ἐς Δίκας βάθρον
προσέπεσες, ὦ τέκνον, πολύ.

Sophocles Antigone 853-855

Advancing to the limit of daring,
you struck the high throne
of Justice, my child, hard.[37]

"The words mean," D. A. Hester asserts, "what they say: Antigone's rashness has brought her into collision with justice."[38] Hester perceives the admonishment for a rebellious young woman that the Coryphaeus intends for Creon's ears. Creon's Antigone, his Amazon, is a woman defined by daring, an attribute always reprehensible when displayed by a woman. The Coryphaeus admonishes this Antigone, but his words understood as a subtext of funeral oratory praise her. For daring to rescue the exposed corpse of her *philos*, Sophocles graces her with the

---

35. Walter Burkert, *Greek Religion*, trans. John Raffan (Cambridge: Harvard University Press, 1985), 180, and *Griechische Religion* (Stuttgart: W. Kohlammer, 1977), 280: *das verhüllte Gesicht göttlichen Wirkens*.

36. Silence is so strong an indicator as to deny the possibility of death. The citizens of Pherae assume that Alcestis is still alive since there are no sounds of beating or wailing heard from Admetus' house: "They would not be silent, if she were dead" (οὐ τἂν φθιμένης γ᾽ ἐσιώπων Euripides *Alcestis* 93).

37. The apparent contradiction between the paternal tone and the harshness of the reproach has caused difficulties and aroused suspicions that the text is corrupt. See Brown, *Sophocles: "Antigone,"* 195-196. Read as we propose, the lines are satisfactory, and the need to emend *polu(n)* to *podi* (that is, Antigone stubs her foot) vanishes.

38. Hester, "Sophocles the Unphilosophical," 35.

orator's praise for the men of the *epitaphios* and their Theban Dead exploit.[39] "They fought," Lysias says of the Athenians before Thebes, "and gained victory with justice as their ally" (τὸ δὲ δίκαιον ἔχοντες σύμμαχον ἐνίκων μαχόμενοι *Funeral Oration* 10).[40] This daring is esteemed for itself so that for Antigone, pressing hard against Justice shows her devotion to what is right.

The Coryphaeus reminds Antigone of the fate that has come to her through her father's winning of the throne of Thebes and its queen: "You are perhaps paying for your father's prize" (πατρῷον δ' ἐκτίνεις τιν' ἆθλον Sophocles *Antigone* 856). "You have touched thoughts excruciatingly painful for me," she replies (ἔψαυσας ἀλγει- / νοτάτας ἐμοὶ μερίμνας 857-858). Antigone acknowledges the "savagery" of her family and that her piety toward them has brought her to this end. Piety has merit, the Coryphaeus responds with an eye toward Creon, but power is not to be transgressed (872-875). As it turns out, his last line to her, "Your self-knowing temper destroyed you" (σὲ δ' αὐτόγνωτος ὤλεσ' ὀργά 875), summarizes Antigone's actions from the moment she first hears of Creon's edict, and assimilates her to the Athenians of Pericles' funeral oration:

> διαφερόντως γὰρ δὴ καὶ τόδε ἔχομεν ὥστε τολμᾶν τε οἱ αὐτοὶ μάλιστα καὶ περὶ ὧν ἐπιχειρήσομεν ἐκλογίζεσθαι· ὃ τοῖς ἄλλοις ἀμαθία μὲν θράσος, λογισμὸς δὲ ὄκνον φέρει. κράτιστοι δ' ἂν τὴν ψυχὴν δικαίως κριθεῖεν οἱ τά τε δεινὰ καὶ ἡδέα σαφέστατα γιγνώσκοντες καὶ διὰ ταῦτα μὴ ἀποτρεπόμενοι ἐκ τῶν κινδύνων.

> Thucydides 2.40.3

> In this respect, we are also different so that the same people are especially daring and especially reflective about what we attempt. Whereas for others, ignorance is boldness, calculation encourages hesitation. The strongest in courage would be rightly judged to be those who know dread and joy very clearly and for that reason do not turn away from dangers.

Creon breaks his long silence to stop Antigone's *kommos*: "Don't you know that in preference to dying no one would stop pouring out songs, if allowed?" (ἆρ' ἴστ' ἀοιδὰς καὶ γόους πρὸ τοῦ θανεῖν / ὡς οὐδ' ἂν εἷς παύσαιτ' ἄν, εἰ χρείη,

---

39. The Scholiast perceives this praiseworthy daring in the Coryphaeus' words: "Advancing to the highest throne of justice with daring, wishing to do something holy concerning your brother, you underwent the opposite, for you fell into an empty tomb" (προβᾶσα ἐπὶ τὸ τῆς δικαιοσύνης ἔσχατον βάθρον μετὰ θράσους, βουλομένη τε ὅσιόν τι δρᾶν περὶ τὸν ἀδελφὸν, τὰ ἐναντία πέπονθας· ἔπεσες γὰρ εἰς τὸ κενοτάφιον). He uses the *epi* of Sophocles' text (*Antigone* 853), which is usually translated to bring out a hostile collision, in a positive sense of attaining or reaching the altar.

40. Similar praise of the dead for their daring in other exploits abounds in oratory. Other examples include: "They were bold when it counted" (αὐθάδεις πρός τὸ συμφέρον Gorgias fr. 6 Diels-Kranz); "Who could not have admired them for their boldness?" (τίς τῆς τόλμης αὐτοὺς οὐκ ἂν ἡγάσθη; Lysias *Funeral Oration* 40); "They dared . . . not only to run risks for

χέων; Sophocles *Antigone* 883-884). When Theseus returns from defeating the Thebans, he approaches Adrastus and the mothers of the slain champions as they are singing laments. He waits silently, afterward explaining: "I hesitated to ask, while you were exhausting your wailing for the army" (μέλλων σ' ἐρωτᾶν, ἡνίκ' ἐξήντλεις στρατῷ / γόους... Euripides *Suppliant Women* 837-838). Evidently, mourning by the women had its own rhythm and duration, and interruption was something not done. But a Theban Creon of Athenian mythmaking cannot be sensitive to such things, and with his orders to his slaves, Antigone's *kyrios* reiterates his arrangements for her funeral procession and entombment (*Antigone* 885-888). When Antigone speaks again, she has stopped her lamentation and employs the iambics of speech:

ὦ τύμβος, ὦ νυμφεῖον, ὦ κατασκαφὴς
οἴκησις ἀείφρουρος, οἷ πορεύομαι
πρὸς τοὺς ἐμαυτῆς, ὧν ἀριθμὸν ἐν νεκροῖς
πλεῖστον δέδεκται Φερσέφασσ' ὀλωλότων.

Sophocles Antigone 891-891

O tomb, O wedding chamber, O hollowed
abode ever guarding, where I am walking
to my own, the greatest number of whom has perished
and Persephassa has received among the dead.

The enclosure awaiting Antigone has three identities for her: it is the grave of Creon's penalty for violating his decree by attempting burial rites for someone he deems an *ekhthros*; it is the nuptial bedroom with her groom, Hades, to whom Creon believes she is excessively devoted (Sophocles *Antigone* 524-525); it is a hollow where she will dwell with her parents and brothers who have perished before her. Antigone recalls her actions and insists upon their rightness among "those thinking rightly." Her implicit challenge flies in the face of Creon's disregard for a dead *philos*, and the form of her death marks her overevaluation of *philotês* and her concomitant underevaluation of the community and marriage. By shutting her away, Creon simultaneously punishes the rebellious woman and defeats a rival for his son's affections by sending her back to her parents. Enclosure in an underground cell befits her devotion to Hades and, in Seaford's terms, expresses symbolically "the retention of a girl by her natal family."[41] Both measures end the marriage, one by giving her out to the god of the dead, which Creon intended (575),

---

their own safety but also to die for the freedom of their enemies" (ἐτόλμησαν . . . οὐ μόνον ὑπὲρ τῆς αὐτῶν σωτηρίας κινδυνεύειν, ἀλλὰ καὶ ὑπὲρ τῆς τῶν πολεμίων ἐλευθερίας ἀποθνήσκειν Lysias 68); "Noble and marvelous the daring accomplished by these men" (κάλης μὲν καὶ παραδόξου τόλμης τῆς πραχθείσας ὑπὸ τῶνδε τῶν ἀνδρῶν Hyperides *Funeral Oration* 40).

41. Seaford, "Imprisonment of Women," 76.

the other by returning the nubile girl to her parents where she is denied marriage to an outsider. Both myths (the bride, the return) derive from thinking about marriage, but the idea of Antigone's transition through marriage to a "wedding chamber" with Hades brings her to the point of aggregation into a normal (i.e., not incestuous) family, so that Sophocles can have her speak from the experience of a wife and mother:

οὔτ' εἰ πόσις μοι κατθανὼν ἐτήκετο,
βίᾳ πολιτῶν τόνδ' ἂν ἠρόμην πόνον.
τίνος νόμου δὴ ταῦτα πρὸς χάριν λέγω;
πόσις μὲν ἄν μοι κατθανόντος ἄλλος ἦν,
καὶ παῖς ἀπ' ἄλλου φωτός, εἰ τοῦδ' ἤμπλακον,
μητρὸς δ' ἐν Ἅιδου καὶ πατρὸς κεκευθότοιν
οὐκ ἔστ' ἀδελφὸς ὅστις ἂν βλάστοι ποτέ.
τοιῷδε μέντοι σ' ἐκπροτιμήσασ' ἐγὼ
νόμῳ.

Sophocles Antigone 905-914

Not even if I were the mother of children,
not if my husband were dead and rotting,
would I have taken up the labor in violence of citizens.
For the sake of what law do I say this?
A husband dead, there would be another for me,
and a child from another man, if I lost this one,
but with my mother and father both hidden in the house of Hades,
there is no brother who would ever be produced, ever.
I honored you [Polyneices] by such
a law.

That this experience is hypothetical does not detract from its power to convey meaning or to impact upon the audience, since the Greeks spoke positively about their circumstances by postulating situations that were contrary to fact.[42]

This is Antigone's *nomos*, the law that governs her actions. It has two provisions, as it were. One is the uniqueness of a brother after one's parents' deaths, and the other, the replaceability of a husband or son. Her *nomos* has been an impediment to unified interpretations of the *Antigone* since the publication in 1848 of Eckerman's conversations with Goethe one Wednesday in 1827 on the nature of ancient tragedy.[43] Goethe lamented: "There is a passage in *Antigone* which I always look upon as a blemish, and I would give a great deal for an apt philologist to prove that

---

42. Smyth, *Greek Grammar*, 518-522.

43. John Oxenford, trans., *Conversations of Goethe with Eckerman and Soret*, (London: G. Bell and Sons, 1901), 227-228. For a discussion of these conversations, see Steiner, *Antigones*, 49-51. The quest for unity as well as the certainty that such unity exists *in* the text motivates much of the criticism of the ancient world. Neuburg ("How Like a Woman," 63) rightly observes

it is interpolated and spurious."[44] It is "unworthy," Goethe asserted, "almost borders upon the comic," "appears to me very far-fetched—to savour too much of dialectical calculation." Goethe did not justify his apperception. His is the reaction of a major figure of the Romantic period in Germany, and his *auctoritas* created a problem, not for Sophocles' play enacted in 438 B.C. but for how Sophocles' play henceforth would be read. That problem, which remains an obstacle today, prompted a controversy that has stigmatized these lines as unworthy of Sophocles. Nevertheless, nothing in their transmission or language sets them apart; only the distaste that they have aroused has spurred efforts to remove them.[45] An Antigone who is willing to leave a husband or son exposed and decomposing should not be one with the Antigone who is willing to die to bury a brother in fulfillment of divine laws. This is the traditional impasse of lines 904ff. In her 1986 study, Sheila Murnaghan made decisive steps toward resolving it by contextualizing the lines in the unsaid reality of marriage as an institution of the *polis* in which partners are replaceable and different individuals may serve equally well as husbands or wives.

Murnaghan begins by noting that Antigone has come face-to-face with the consequences of a decision made in haste.[46] Antigone must deal with the loss of marriage and childbearing. The one constant in her actions has been the desire to bury her brother. As she is forced to confront different situations caused by her desire, she changes her thoughts and offers what are conflicting rationalizations. The spectator is not expected to gather them together but to regard them diachronically in the "shifting evolution" of her thoughts. (This is, in fact, the way one watches a play as opposed to the way one thinks about it critically afterwards.) Thus, the inconsistency between what Antigone says now about husbands and sons and her earlier statements about unwritten laws may be dismissed as part of Antigone's development and not a flaw in Sophocles' text. In this speech, then,

---

that "we [scholars; readers] do not like inconsistency." Our desire for unity and consistency as we define them has made of the ancient world a metaphor that resists attempts to see through to the perspective of the ancients.

44. Unbeknownst to Goethe, August Ludwig Wilhelm Jacob (*Quaestiones Sophocleae* [Varsaviae: impensis Auctoris, 1821]) had already argued the spuriousness of the passage. See Steiner, *Antigones*, 50.

45. For bibliography and a survey of interpretations of these lines, see Hester, "Sophocles the Unphilosophical," 55-58; Winnington-Ingram, *Sophocles: An Interpretation*, 145; T. A. Szlezák, "Bermerkungen zur Diskussion um Sophokles, *Antigone* 904-920," *Rheinisches Museum* 124 (1981), 108-142; Murnaghan, "*Antigone* 904-920," 192 n. 1; Neuburg, "How Like a Woman," 54 nn. 2, 3, 57-61.

46. Murnaghan, "*Antigone* 904-920," 195. Neuburg ("How Like a Woman," 75-76) discusses the passage and its problems for readers along the same lines and comes to essentially the same conclusion: "The rationale, the 'calculus' which Antigone expresses in 909-12 is not some irrelevant sophistic hypothesising on her part; it expresses grimly the nature of the choice forced upon her by Creon . . . she is forced to choose the blood-family at the expense of the marriage-family, ending up in a void between them, which for a woman is also death" (75-76).

Antigone is "groping for a way to reconcile herself to the renunciation of marriage."[47] She mounts an argument that recalls that of Creon to Haemon: "The fields of others are fit for the plow" (ἀρώσιμοι γὰρ χἀτέρων εἰσὶν γύαι Sophocles *Antigone* 569), which is to say that the parties in marriage are replaceable, and its ties, unlike those of blood kinship, can be made and unmade. "Antigone is defining 'husband'," Murnaghan concludes, "not as the unchanging identity of a specific individual but as an abstract role that could be played by several different men."[48] From the viewpoint of marriage as an institution, one husband is as satisfactory as another. This is a rationale behind Pericles' law on citizenship of 451 B.C.: the *dēmos* cares nothing for the emotional bonds in marriage but only that the man and the woman be Athenians.[49] Pericles expresses the same social conception of marriage in the Thucydidean funeral oration:[50]

καρτερεῖν δὲ χρὴ καὶ ἄλλων παίδων ἐλπίδι, οἷς ἔτι ἡλικία τέκνωσιν ποιεῖσθαι· ἰδίᾳ τε γὰρ τῶν οὐκ ὄντων λήθη οἱ ἐπιγιγνόμενοί τισιν ἔσονται, καὶ τῇ πόλει διχόθεν, ἔκ τε τοῦ μὴ ἐρημοῦσθαι καὶ ἀσφαλείᾳ, ξυνοίσει.

Thucydides 2.44.3

Those of you who are of an age for producing children should take strength in the hope of other ones. New children, for you personally, will be forgetfulness for those who are no longer, and for the city, will bring two advantages in the form of not being deserted but on firm ground.

Understood as consolation for parents, Pericles' advice is not comforting. Even those parents of children slain in war who were young enough to have other children would not be likely to forget the one(s) they had lost. Pericles is speaking not to individuals qua individuals, however, but to individuals in their social role as parents, bearers of social status and responsibility. Murnaghan expresses what is assumed: parents do not have children solely for their own benefit; from the viewpoint of the *polis* and its orator, they have them for the city's salvation. The *polis* needs warriors for its defense; in this respect, individuals are interchangeable,

---

47. Murnaghan, "*Antigone* 904-920," 195.

48. Murnaghan, "*Antigone* 904-920," 198. Penelope puts off the suitors and gives Odysseus his homecoming because she values him as her husband, even though he has been long absent and could have been replaced by any one of numerous suitors. Aeschylus' Clytemnestra prefers another man and terminates her marriage with Agamemnon by slaying him. See Sheila Murnaghan, "Penelope's *agnoia*: Knowledge, Power and Gender in the *Odyssey*," *Helios* 13 (1986), 103-115.

49. For Pericles' citizenship law of 451 B.C., see Cynthia Patterson, *Pericles' Citizenship Law of 451-50 B.C.* (New York: Arno Press), 1981.

50. Murnaghan, "*Antigone* 904-920," 199-200.

replaceable, and of less worth than the welfare of all. To that end, parents must surrender their children to fight and die on its behalf.

To summarize, lines 904ff. are not inconsistent with Antigone's earlier stance because at that time she was supporting her position toward Polyneices with an argument from unwritten laws, and now she has become aware that blood ties have robbed her of ties of marriage. The lines are also consistent on the subtextual level in that the orator speaks of both unwritten law (Thucydides 2.37.3) and the replaceability of the parties in marriage (Thucydides 2.44.3). Similarly, for the *polis,* one hoplite is as good as another as long as the city has hoplites to defend it. Manifesting this belief were the rituals of the third day of the public funeral when the individual dead lost their separate identities to be buried together in chests organized by the tribes of the city whose interests they died aiding. Still, questions remain. How can one figure express such different attitudes toward an unburied corpse? How can she be so brutal toward a son when she is willing to die for a brother? Antigone does not maintain contradictory attitudes toward the dead because she does not espouse them as the same person. She has undergone a transition, dying as her old self as Jocasta's daughter to be reborn as a new self as Hades' bride. The virgin daughter and the married woman have different loyalties and perspectives. The theme of marriage is thus central to integrating lines 904ff. into the whole, but we need to accept that and go beyond to ponder how marriage affects what Antigone is saying. We need to examine how Sophocles uses the marriage theme in these lines to make meanings for his audience. This approach provides insight into how marriage rituals function in *Antigone* and how the play itself functioned in the theater of the *dêmos.* More importantly, it promises to redeem a passage that has been an anathema for Sophocles' modern audiences and return it to the ornament (*anathêma*) we believe Sophocles intended it to be.

Antigone's words to her final chamber evoke the consequences of, as well as the reasons for, her enclosure. Besides being the cell that constitutes her grave and natal dwelling, it is the nuptial chamber with her groom, Hades. The transition to death or to the home of dead parents is final and barren; however, transition to marriage, even marriage to Hades, affords the imagination a state of aggregation of the bride into the statuses of wife and mother. As we have noted, Antigone conducts her own wedding ceremony. She is penetrated by the eyes of the Theban men who substitute for her unseen groom. Unlike the girl who died unmarried, Antigone as Hades' bride on the tragic stage can have the experiences of a bride. This potential for the imagination, predicated by the rituals of marriage itself, gives Sophocles the opportunity to have Antigone picture how she would have acted as a wife and mother.

When Antigone pronounces her "unwritten usages" speech, she is acting on behalf of Polyneices, like herself a *philos* and child of her mother, Jocasta. Her resistance to Creon is comparable to that of the Athenians in the exploit of the Theban Dead. Although her devotion to her mother rather than her father perverts the Greek norm, Antigone otherwise reproduces the daughter's intense loyalty to her parental household.[51] In the scene before 904 ff., she is given out by her *kyrios* to a groom, Hades. "We are pure as far as this girl goes" (889), Creon announces. She undergoes the transition from girlhood to adulthood that marriage effects, and, although yet to enter her husband's bed chamber, the defiant virgin has died in marriage to Hades and been reborn as a married woman. Marriage provides the mechanism that allows Sophocles to have her embrace things so different. The married Antigone no longer represents Athenian men of funeral oratory; she represents Athenian women. For these women, the cost of the public funeral is the sacrifice of husbands and sons both in war and in the rituals of burial. Once a married woman, Antigone broadens her loyalties to encompass both parents. She speaks of father and mother as parents in a normal family. More significantly, she has transferred her loyalty from her family, whose members are irreplaceable, to the city that values husbands and sons as interchangeable—and her obedience from the first provision of her *nomos* to the second. Antigone does devalue marriage, as Murnaghan points out, and in the same way as the *polis*.

Antigone is again true to her name, *anti-gone*. By the first provision of her *nomos*, she is willing to do anything, including harming the family by depriving it of her fertility, to secure burial of a brother whom she should relinquish to the state and another woman. By its second provision, she is anti-family in the way of the *dêmos* of the public funeral: she hands over to the state her husband and son for its purposes. In so doing, she deprives the family of the institutions, *prothesis* and *ekphora*, that facilitated its reorganization after the death of an important member. She removes from its women the power to establish the composition of the mourning group and therefore of those who could inherit. The new Antigone, echoing her sister's language (Sophocles *Antigone* 79: *biai politôn*), cannot act "in violence of citizens" (907: *biai politôn*). Antigone speaks these lines as the representative of Athenian women whose traditional care for the dead had been usurped when the *dêmos* seized control over those killed in its wars. Women who once mourned and prepared their dead for burial within the confines of their own houses had to submit to the new rituals of the state funeral. Women had never "owned" their sons and husbands but always had to surrender them to the ambitions of men, their one consolation being that they could care for their bodies. By yielding the corpses of husband and child to the citizens, Antigone surrenders the last hold of the *polis'* women upon their children, conferring upon the citizens a founding charter of their women's approval for their public funeral. That is Sophocles' ornament for his audience.

---

51. Redfield, "Notes on the Greek Wedding," 187: "The daughter is the member of the family closest to the father." On Electra as a perversion of the daughter's loyalty to the father, see Jean-Pierre Vernant, "Hestia-Hermès: Sur l'expression religieuse de l'espace et du mouvement chez les Grecs," in *Mythe et pensée chez les Grecs: Etudes du psychologie historique*, vol. 1 (Paris: François Maspero, 1974), 137-139.

Excessive devotion to a *philos* manifested the forces of family and household that were opposed to the interests of the group or *polis*. They were espoused most often and profoundly by women in lamentation for the dead. Antigone takes grief for her brother to the extreme of losing her life. Her living counterparts were women mourners whose grief for their personal losses detracts from the need for women to support the war effort and the aggressive policies of their *polis*. Accordingly, Athenian women surrendered their men to the citizens; it was a reality of their lives during the decade of *Antigone*.

The public funeral, in part, was intended to ease the situation (for men, at least) by substituting a man's spoken and formulaic eulogy of the dead for the women's personal lamentations. But it caused a rent in the cultural fabric and assaulted the traditional privileges of women that, although largely invisible today in the words left by Athenian men, was deeply felt. Pericles' funeral oration, recorded by an Athenian extremely reluctant to speak of extraneous issues, among them the women of his world, exposes the tensions enveloping the public funeral's intrusion into the lives and spheres of women. Antigone is a construct of a man speaking in a medium administered by men, and *Antigone* was but a moment in trying to gloss over the wound that was there before its production and remained when those in the audience exited the theater. Antigone's charter, however, breaks the dramatic illusion with a message of mediation. With her lines, the woman Antigone grants Athenian men control over the bodies of those killed in war and the right to praise the dead rather than mourn them. Though less obvious because of Sophocles' skill at suggesting character, it is the message conveyed by Theseus in Euripides' *Suppliant Women*.

When the mothers of the slain champions win Theseus' consent to recover the bodies of their sons, they in effect entrust them to the *dêmos*. The women finish their lamenting, and Theseus asks Adrastus, the Argive king, to laud the dead, to deliver over them a funeral oration (Euripides *Suppliant Women* 857-859). At its conclusion, when the corpses are being carried away for cremation, Adrastus urges the women to approach their sons, and Theseus demurs: "Adrastus, you are suggesting something not at all fitting" (ἥκιστ', Ἄδραστε, τοῦτο πρόσφορον λέγεις 942). The women, Theseus argues, would be tormented with pain at the sight of the blood and wounds of the corpses. Theseus' stance is palpable nonsense, for death concerned women, but with its caution, he maintains male political control over the corpses by forestalling renewed lamentation by the women, which would undo the spoken praise that Adrastus has conferred with an oration. Instead, for the first time, the women acknowledge their sons, "the most glorious among Argives" (κλεινοτάτους ἐν Ἀργείοις 965), in a civic context. "[T]hey recognize at last the rights of the city over the children whom they had wanted entirely for themselves."[52] The mothers, like Antigone, yield burial of those killed in war to the city—the imperative enabling the public funeral. What Euripides does by an

---

52. Loraux, *Invention*, 49.

assertion of male will, Sophocles achieves by marriage. The Athenian hero Theseus usurps dominance from the mothers under the guise of his selfless care for the dead. Anti-Athenian Antigone relinquishes husband and child to the citizens, an anonymous group who represent the Athenians of the subtext.

Antigone has celebrated her own lifting of the veil, and, with her *nomos* explained, she resumes the wedding ceremony: "He is now taking me by the hand and leads me away" (καὶ νῦν ἄγει με διὰ χερῶν οὕτω λαβὼν Sophocles *Antigone* 916). After the *anakalyptêria*, the bride's husband moved from where he was dining with the men, across the room, to the women's tables. He brought his wife "the gifts of the unveiling" that compensated her for what she had surrendered. He took her by the wrist in a gesture known as *cheira epi karpôi* (hand on wrist) that symbolized his abduction of her into marriage.[53] Firmly in his grip, she was guided across the threshold of the house of her father and of her childhood to the procession and chariot waiting to escort her to her new home and its threshold into maturity. Antigone's groom, Hades, as invisible before the audience as in her language, is claiming her as his bride.[54] She begins walking slowly toward the country:

ἄλεκτρον, ἀνυμέναιον, οὔτε του γάμου
μέρος λαχοῦσαν οὔτε παιδείου τροφῆς,
ἀλλ᾽ ὧδ᾽ ἐρῆμος πρὸς φίλων ἡ δύσμορος
ζῶσ᾽ ἐς θανόντων ἔρχομαι κατασκαφάς

Sophocles *Antigone* 917-20

Unbedded, unhymned, and ungraced
by a share of bridal coupling and nurturing a child,
but in this way deserted of *philoi* and ill-fated,
I am going alive into the hollowed abodes of the dead.

Some kind of movement here, suggested by "I am going," would make visual her situation: Antigone has departed from the living. This fate has befallen her despite her conviction, expressed in a rhetorical question (921), that she has not transgressed any law of the gods. She no longer looks to the gods—her only remaining allies— for self-justification, not from doubts about their justice but because she is "dead"

---

53. For this rite, see George E. Mylonas, "A Signet-Ring in the City Art Museum of St. Louis," *American Journal of Archaeology* 49 (1945), 564-565; Jenkins, "Is There Life After Marriage?" 140.

54. The Scholiast remarks that *agei* (he leads; Sophocles *Antigone* 916) is "more expressive, since she did not say that he ordered me to be led, but he leads me himself" (ἐμφατικώτερον τὸ ΑΓΕΙ. οὐ γὰρ εἶπε, ὅτι ἐκέλευσέ με ἀχθῆναι, ἀλλ᾽ αὐτὸς ἄγει). The Scholiast evidently infers that Creon is the unexpressed subject of *agei*. Syntactically, this is possible, since no agent intervenes between Creon in 914 and the verb *agei* (916). But Creon has just declared himself "pure" of Antigone (889). As her *kyrios*, he sends her forth from the house. He cannot then take her by the wrist, for that is the groom's part to perform—the Unseen One.

and no longer has any need for gods. As she is led away, her words look to the future:

τί χρή με τὴν δύστηνον ἐς θεοὺς ἔτι
βλέπειν; τιν' αὐδᾶν ξυμμάχων; ἐπεί γε δὴ
τὴν δυσσέβειαν εὐσεβοῦσ' ἐκτησάμην.
ἀλλ' εἰ μὲν οὖν τάδ' ἐστιν ἐν θεοῖς καλά,
παθόντες ἂν ξυγγνοῖμεν ἡμαρτηκότες·
εἰ δ' οἵδ' ἁμαρτάνουσι, μὴ πλείω κακὰ
πάθοιεν ἢ καὶ δρῶσιν ἐκδίκως ἐμέ.

Sophocles Antigone 922-928

Why should I in such misery look further to the gods?
What ally of those who are allies should I look to, seeing
that by acting piously, I have come to possess impiety?
If this is good and beautiful before the gods,
then I would realize my mistake after suffering my doom.
But if these men are making mistakes, may they suffer no more
evils than they unjustly are doing to me.

Although the piety of her deed was fixed by the myth, Sophocles' Antigone might have doubts, as Linforth suggests, about the gods' approval of her deed.[55] Certainly, Sophocles has already taken dramatic license in making the mortal Niobe a god. But to draw such a conclusion about Antigone goes against everything the audience has heard from her. From beginning to end, her protestations that she has acted piously are consistent and affirm her conviction—if only by their frequent repetition. Her last words speak to it redundantly: "having piously rendered piety" (τὴν εὐσεβίαν σεβίσασα 943). Thus, rather than doubts about the gods' approval of her deed, Sophocles' audience may have heard a defiant piety in her deference to them. And the impiety she now "possesses" can only be an impious reputation for which Creon must be held accountable.

"These men" against whom she hopes for vengeance may include those anonymous citizens and Theban elders who do not dare to come to her defense, but it is surely directed at Creon, since it is he who has slain her "unjustly," he who has murdered her. Although restricted by the Athenian legal system, the obligations to avenge murdered kin fell upon family members.[56] But Antigone has no ally among those who are normally allies; she has no family members, no *philoi*, to execute such revenge. She has banished Ismene, and Creon is her murderer. In this, her penultimate speech, she cries out for vengeance that presumably could come, in her thinking, only from the gods. She is dead when Eurydice assumes the role of her

---

55. Linforth, "Antigone and Creon," 230.
56. Obligations of this sort could lead to aggressive funerals in which the promise of vengeance was displayed by carrying weapons in the rituals and to a vendetta between families that spread

avenger. The "storms" and "blasts" of the Coryphaeus' next line evoke the violence of the divine-sent storm and of Antigone the *teras* concealed within it that foretells the loss of the last root of Creon's house and harbingers the form that vengeance for Antigone will take: Eurydice's refusal to mourn his son for him, a refusal that bears out the subtext, as Sophocles strengthens the coincidence between what is happening in the theater and what is happening in the world of his audience.

The Coryphaeus again sees the signs of the savagery that Antigone has taken from her father: "The same blasts of the same winds of her essence (*psychê*) grip her still" (ἔτι τῶν αὐτῶν ἀνέμων αὐταὶ / ψυχῆς ῥιπαὶ τήνδε γ' ἔχουσιν Sophocles *Antigone* 929-930). His earlier comment (471-472), which was elicited by her defiance of Creon, ended with her denouncing Creon as a fool. The reference that concludes this speech is directed more pointedly at her slayer, and he seems to catch its implications. He threatens his slaves for their slowness in leading Antigone off. Creon will soon send slaves to conduct burial rites for his *philos*, Polyneices. His willingness to inflict upon slaves the "weeping and wailing" (*klaumata* 932) that he should have allowed Antigone to bestow upon their *philos* manifests the dysfunction of burial rites displayed by Thebans in Athenian mythmaking.

The line following Creon's threat against the slaves, "Alas, what you said is very near death" (οἴμοι, θανάτου τοῦτ' ἐγγυτάτω / τοὔπος ἀφῖκται Sophocles *Antigone* 933-34) is attributed to Antigone in the manuscripts but should be given to the Coryphaeus. The subtext to Creon's response offers support for the shift to the Coryphaeus: "I offer no consolation to take heart that these arrangements will not be carried out as proposed" (θαρσεῖν οὐδὲν παραμυθοῦμαι / μὴ οὐ τάδε ταύτῃ κατακυροῦσθαι 935-936). The Scholiast supplies Creon's thoughts:

> οὐ παραμυθοῦμαι σε θαρρεῖν, ὡς μὴ κεκυρωμένου σοι τοῦ ἀποθανεῖν. Τοῦτο δέ φησιν, ὡς οὐκ ἐνδιδοὺς, ἵνα μὴ ὑπονοήσῃ ἐκείνη μεταπεπεικέναι αὐτὸν δακρύουσα.

Scholiast ad Sophocles Antigone 935

I don't console you [Antigone] to take heart because death has been determined for you. He says this because he is not yielding so that she not suspect that she has won him over by crying.

Antigone, however, wishes for vengeance on Creon in his presence and shows no desire to sway him. Creon himself refuses to console Antigone, but his word for consoling (*paramythoumai*) moves what he is saying beyond its surface. With it, Sophocles clearly signals the *paramythia*, consolation intermingled with threnetic elements that the funeral orator offered the living after the *epainos* of the dead:[57]

---

pollution throughout the community. W. K. Lacey (*The Family in Classical Greece* [London and Southampton: Thames and Hudson, 1968], 48, 53-54, 148) discusses this in the Homeric poems. See also Garland, *Greek Way of Death*, 93-94; Seaford, *Reciprocity and Ritual*, 93-94.

57. Ziolkowski, *Thucydides and the Tradition*, 49.

"I do not pity the parents of these men . . . Rather, I will offer them consolation (*paramythêsomai*)" (οὐκ ὀλοφύρομαι μᾶλλον ἢ παραμυθήσομαι Thucydides 2.44.1).[58] The orator comforted the parents because they were alive to benefit from it. Antigone is dead, and Creon refuses to console the Coryphaeus concerning her. The line belongs to the Coryphaeus.

Antigone calls out for the last time: "I am being led away, I delay no longer" (ἄγομαι δὴ 'γὼ κοὐκέτι μέλλω Sophocles *Antigone* 939). The slaves, we imagine, have surrounded her, and the procession is underway. Again, she insists on being seen: "Look, O magnates of Thebes, at me" (λεύσσετε, Θήβης οἱ κοιρανίδαι 940). Vase painters usually represent the bride unveiled; it is a far more arresting image than the reality. In practice, however, the bride probably replaced her veil before joining the procession.[59] At this cry, Antigone also replaces her veil and joins the slaves, Creon's ersatz *philoi*.

---

58. Other examples include Plato *Menexenos* 236 E: "Needed is the sort of oration that will praise the dead adequately and encourage the living graciously by exhorting their sons and brothers to imitate their bravery and by consoling their fathers and mothers and whoever of their elders still left alive" (δεῖ δὴ τοιούτου τινὸς λόγου ὅστις τοὺς μὲν τετελευτηκότας ἱκανῶς ἐπαινέσεται, τοῖς δὲ ζῶσιν εὐμενῶς παραινέσεται, ἐκγόνοις μὲν καὶ ἀδελφοῖς μιμεῖσθαι τὴν τῶνδε ἀρετὴν παρακελευόμενος, πατέρας δὲ καὶ μητέρας καὶ εἴ τινες τῶν ἄνωθεν ἔτι προγόνων λείπονται, τούτους δὲ παραμυθούμενος; Hyperides, *Funeral Oration* 41: "It is perhaps difficult to console those who are in such sufferings" (Χαλεπὸν μὲν ἴσως ἐστὶ τοὺς ἐν τοῖς τοιούτοις ὄντας πάθεσι παραμυθεῖσθαι).

59. See Oakley and Sinos, *The Wedding in Ancient Athens*, 31-32 on their vase 79, an Attic red-figure salt cellar. In this painting, the groom is about to lead away his bride by the wrist. She is completely veiled, her face covered by her mantle. The artist, it seems, has opted for realism at the expense of aesthetic appeal.

7. The Prophet Speaks
Fourth Stasimon and Fifth Episode (944-1114)

As Creon's slaves lead Antigone away, the elders begin to move rhythmically across the orchestra. The sounds of their lyrics and the *aulos* (a clarinet- or oboe-like instrument) coincide with those heard in actual practice in the rituals of both wedding and funeral when the participants formed their procession and set out to escort their charge to its destination. The bride departs for the *thalamos* (bridal chamber) in her groom's house; the corpse, for the grave and integration with the dead. Creon's slaves escort Antigone to an underground chamber (*thalamos*) where she will reside with the family of her birth. Imprisonment underground is the thread that binds the exempla of the fourth stasimon, but the link is progressively complicated with other elements in the myths.[1] The ode does more, however, than speak of the past. Antigone has played her part and paid its price. The stasimon looks forward to the message that Tiresias will bring and to his confrontation with Creon. The audience, of course, does not know Tiresias is coming, but any group of experienced theatergoers senses when "the axe is about to fall." In the funeral orator's myth, persuasion fails to motivate the Thebans to desist from their impiety. The Athenian army must beat them into submission. This element, suitably altered for the context, awaits—and its impending presence must have been almost tangible.

Antigone remains within earshot throughout the stasimon, for the elders address her directly as *pais* at its beginning and end (Sophocles *Antigone* 949, 987). They call out to her to hear Danaë's fate:

ἔτλα καὶ Δανάας οὐράνιον φῶς
ἀλλάξαι δέμας ἐν χαλκοδέτοις αὐλαῖς·
κρυπτομένα δ' ἐν τυμβή-

---

1. Seaford, "Imprisonment of Women," 85-86. The myths of the fourth stasimon have been much discussed. Christiane Sourvinou-Inwood has done a masterful study of the fourth stasimon in "The Fourth Stasimon of Sophocles' *Antigone*," *Bulletin of the Institute of Classical Studies of the University of London* 36 (1989), 141-165. We have benefited in our analysis from her insights, which are too detailed to be summarized here.

ρει θαλάμῳ κατεζεύχθη·
καίτοι ⟨καὶ⟩ γενεᾷ τίμιος, ὦ παῖ παῖ,
καὶ Ζηνὸς ταμιεύεσκε γονὰς χρυσορύτους.
ἀλλ᾽ ἁ μοιριδία τις δύνασις δεινά·
οὔτ᾽ ἄν νιν ὄλβος οὔτ᾽ Ἄρης,
οὐ πύργος, οὐχ ἁλίκτυποι
κελαιναὶ νᾶες ἐκφύγοιεν.

Sophocles *Antigone* 944-954

Even Danaë's beauty endured exchanging the light
of the heavens for chambers bound in bronze.
Hidden in a tomb-
like chamber, she was bent to the yoke.
And yet, honored in birth, O child, child,
she became keeper of the gold-streaming seed of Zeus.
But the power of fate (whatever it may be) is terrible.
Neither wealth nor Ares,
no tower, no dark ships
beaten by the sea can escape it.

Danaë was imprisoned by her father in an underground chamber where she was visited by Zeus in the shape of a stream of gold and impregnated with their son, Perseus. The fateful circumstances leading to her enclosure, the oracle that her father, Acrisius, would perish at her son's hands, and Acrisius' plan to escape this end by entombing his daughter, are taken as known.[2] The *thalamos* becomes for Danaë a bridal chamber with a god and a storeroom analogous to her womb in that both shelter the god's wealth.[3] By giving birth to the son of a god, she is compensated for her undeserved imprisonment. But in wanting Antigone to hear what happened to Danaë, the elders, despite their paternalistic address, are hardly seeking to console her. There can be no such happy outcome for Antigone. This difference, that Danaë is innocent, while Antigone, although fated by the doom overhanging her house, has acted on her own in fulfilling that doom by opposing Creon, is all too precise, even cruel, in its accuracy.[4] That is the way she and Creon, still visible to the elders, must hear their words. But Sophocles' audience would be sensitive as well to Acrisius' deed and his fate and reflect on Creon who has also

---

2. For the myth of Danaë, see Apollodorus, *The Library* 2.4.1, 4; Jebb, *Antigone*, 169; Brown, *Sophocles: "Antigone,"* 203. For the fragments of Sophocles' *Acrisius* and *Danaë*, see Radt, *Sophocles*, 136-140, 173-175, respectively.

3. For *thalamos* as "wedding chamber" and "storeroom," see Liddell, Scott, and Jones, *Lexicon*, 781 s.v. θάλαμος.

4. Sourvinou-Inwood ("Fourth Stasimon," 145) states that the fifth-century audience would have seen the contrast between Danaë's and Antigone's suffering in this way. The elders have criticized Antigone throughout, with their praise coming in a subtextual voice of which they are unaware.

given out a *philê* in marriage to a god, thereby preventing her from marrying and bearing children.

The elders compound their cruelty with another mythic tale where enclosure brings reward:

ζεύχθη δ' ὀξύχολος παῖς ὁ Δρύαντος,
Ἠδωνῶν βασιλεύς, κερτομίοις ὀργαῖς
ἐκ Διονύσου πετρώ-
δει κατάφαρκτος ἐν δεσμῷ.
οὕτω τᾶς μανίας δεινὸν ἀποστάζει
ἀνθηρόν τε μένος. κεῖνος ἐπέγνω μανίαις
ψαύων τὸν θεὸν ἐν κερτομίοις γλώσσαις.
παύεσκε μὲν γὰρ ἐνθέους
γυναῖκας εὔιόν τε πῦρ,
φιλαύλους τ' ἠρέθιζε μούσας.

Sophocles Antigone 955-965

Dryas' hot-headed son was yoked,
King of Edonians, for his heart-stinging rage.
Shut away at Dionysus'
command in a rocky bondage.
Thus his madness' flowering might, terrible and wonderful,
trickles away. That one in madness touched the god
with heart-stinging tongues and came to know him.
He would stop the women taken by god
and the fire of the god's holy *Eu-oi-oi-oi.*[5]
He would anger the Muses who love the flute.

Sophocles' version seems to concur, as far as it goes, with what little is known about Aeschylus' treatment of the myth in *Edonians*, the first play of his *Lycurgeia* trilogy.[6] Both versions have Lycurgus' verbal insolence and mad rage toward Dionysus, his imprisonment in a rocky cave, and his acceptance of Dionysian madness induced by the god.[7] Aeschylus' tragedy probably included Lycurgus' murder of his son whom, in his madness, he prunes as if a vine branch, and ended with Dionysus' pronouncement that the land would be restored to fertility only if the Edonians bound Lycurgus in a cave in the mountains. Sophocles, however, is silent about the son's fate; his Lycurgus is shut away for his rage against Dionysus and for interfering with the Muses who, in this context, would appear to be the

---

5. For this cry, which we use to translate εὔιον (Sophocles *Antigone* 964), see C. S. Lewis, *Prince Caspian: The Return to Narnia* (1951; reprint, New York: Macmillan, 1970), 152. The full cry is "Euan, euan, eu-oi-oi-oi."

6. West, "Tragica VI," 63-64.

7. For Aeschylus' *Edonoi*, see the fragments 57-67 in Radt, *Aeschylus*, 178-185. For the Lycurgus myth, see also Apollodoros, *The Library* 3.5.1.

enthused women of Dionysus whose instrument in cult and tragedy is the *aulos*. Pent up in the cave, Lycurgus slowly overcomes his madness and "comes to know" the god. Rather than a punishment, imprisonment in Sophocles brings knowledge of the god and release from madness. If, as M. L. West conjectures, Sophocles' audience received this antistrophe through the version of the myth presented by Aeschylus' *Edonians,* they knew that Lycurgus had realized his mistake in rejecting Dionysus and had become the god's servant and prophet.[8] They knew, in short, that his imprisonment had brought about healing.[9]

The contrast between Antigone's and Lycurgus' fates parallels and reinforces the harshness of the difference between Antigone and Danaë. Unlike Lycurgus, who learns the need in society for Dionysus, Antigone will attain no such understanding of the consequences for society of her act done in violence of the citizens. Her chamber will bring no healing. But Sophocles' audience might well have seen Antigone in the role of a Maenad, beyond the control of men because she is in the service of the gods. And in so far as she serves the gods, Creon, by opposing her deed, is in error, though not unreasonably, since the madness of Dionysus comes as savage and foreign, and its benefits are difficult for mortals to comprehend.[10] The first antistrophe hints, then, that Antigone's imprisonment opens the possibility for Creon to relent and accept the disorder that she has introduced into the city by disobeying his edict.[11] Even so, the audience would not miss the relevance of Lycurgus' son, victim of his father's madness, to Haemon's fate at the hands of his father.

The second strophic pair concern a single myth, the blinding of the Phineidai (sons of Phineus):

παρὰ δὲ κυανέων †πελαγέων πετρῶν† διδύμας ἁλὸς
ἀκταὶ Βοσπόριαι ‹·-·–› ὁ Θρηίκων
Σαλμυδησσός ἵν' ἀγχίπτολις Ἄ-
ρης δισσοῖσι Φινεΐδαις
εἶδεν ἀρατὸν ἕλκος
τυφλωθὲν ἐξ ἀγρίας δάμαρτος
ἀλαὸν ἀλαστόροισιν ὀμμάτων κύκλοις
ἀραχθέντων ὑφ' αἱματηραῖς
χείρεσσι καὶ κερκίδων ἀκμαῖσιν.

κατὰ δὲ τακόμενοι μέλεοι μελέαν πάθαν
κλαῖον, ματρὸς ἔχοντες ἀνυμφεύτου γονάν·

8. West, "Tragica VI," 64.

9. Sourvinou-Inwood ("Fourth Stasimon," 148) appreciates that "the emphasis here is on learning and healing; the context of both mentions of Lykourgos' *mania* is its healing."

10. For a recent study of Dionysus in the *polis*, see Seaford, "Reciprocity and Ritual," 235-280, and in tragedy, 340-367.

11. Sourvinou-Inwood, "Fourth Stasimon," 151.

ἁ δὲ σπέρμα μὲν ἀρχαιογόνων
⟨ἦν⟩ ἄνασσ' Ἐρεχθεϊδᾶν,
τηλεπόροις δ' ἐν ἄντροις
τράφη θυέλλησιν ἐν πατρῴαις
Βορεὰς ἄμιππος ὀρθόποδος ὑπὲρ πάγου
θεῶν παῖς· ἀλλὰ κἀπ' ἐκείνᾳ
Μοῖραι μακραίωνες ἔσχον, ὦ παῖ.

Sophocles *Antigone* 966-987

Beside the expanse of the twin seas' Dark Rocks,
lie the shores of the Bosporus . . . and Thracian
Salmydessus where its neighbor Ares
saw upon Phineus' two sons
an accursed wound
of blindness dealt by his savage wife,[12]
a wound blinding upon orbs
appealing for vengeance from eyes pierced
by bloody hands and pointed shuttles.
Wretchedly wasting away, they weep their miserable
suffering, having birth from a mother ill-wed.[13]
The queen is the seed of
the sons of Erechtheus, an ancient lineage,
and in far-off caves
she was reared amid paternal storms,
daughter of Boreas, swift with the horses across the steep hills,
child of gods. But even over that one
the long-lived Fates wielded power, child.

By locating the blinding in a savage part of Thrace, Sophocles adds to the savagery of the crime. But the key to the passage, Sourvinou-Inwood points out, lies in the phrase *agria dama* (Sophocles *Antigone* 973), "'wild tamed-wife', an oxymoron which expresses the notion of breakdown of normality, the failure of the taming that should have been achieved through marriage."[14] The question is whether the "savage wife" is Cleopatra, Phineus' first wife and mother of the children, or his second wife and their stepmother. If the reference is to Phineus' second wife, the children are exposed to their stepmother's savagery by the absence of their mother and perhaps by the failure of their father to protect them from her false allegations of rape. Their weakness evokes Antigone's vulnerability before Creon, the *kyrios* who should be her "caring kin" (549: *kêdemôn*). On the other hand, maintaining Cleopatra as the savage, untamed mother bears on Antigone as a woman who,

---

12. Sophocles rules out the version of the myth that Phineus blinded his sons after his second wife, Idaea, falsely accused them of attempting to rape her (Apollodorus, *The Library*, 3.15.3).

13. Alliteration of w and m imitates Sophocles' alliteration of pi and kappa.

14. Sourvinou-Inwood, "Fourth Stasimon," 154.

through support of her brother, harmed her children by not allowing herself the opportunity to become a wife and mother.[15] The latter reading of the comparison with Cleopatra, coming so soon after Antigone's *anathêma*, supports our reading of 904 ff. in that Sophocles is provoking meanings from *philoi* by marriage, in those lines, a husband and son, and in these, children for her father's household—all of whom belong to the unreal.

More apt in its reference to Antigone than the accounts of Danaë and Lycurgus, this myth outlines a comparison between Antigone and Cleopatra as women destroyed by fate for destroying their children. It serves as a powerful, albeit implicit, reminder of the consequences of Antigone's devotion to granting Polyneices burial rites—the essential subject of the play. Its thematic centrality may explain why Sophocles gives to this third myth both strophe and antistrophe, a structure that has long puzzled scholars.

In sum, the fourth stasimon would prompt Sophocles' audience, with its storehouse of mythic associations, to think of Creon's action in terms of Acrisius' thwarted imprisonment of Danaë, Lycurgus' impiety toward a god's devotees, and a savage woman's ruin of a man's household. Destruction, although late coming, awaits Acrisius, Lycurgus changes his mind about the god and is saved, and Phineus' loses his household at the hands of a woman not domesticated by marriage. The Lycurgus exemplum, alone not marked by fate, allows for the possibility that Creon could change his mind. This in itself tempers somewhat the finality of Antigone's departure that must have been felt as the fifth episode gets underway with a scene that is theater for willingness to yield to another's advice.

An actor enters from the city with the solemnity of an elderly man of importance. He is guided by a boy, his guide as he is a guide for others (Sophocles *Antigone* 1014). The scene visually enacts the heeding of advice. The actor's costume, the *agrênon,* or "netlike mesh of wool around the whole body" (τὸ δ᾽ ἦν πλέγμα ἐξ ἐρίων δικτυῶδες περὶ πᾶν τὸ σῶμα Pollux *Onomasticum* 4.116), shows that he is impersonating a prophet.[16] The audience would assume that he is the famous Theban Tiresias. He is being played by either of the actors not playing Creon. If he is the actor who spoke Antigone, then Tiresias would seem to be the instrument of her vengeance. Joining Tiresias with Ismene and Haemon reinforces the stability and loyalty of the woman and the ephebe with the authority of the seer. It is time for intervention from the gods, and the spectators have probably surmised that Tiresias will say something about Polyneices' corpse. As the scene of a holy man appealing

---

15. Sourvinou-Inwood, "Fourth Stasimon," 159-160.

16. There is no evidence for Tiresias' costume in Sophocles' *Antigone*; according to Pollux (*Onomasticum* 4.116), "Tiresias put one on, or some other seer" (ὃ Τειρεσίας ἐπεβάλλετο ἢ τις ἄλλος μάντις). No illustration of the *agrênon* is extant (Pickard-Cambridge, 203). For the suggestion that Cassandra also wears an *agrênon*, see Fraenkel, *Agamemnon*, 3.584.

to a strong man to release a body for burial enfolds, the spectators must have read it intertextually with the third act of Homer's myth of the exposed corpse (*Iliad* 24.77-140). In this reading, Tiresias corresponds to Thetis.

Zeus sends Thetis with his message for Achilles:

σκύζεσθαί οἱ εἰπὲ θεούς, ἐμὲ δ' ἔξοχα πάντων
ἀθανάτων κεχολῶσθαι, ὅτι φρεσὶ μαινομένῃσιν
Ἕκτορ' ἔχει παρὰ νηυσὶ κορωνίσιν οὐδ' ἀπέλυσεν.

Homer *Iliad* 24.113-115

Tell him that the gods are angry at him and that I above all
the immortals am wrathful that, in his mind's fury,
he keeps Hector beside the curved ships and did not release him.

Achilles complies without hesitation: "Let it be so. May he who brings the ransom take away the corpse, if the Olympian himself orders this eagerly in his heart" (τῇδ' εἴη· ὃς ἄποινα φέροι καὶ νεκρὸν ἄγοιτο, / εἰ δὴ πρόφρονι θυμῷ Ὀλύμπιος αὐτὸς ἀνώγει Homer *Iliad* 24.139-140). Yet, with Zeus's words to Thetis, "if somehow he may fear me and ransom Hector" (αἴ κέν πως ἐμέ τε δείσῃ ἀπό θ' Ἕκτορα λύσῃ 24.116), Homer suggests a different outcome for the third act of his myth of the exposed corpse, namely, the refusal to obey the gods. This scene of dispatching a messenger and compliance with Zeus's request, repeated countless times in manifold forms in the audience's experiences of epic song, strengthens the lesson to be learned, obedience to Zeus.

Tiresias appeals to Creon to obey by reminding him of their past experience. On another occasion of public importance, Tiresias counseled him, and Creon followed the seer's advice and saved the city (Sophocles *Antigone* 993-994, 1058). But Creon's acknowledgment, "I can bear witness to your aid from experience" (ἔχω πεπονθὼς μαρτυρεῖν ὀνήσιμα 995), also yields the embittered: "I can bear witness, having suffered your help."[17] Sophocles surely expected his audience to ponder this occasion, and without grasping at imaginary figments, it would only have recourse to the death of Creon's other son. Aeschylus identifies him as Megareus, "the offspring of Creon, of the race of Sown Men" (Κρέοντος σπέρμα τοῦ σπαρτῶν γένους *Seven Against Thebes* 474), who joins others in defending the gates of Thebes. Had Creon's son died defending the city, his death would have fulfilled a man's purpose, and there would be no reason for Creon's antagonistic tone toward a former benefactor. Creon seems to resent Tiresias from the first. Euripides in *Phoenician Women* preserves a different death for the youth, here named for his grandfather, Menoeceus.[18] In this version, Tiresias prophesies that the Thebans

---

17. Kamberbeek, *Antigone*, 172-173.
18. See Euripides *Phoenician Women* 911-1018; Pausanias 9.25.1; Cicero *Tusculan Disputations* 1.116; Hyginus *Fabulae* 68. See Foley (*Ritual Irony*, 106-146) for the sacrifice of Menoeceus in Euripides' *Phoenician Women*. It is not without interest that the Coryphaeus

will defeat the Argives if Creon sacrifices his son to Ares. Creon refuses and urges the boy to flee, but hearing the prophesy, Menoeceus sacrifices himself in front of the city gates. The death in Euripides' version goes far in explaining not only Creon's resentment toward a prophet who gave him salutary advice in the past but in justifying for Creon his wrath toward Polyneices whose assault cost him his son. The audience hears Tiresias' declaration to Creon. It cuts through the edginess of their initial pleasantries: "Start thinking, now that you have once more come onto the razor's edge of chance" (φρόνει βεβὼς αὖ νῦν ἐπὶ ξυροῦ τύχης Sophocles *Antigone* 996).

Tiresias twice appeals to Creon to think, with words derived from the same verbal root as Creon's "thought" (*phronêma* Sophocles *Antigone* 207). He begins with a present imperative, *phronei* (Sophocles *Antigone* 996), to prod Creon into thinking about the consequences for the city of his *phronêma* concerning corpses: chaos at Tiresias' augury, failure of burnt offerings, and the gods' refusal to accept sacrifices (999-1013). The city is sick from the mutilation of the corpse by birds and dogs and their spreading of Polyneices' meat (1017), no longer deemed human flesh, throughout its altars and hearths (1015-1022). The gods first disclosed their wrath over the exposed corpse through dust and Antigone, the bird of omen. Now, through Tiresias, they initiate a direct appeal to the human responsible for exposing a dead body and for dishonoring, to use Apollo's words, "mute earth" (κωφὴν ... γαῖαν Homer 24.54).

The seer next implores Creon with the more vivid and pressing aorist imperative, *phronêson* (φρόνησον Sophocles *Antigone* 1023): "think once [and never again about these things]." Creon is not unintelligent; he once realized that Polyneices and Eteocles were kinsmen and that both were dead. He has since thought and acted foolishly in distinguishing between their corpses. But Tiresias tells him that a man who has fallen into trouble may still repair his situation if he accepts advice and yields: "Self-will incurs a charge of stupidity (αὐθαδία τοι σκαιότητ' ὀφλισκάνει 1028). Give in to the dead. Do not goad the deceased. What valor this—to kill the dead again?" (ἀλλ' εἶκε τῷ θανόντι, μηδ' ὀλωλότα / κέντει. τίς ἀλκὴ τὸν θανόντ' ἐπικτανεῖν; 1029-1030). By yielding, he may restore his relationship with the gods. Lycurgus, when shut away, recovered from his madness and his ignorance of Dionysus' divinity. The exemplum implies the same is possible for Creon and anticipates his first exchange with Tiresias. Creon is now faced with a crisis much like Achilles' after Thetis delivered Zeus's message. Linforth observes that "the course of events was already in train, and would have gone the same if

---

addresses Creon as "son of Menoeceus" at Sophocles *Antigone* 1098. Mention of Menoeceus, cited before as Creon's father (156) and implying that Creon is not of the royal line of Thebes, now may be intended to remind those in the audience of the name given elsewhere to Creon's son. In *Antigone*, Creon's son is identified as Megareus (1303).

19. Linforth, "Antigone and Creon," 236.

Creon had yielded immediately after the first speech."[19] Be that as it may, the scene depends, in fact, upon the possibility of Creon's yielding for its tension and for any hold it might have had on its audience.

Tiresias characterizes the Creon whom he is addressing as a man who has made a mistake over a corpse and when offered a remedy in the form of good advice, would heed it and change his mind. Creon has appropriated the body of a man slain in war. In this, as we have seen, he resembles Athenians themselves. Even before the inauguration of the public funeral, Athenians intervened in the burial of the dead through funeral legislation. Aggrandizing burial or withholding it offered an avenue to power, because due and proper burial was the norm.[20] At Athens, the culture hero Bouzygos placed a curse upon "those who neglect an unburied body" (τοῖς περιορῶσιν ἄταφον σῶμα Scholiast ad Antigone 255). Aelian seems to refer to Bouzygos' curse with "an Attic law," which states that "whoever comes upon an unburied corpse of a human, by all means throw earth upon it, and then bury it looking to the sunset" (ὃς ἂν ἀτάφῳ περιτύχῃ σώματι ἀνθρώπου, πάντως ἐπιβάλλειν αὐτῷ γῆν, θάπτειν δὲ πρὸς δυσμὰς βλέποντα Aelian Miscellaneous Stories 5.14). Some token act of burial, "this minimum human obligation," was required by virtue of the body's being that of a human.[21] Yet burial within the territory of Attica was never automatic, and its denial included punishments for particularly odious transgressions. Plato reserved ignominious burial outside the borders, the kind that made the perpetrator "vanish," for citizens who had committed unspeakable crimes (Laws 854 E; 873 C-D; 909 C). The bodies of tyrants, traitors, and temple-robbers, by panhellenic practice, were cast beyond the borders of the territory (Xenophon Hellenica 1.7.22). The remains of such offenders could be dug up and cast from Attica "so that there not lie in the country the bones of someone who betrayed the country and the city" (Lycurgos Against Leocrates 113). Nevertheless, it was generally understood that the bodies of such men would be retrieved by their philoi and, if possible, buried secretly in Attica. Although "it was not permitted to bury the bones of one exiled for treason" in Attica, the body of Themistocles was retrieved and buried secretly in his mother earth (Thucydides 1.138.6). From historical practice, it seems, Athenians would have allowed Polyneices' family to bury him in Attica, although not publicly. Athenians of funeral oratory did what Creon cannot. They discounted what the Argives did when alive and removed their bodies for burial:

> Ἀθηναῖοι ἡγησάμενοι ἐκείνους μὲν, εἴ τι ἠδίκουν, ἀποθανόντας δίκην
> ἔχειν τὴν μεγίστην ... τοὺς τεθνεῶτας ἐν τῷ πολέμῳ ἀξιοῦντες τῶν
> νομιζομένων τυγχάνειν πρὸς τοὺς ἑτέρους.

---

20. Parker, Miasma, 46; Whitehorne, "Background," 135-136; Garland, Greek Way of Death, 101-103.

21. Parker, Miasma, 44.

Lysias Funeral Oration 7, 9

The Athenians judged that those men, if they had done some wrong, paid the utmost penalty by dying. . . .Rather, considering it right that those killed in war receive the customary rites, they underwent dangers against others.

By their own admission, Athenians would have relented. So they may have thought about a man in Creon's position. But Creon is a Theban leader of their public myth, and his failure to act for Polyneices upon what he admits in other circumstances is pious is not a personal failing alone but a variation in anti-Athens mythmaking. Tiresias qua Thetis will not be able to advise, much less persuade, Creon. In the tragic theater, Creon must fail on his own.

Creon has listened to Tiresias before and fears what he is about to say: "How I tremble at your voice" (ὡς ἐγὼ τὸ σὸν φρίσσω στόμα Sophocles *Antigone* 997). The seer punctuates his words with his authority as a prophetic interpreter of signs. His demeanor on stage seems calm as befits the wise adviser who counsels his leader. Tiresias reports the signs, interprets their meaning for the will of the gods, cautions against stubbornness, and calls for Creon to yield. His message, the same in an Athenian version of the myth (Euripides *Suppliant Women* 543-548), would seem self-evident to the audience, even without the Homeric subtext. But not to Creon. The man who admitted his fear and who speaks often of Zeus (*Antigone* 184, 304, 487, 658), when faced by a messenger from the gods, resorts to violence. He responds by turning his counselor into a hostile bowman and resented prophet: "Old man, you all shoot your arrows at me like bowmen at their target, and I am not lacking experience of that prophetic art of yours" (ὦ πρέσβυ, πάντες ὥστε τοξόται σκοποῦ / τοξεύετ' ἀνδρὸς τοῦδε, κοὐδὲ μαντικῆς / ἄπρακτος ὑμῖν εἰμι 1033-1035). He accuses Tiresias of venality, a charge against prophets that Sophocles' audience would recognize as a commonplace but one that recalls Antigone's claim to profit from her deed, a claim that distances her from the selfless and altruistic Athenians of the subtext. Unspoken till now but surely not unrecognized by the spectators is the "profit" Theban Creon has sought—in turn, superiority as a leader, as a man, and as a father—to which Tiresias soon gives voice: "the family of absolute rulers holds disgraceful profiteering as its *philos*" (τὸ δ' αὖ τυράννων αἰσχροκέρδειαν φιλεῖ 1056).

In the face of Tiresias' serenity, Creon's violent outburst might seem surprisingly disproportionate were it not that the audience has witnessed his quick rage in his confrontations with the Watchman, Coryphaeus, Antigone, Ismene, and Haemon. To Creon, Tiresias is a rival in a contest for the body of Polyneices. He has had other rivals—men bribing other men, Antigone, Haemon—and each rival has provoked a violent reaction from Creon. Tiresias is no exception to this. But he is unique in that he speaks on the basis of "the marks of my craft" (τέχνης σημεῖα τῆς ἐμῆς Sophocles *Antigone* 998) whose power Creon knows and has reason to fear despite the audaciousness of his tirade.

When Tiresias urges Creon to "yield to the dead" (Sophocles *Antigone* 1029), that is, to surrender the body, Creon responds with vociferous disregard for the concerns of the gods:

τάφῳ δ' ἐκεῖνον οὐχὶ κρύψετε,
οὐδ' εἰ θέλουσ' οἱ Ζηνὸς αἰετοὶ βορὰν
φέρειν νιν ἁρπάζοντες ἐς Διὸς θρόνους·
οὐδ' ὡς μίασμα τοῦτο μὴ τρέσας ἐγὼ
θάπτειν παρήσω κεῖνον.

Sophocles *Antigone* 1039-1043

You will not hide that one with a tomb,
not even if Zeus's eagles want to seize
him for meat and carry him to Zeus's throne.
Not even out of fear for this pollution
would I hand him over to you for burying.

But Creon's attack does end with refusal of the prophet's advice. He goes on to equate his knowledge with that of the gods and to deny the validity of the prophet's seer craft:

εὖ γὰρ οἶδ' ὅτι
θεοὺς μιαίνειν οὔτις ἀνθρώπων σθένει.
πίπτουσι δ', ὦ γεραιὲ Τειρεσία, βροτῶν
χοἰ πολλὰ δεινοὶ πτώματ' αἴσχρ', ὅταν λόγους
αἰσχροὺς καλῶς λέγωσι τοῦ κέρδους χάριν.

Sophocles *Antigone* 1043-1047

I know well that
none among men has the power to pollute gods.
They fall shameful falls, old man Tiresias, those mortals who
are very clever, whenever they utter shameful
words nobly for the sake of profit.

Creon's rage and his insistence on the rightness of his actions have now gone too far, making the gods—if only verbally—explicit victims of his arrogance and self-interest. Sophocles' audience could not doubt that Creon would be punished—although they did not know how—since, as N. R. E. Fisher comments, "[I]n the case of *hybris* the gods tend to get involved either if they are themselves seen as the direct victims (or the perpetrators) of hybristic behaviour, or if they are supposed to object to such behaviour in their role as general defenders of human morality."[22] Following Creon's volley of insults and denials, the men fall into a stichomythia, tragedy's surrogate for the physical violence enacted in a boxing match or hoplite battle. In these exchanges, what is said matters less than the effort of each contestant

---

22. Fisher, "*Hybris* and Dishonour," 178.

to use what is said to land a telling, final blow. Creon and Tiresias spar with one another through truisms—love of money, seeking profit, and speech itself. Neither gains the upper hand in the stichomythia, but their battle of one-liners reverses their positions. Tiresias becomes angry and shoots forth his next words like the shafts of a bowman: "Such bolts like an archer, I let loose in rage at your heart, for you rile me, sure bolts whose heat you will not run out from under" (τοιαῦτά σοι, λυπεῖς γάρ ὥστε τοξότης / ἀφῆκα θυμῷ καρδίας τοξεύματα / βέβαια, τῶν σὺ θάλπος οὐχ ὑπεκδραμῇ Sophocles *Antigone* 1084-1086). A holy man appealing to a leader to surrender a body evokes Chryses, priest of Apollo, but after Creon plays Agamemnon in refusing him, Tiresias seems to have metamorphosed into the god himself, Apollo, Lord of the Silver Bow.

Tiresias lets fly his truths about the object of their rivalry, but the opportunity for counseling has passed. He now sees Creon as an enemy, and this, their second exchange, is comparable to the battle of the Athenians and Thebans for the bodies of the Argives: "When [the Athenians] could not obtain their request [to take up the corpses], they marched against the Cadmeians. . . . They fought and gained victory with justice as their ally" (οὐ δυνάμενοι δὲ τούτων τυχεῖν ἐστράτευσαν ἐπ᾽ αὐτούς. . . . τὸ δὲ δίκαιον ἔχοντες σύμμαχον ἐνίκων μαχόμενοι Lysias *Funeral Oration* 8,10). Creon will repay his action with one from his own loins, corpse for corpse:

ἀνθ᾽ ὧν ἔχεις μὲν τῶν ἄνω βαλὼν κάτω,
ψυχήν γ᾽ ἀτίμως ἐν τάφῳ κατοικίσας,
ἔχεις δὲ τῶν κάτωθεν ἐνθάδ᾽ αὖ θεῶν
ἄμοιρον, ἀκτέριστον, ἀνόσιον νέκυν.

Sophocles Antigone 1068-1071

because you have thrown one of those up here down there
and while domiciling a living being in a tomb without honor,
you have one of those belonging to lower gods up here
a corpse without portion, without burial rites, without holiness.

Creon has pushed himself in, he has indulged himself, by deciding the treatment to be meted out to corpses. But, as Antigone said to Ismene (Sophocles *Antigone* 48), so Tiresias tells Creon: ὧν οὔτε σοὶ μέτεστιν (you have no share in these [corpses] 1073). A god or gods spread dust to protect the body and hide its offensive pollution from their sight. Creon discounts their signs, ignores their warnings, acts "without honor" toward the gods. In so many words, Tiresias confirms what the audience suspects, that Creon has acted hubristically, and such actions provoke his victims, the gods, to seek vengeance:

τούτων σε λωβητῆρες ὑστεροφθόροι
λοχῶσιν "Αιδου καὶ θεῶν Ἐρινύες,
ἐν τοῖσιν αὐτοῖς τοῖσδε ληφθῆναι κακοῖς.

Sophocles Antigone 1074-1076

For this reason, mutilators whose destruction comes afterwards,
lie in ambush for you, the Erinyes of Hades and the gods,
so that you may be caught in those very same evils.

Tiresias exits slowly, led by the boy toward the same gangway through which he entered. The sight visually restores authority to the prophet and, by conceding guidance, rebuffs Creon's challenge to his guidance. Tiresias falls short of his subtextual positioning as the Lord of the Silver Bow. He foresees laments of men and women in Creon's house that, as far as the action of the play goes, do not occur. But he wins the contest for the right to the words defining the gods by fastening his definition of Creon upon his opponent. Creon has been inverted from the strong man back to the fearful man he was when he waited to hear Tiresias' words (Sophocles *Antigone* 997). The seer gone, the Coryphaeus attests his veracity: "not ever did this man cry forth a falsehood to the city" (μή πώ ποτ' αὐτὸν ψεῦδος ἐς πόλιν λακεῖν 1094), and urges Creon "to take good counsel (εὐβουλίας δεῖ . . . λαβεῖν 1098). Frightened, Creon at last seeks advice: "What must I do, then? Tell me. I will obey" (τί δῆτα χρὴ δρᾶν; φράζε· πείσομαι δ' ἐγώ 1099). Like his counterparts in the Theban Dead myth, he has waged a battle over exposing corpses and has lost. The Coryphaeus urges him to release Antigone and entomb Polyneices (1100-1101). He yields: "Alas, it is hard, but I resign my heart's desire to do this. A battle must not be waged against necessity" (οἴμοι· μόλις μέν, καρδίας δ' ἐξίσταμαι / τὸ δρᾶν· ἀνάγκῃ δ' οὐχὶ δυσμαχητέον 1105-1106). The allusion to a "battle," even one standing in an impersonal verbal adjective (*dysmachêteon* 1106), is a graphic clue to the subtext of the orator's myth.

Creon finally tries to act like the *kyrios* of his house. He calls for his servants to come with axes (Sophocles *Antigone* 1109) and run to the highlands. The axes are the type used for chopping wood. His request gives the impression that he intends to have a pyre built for Polyneices, and he inspires confidence that he has learned his lesson:

δέδοικα γὰρ μὴ τοὺς καθεστῶτας νόμους
ἄριστον ᾖ σῴζοντα τὸν βίον τελεῖν.

Sophocles Antigone 1113-1114

For I fear that it is best for one to end
his life preserving the established customs.

It may also have been a lesson received with trepidation among Athenians who had been altering customs and inventing new ones for generations.

8.Creon's Defeat
Fifth Stasimon and *Exodos* (1115-1352)

The elders invoked Dionysus in their entrance song to come and lead their all-night dances in celebration of the city's escape from the Argives (Sophocles *Antigone* 148-154). Once again the city is in danger—this time from within—and their prayers turn to the patron god of their city. Creon's refusal to bury the corpses of Polyneices and the Argives (1080-1083) has sickened the city with pollution, and the gods are no longer accepting its sacrifices. The old men are more concerned for their city's welfare than for Creon's. They have stood by and watched him as he ruled, but they remain loyal to Thebes. In this, they reflect the function of tragedy itself to promote through its spectacle and plots the triumph of the city over its distinguished families.[1] Only in this way could the *pandamos polis*, "the city and its citizens" (1141), be safe and prosper. To this end, the elders appeal to Dionysus to appear with "a cleansing foot" (καθαρσίῳ ποδὶ 1144). Dionysus purifies through violence that will sweep away the pollution caused by the unburied corpse, and, at the same time, liberates women from intolerable situations, so that Eurydice will be released from Creon's wreckage of her motherhood. In the destruction suffered in the *exodos*, the hand of Dionysus Katharios and Dionysus Lysios is revealed.

A man enters from the country. The audience has not seen him before, but they would guess that he is a messenger with news. He is played by either the Antigone or Ismene actor. Our preference leans toward the actor who impersonated Antigone, as this distribution imparts to the Messenger's speech the function of reporting a drama in Antigone's *thalamos* that seems orchestrated by Antigone. The Athenian audience, however, would probably have focused on the fact that the Messenger presents the view of the ordinary man that Creon has labored to oppose and struggled to reject, all to no avail, for "mortals have no prophet at all for what is established" (καὶ μάντις οὐδεὶς τῶν καθεστώτων βροτοῖς Sophocles *Antigone* 1160). The Messenger delivers his message: "They are dead. The living are responsible for their dying. . . . Haemon is dead, his blood drawn by a hand . . . by his own hand in

---

1. Seaford, *Reciprocity and Ritual*, 341-355.

wrath at his father for the murder" (τεθνᾶσιν· οἱ δὲ ζῶντες αἴτιοι θανεῖν 1173, Αἵμων ὄλωλεν· αὐτόχειρ δ᾽ αἱμάσσεται 1175, αὐτὸς πρὸς αὐτοῦ, πατρὶ μηνίσας φόνου 1177).

The exchange between the Coryphaeus and Messenger is interrupted as the door to the house swings inwardly. The audience may have anticipated the return of Ismene. Instead, an older woman appears whom the Coryphaeus immediately identifies as Creon's wife:

κοὶ μὴν ὁρῶ τάλαιναν Εὐρυδίκην ὁμοῦ
δάμαρτα τὴν Κρέοντος· ἐκ δὲ δωμάτων
ἤτοι κλυοῦσα παιδὸς ἢ τύχῃ περᾷ.

Sophocles Antigone 1180-1182

Here I see wretched Eurydice close by,
wife of Creon. She comes from the house,
because she has heard about her son, or by chance.

Nothing has prepared the audience for the presence of a wife in the house. The silence enshrouding her testifies to her enclosure in the inner spaces of the woman's world away from the talk of (and with) others. Like Deianeira (Sophocles *Women of Trachis* 40-43), Eurydice remains ignorant of events transpiring outside her house. When she decides to leave the house, it is for a task duly conducted in public by women (Sophocles *Antigone* 1185). She is going to invoke Athena in prayer at the goddess's temple. Perhaps like Hecuba and her old women (Homer *Iliad* 6.286-296), she means to implore the daughter of Zeus for the sake of the city. She is accosted by sounds of an *oikeion kakon* (misfortune for my house 1187), and, without realizing it, Creon prevents another woman from carrying out rituals that benefit his city and household.[2] Overhearing the Messenger's dread words, Eurydice comes out to hear them again as one not without experience in misfortunes (1190-1191). The Messenger recounts in detail what he has witnessed:

ἐγὼ δὲ σῷ ποδαγὸς ἑσπόμην πόσει
πεδίον ἐπ᾽ ἄκρον, ἔνθ᾽ ἔκειτο νηλεὲς
κυνοσπάρακτον σῶμα Πολυνείκους ἔτι·
καὶ τὸν μέν, αἰτήσαντες ἐνοδίαν θεὸν
Πλούτωνά τ᾽ ὀργὰς εὐμενεῖς κατασχεθεῖν,
λούσαντες ἁγνὸν λουτρόν, ἐν νεοσπάσιν
θαλλοῖς ὃ δὴ 'λέλειπτο συγκατήθομεν,

---

2. Barbara Goff ("The Women of Thebes," *The Classical Journal* 90 [1995], 358) observes that in the Thebes of anti-Athens mythmaking "[a]ll those actions that may be understood as belonging to the sphere of ritual—such as prayers, libations, dancing in honor of a god, or discharging funeral duties—are obstructed."

καὶ τύμβον ὀρθόκρανον οἰκείας χθονὸς
χώσαντες . . . .

Sophocles Antigone 1196-1204

I followed your husband as his guide
to the edge of the plain where was lying, unpitied
and rent by dogs, Polyneices' body, still.
We asked the Goddess of the Road and
Plouton to maintain a kindly disposition.
We bathed him with purifying bath and burned
what was left on newly plucked branches.
A lofty crowned mound of his own earth,
having heaped upon him. . . .

Creon called for axes of the type used for chopping wood (Sophocles *Antigone* 1109). As we have suggested, spectators might assume they would be used to construct a pyre. Yet none is constructed, and Creon's slaves break off light branches for the bedding of Polyneices' remains. This revelation surely left Sophocles' audience to wonder why he has Creon call for an inappropriate tool.[3] With a deft stroke, Sophocles prepares the expectation among the audience that Creon has not only learned the lesson of customs but also intends to implement custom in proper fashion. But the impression proves to be false; instead, the wrong kind of axes prefigures the stupidity over burial predicated by anti-Athens mythmaking. For the same reason, Creon cannot take good advice about caring for the dead. Despite his apparent intention to release Antigone while his slaves go to the corpse (1109-1112), he reverses the order of things, going first to Polyneices' body and arriving too late to save Antigone. Even so, he cannot care for the corpse of his *philos* in the proper manner. "It is disgraceful," Helen admonishes Electra, "for servants to bring these [liquid offerings]" to your mother's grave (αἰσχρόν γε μέντοι προσπόλους φέρειν τάδε Euripides *Orestes* 106). Creon, indifferent to such niceties, permits slaves and strangers to the dead to touch his nephew's body. They bathe and cremate the body and heap a mound over the remains. They confer upon it the care that it should have received in the house from kinswomen. By contrast, in anti-Athens mythmaking set in Attica, King Theseus buries the mass of the dead at Eleutherae (Eurides *Suppliant Women* 757) and tends to the bodies of the five remaining champions himself. Although they are disfigured by wounds and putrefied,

---

3. Jebb (*Antigone,* 197) suggests Sophocles had in mind "some kind of axe which could serve like the γενής [pick] of v. 249." Brown (*Sophocles: "Antigone"* 213) thinks picks "for rescuing Antigone or for burying Polynices." A comparably inappropriate use of language occurs when Sophocles calls the robe Deineira sends to Heracles a *peplos* (woman's dress) (*Women of Trachis* 602) instead of a *khiton* (man's tunic). Loraux ("Herakles," 39) cautions against reducing these apparent misuses of language to "anomalies" or "approximations" rather than "coming to terms" with them because "it does not do justice to the precision and rigor of Sophokles' language" to explain them away.

he keeps the slaves from touching the bodies. He washes and clothes them and spreads their beds himself (763-766). Theseus treats the champions as if they were his *philoi*. He replaces their mothers in duties men outside their mythmaking were eager, it would seem, to leave for the women of the family.[4]

The Messenger continues his disturbing account:

αὖθις πρὸς λιθόστρωτον κόρης
νυμφεῖον "Αιδου κοῖλον εἰσεβαίνομεν.
φωνῆς δ᾽ ἄπωθεν ὀρθίων κωκυμάτων
κλύει τις ἀκτέριστον ἀμφὶ παστάδα,
καὶ δεσπότῃ Κρέοντι σημαίνει μολών·
τῷ δ᾽ ἀθλίας ἄσημα περιβαίνει βοῆς
ἕρποντι μᾶλλον ἆσσον, οἰμώξας δ᾽ ἔπος
ἵησι δυσθρήνητον, "ὦ τάλας ἐγώ,
ἆρ᾽ εἰμὶ μάντις; ἆρα δυστυχεστάτην
κέλευθον ἕρπω τῶν παρελθουσῶν ὁδῶν;
παιδός με σαίνει φθόγγος."

                                               Sophocles *Antigone* 1204-1214

Then we left for the maiden's hollow
bridal chamber of Hades with its bedding of stone.
From afar, someone hears the high-pitched keening
of a voice near the bridal chamber unhallowed
by funeral rites. He comes and reports this to our master.
Senseless sounds of a cry of suffering
come over Creon as he draws nearer.
Crying out, he sent forth a mournful word:
"Oh, miserable me, am I a seer? Am I going
that most unfortunate road of all those traveled?
My son's voice touches me."

Although women were associated in both life and mythmaking with the inner spaces of the household, it was the son who remained at home to initiate a strange woman into the rites of his household at its hearth, and the daughter who left for another household.[5] When Creon drives Haemon into the cave that is Antigone's bridal chamber, their *kyrios* perverts the *ekdosis*, the "giving out" of the daughter in marriage. He sends his son into Antigone's bridal chamber in the way of a bride. Funeral sounds that emanate from a bridal chamber unhallowed by funeral rites mark the blending of rites and sexual roles Creon has inflicted upon those under his *kyrieia*. They are the wails of Haemon's keening that Creon answers with cries of

---

4. Vase painters depict men at a distance from the body. See plates in Boardman, "Painted Funerary Plaques," 1995; Shapiro, "Iconography," 630, Figure 1.
5. Vernant, *Mythe et pensée*, 1.131-132.

mourning. By forbidding the women of his household to mourn a man of their own, Creon causes the men of his household to mourn antiphonally like women. He knows his son's voice; he is touched with love by its sound.[6] The image of the road lying forth before Creon expresses succinctly and poignantly the suffering he must traverse.

Whatever Creon suspects, he desperately wants to retrieve Haemon from the cave with its sounds of death: "Come out, son, I beg you in supplication" (ἔξελθε, τέκνον, ἱκέσιός σε λίσσομαι Sophocles *Antigone* 1230). He humbles himself before his son, a suppliant to the stronger person. But Haemon has quit the civilized world of language and communication (354) claimed for man in the first stasimon as something he taught himself. Creon has driven his son into "the savage" (*to agrion*).[7] Catching sight of his father "with savage eyes" (ἀγρίοις ὄσσοισι), Haemon spits in his face and lunges at him with his sword (1231-1234). The son, whose "Father, I am yours" (635) expressed such filial devotion, has been brought to this by the father. Creon dismisses a loyal youth to find him again a patricidal man, an encounter reminiscent of Laïus' meeting with his grown son at the crossroads in Phocis. Both fathers incur a bestial violence that harbors no filial affection, for both have eradicated "the human."[8]

Creon's slaves insinuate themselves through the gap Haemon opened in the rocks and, in the most remote part of the cave, behold the scene:

> ἐν δὲ λοισθίῳ τυμβεύματι
> τὴν μὲν κρεμαστὴν αὐχένος κατείδομεν,
> βρόχῳ μιτώδει σινδόνος καθημμένην,
> τὸν δ' ἀμφὶ μέσσῃ περιπετῆ προσκείμενον,
> εὐνῆς ἀποιμώζοντα τῆς κάτω φθορὰν
> καὶ πατρὸς ἔργα καὶ τὸ δύστηνον λέχος.

> Sophocles *Antigone* 1220-1225

In the furthest part of the tomb,
we saw her hanging by the neck,
suspended by a noose of fine linen,
and him lying beside her, his arms about her waist,
bewailing the destruction of his nuptial bed departed below,
his father's deeds, and his wretched marriage bed.

---

6. W. S. Barrett (*Euripides: "Hippolytos"* [Oxford: Oxford University Press, 1964], 328) notes that "σαίνειν is properly 'fawn', of a dog showing fondness or gladness; it is then used (chiefly in tragedy) of a person or thing which attempts to rouse, or which in fact rouses, a person's favourable emotion." Creon hears Haemon's voice with trepidation, "yet it σαίνει [1214] because it is the voice of one he loves."

7. For *agrios*, see Segal, *Tragedy and Civilization*, 30-33.

8. Charles Segal's pages (*Tragedy and Civilization*, 222-223) on the "primal scene" between "two men of kingly rank" are indispensable.

Antigone is hanging, erect and raised from the ground; her head and upper body project above Haemon who is grasping her at the waist. The "noose of fine linen," her veil in our theater of the mind, evokes the *anakalyptêria* and Antigone's moment of consent. She has become Hades' bride. The audience is not to wonder how she attached the noose to the roof of the cave. The scene is not realistic but suggestive of the groom's lifting of his bride into the chariot at the inception of the wedding procession. Aristophanes' son, the comedian Araros, refers to this rite: "When the time comes, you will lift the bride into the air and place her in the cart.[9] An Attic red-figure *loutrophoros* depicts the rite that is itself a vestige of bridal abduction.[10] The bride holds herself rigidly erect. The groom stands behind her and gently raises her straight up and into the cart. His left foot is raised as his leg balances and supports her weight. The effort of this rite may explain why more than one groom preferred to send a *nymphagogos* to "lead his bride from her father's house" (ἄγων τὴν νύμφην ἐκ τῆς τοῦ πατρὸς οἰκίας Pollux *Onomasticum* 3.41). The driver waits in the chariot, looking back at the bridal couple as an Eros flies above. The groom's act demonstrates his physical strength and health and his dominance over his bride who submits with dignity and compliance by stiffening her body in an act she may never have attempted before or need again. The moment embodies Aristotle's prescription for a marriage as a relationship between the husband who rules and the wife who is ruled (*Politics* 1259 A 39-B 10). As Oakley and Sinos point out, "the groom plays the active role, the one who marries (*ho gamon*), while the bride is the object of his action, the one who is married (*hê gamoumenê*)."[11] The tableau blends the lifting of Antigone the bride with the lifting of Antigone the corpse, and the fine linen that veiled the bride with the linen that shrouded corpses.[12] Sophocles' original audience had seen and participated in wedding ceremonies; they would not miss the clues in this vignette in reported speech.

Haemon lunges at his retreating father, and, angry with himself for missing, falls upon his sword (Sophocles *Antigone* 1233-1236). The brutality of what is happening almost slips by as the Messenger delivers his report. A son, enraged at himself for not killing his father, slays himself. Under the normal conditions that underlie tragedy, Haemon should have left his father for his comrades in the hoplite formation where he would draw the blood of his enemy or shed his own in the killing zone. He should

---

9. Araros, *Hymnaios* in J. M. Edmonds, *Fragments of Attic Comedy*, 3 vols, Leiden: E .J. Brill, 1959), fr. 17: ὅπως τε τὴν νύμφην ἐπειδὰν καιρὸς ᾖ, / μετεώρον ἐπὶ τὸ ζεῦγος ἀναθήσεις φέρων.

10. Collignon, "Cérémonies du marriage," 1652, Figure 4866; Jenkins, "Is There Life After Marriage," 137-138 and Figure 1; Oakley and Sinos, *The Wedding in Ancient Athens*, 30-31 and figure 72.

11. Oakley and Sinos, *The Wedding in Ancient Athens*, 31.

12. Sophocles uses *sindôn*, the linen of Antigone's noose/veil (1222), to denote a shroud in *Eurypylos*, fr. 210 (Radt, *Sophocles*, 203), as does Aeschylus in *Nereiads*, fr. 153 (Radt, *Aeschylus*, 264).

have remained in his father's house and as Antigone's bridegroom caused the blood of Antigone's virginity to flow in marriage.[13] Indeed, he embraces (προσπτύσσεται 1237) the maiden, accepting her into his enfolding arms. Sophocles' verb, based on a root for "fold," does not itself bear sexual connotations. Homer uses it for a son embracing his father in his arms (*Odyssey* 11.451). However, the context of the consummation of Haemon's "marriage rites" (τὰ νυμφικὰ . . . τέλη *Antigone* 1240-1241) renders such connotations unavoidable here:

> ἐς δ' ὑγρὸν
> ἀγκῶν' ἔτ' ἔμφρων παρθένῳ προσπτύσσεται·
> καὶ φυσιῶν ὀξεῖαν ἐκβάλλει ῥοὴν
> λευκῇ παρειᾷ φοινίου σταλάγματος.
> κεῖται δὲ νεκρὸς περὶ νεκρῷ, τὰ νυμφικὰ
> τέλη λαχὼν δείλαιος ἔν γ' "Αιδου δόμοις.

Sophocles Antigone 1236-1241

> Still conscious,
> he enfolds the girl in his faint embrace.
> He was panting and streaming a swift flow
> of blood upon her white cheek.
> He lies there, corpse around corpse.
> The wretched received marriage rites in Hades' house.

Stone as a metaphor for the female body is identified "with virginity, as in Antigone's case, or with the end of fertility, as in Niobe's."[14] Niobe is tamed, conquered by rock and clinging ivy. Petrification denies sexual access to a woman's body and so dispossesses it of erotic power over men or procreative usefulness for them. Creon would not give Antigone to Haemon to be his "field for plowing," a metaphor that expresses the fertility of the female body as lying open to be enhanced by the work of men. The audience can now glean another meaning in the comparison of Antigone's enclosure to Niobe's petrification. Sophocles' imagery conveys the sealing off of Antigone's fertility by Creon's imprisonment. But Antigone retaliates by hanging herself, reifying the virgin's symbolic death in marriage.[15] Other implications are present. In Greek popular belief, the upper cervix (neck) was associated with the lower cervix (uterus). "That a young girl's neck enlarges after

---

13. Jean-Pierre Vernant (*Myth and Society in Ancient Greece*, trans. Janet Lloyd (Sussex: Harvester Press; Atlantic Highlands, NJ: Humanities Press, 23) explains that "[m]arriage is for the girl what war is for the boy: for each of them these mark the fullfiment [*sic*] of their respective natures as they emerge from a state in which each still shared in the nature of the other."

14. DuBois, *Sowing the Body*, 87.

15. Nicole Loraux (*Tragic Ways of Killing a Woman* [Cambridge and London: Harvard University Press, 1987], 17-21) points out that in tragedy, death by hanging affords a means of escape to women whom men have trapped in intolerable situations.

defloration is a projection upward of the widening of her αὐχήν, *cervix*, 'neck,' by the first opening of her uterine mouth."[16] Antigone seizes control over her body, closing off her "lower neck" by strangling its upper analogue and thus determining for herself who will enter her. What Antigone could not do for Polyneices, namely, control his body, she does for her own.

Antigone remains hanging in the rocky marriage chamber. Nothing in lines 1236-1240 justifies Jebb's assertion that "verses 1236-1240 require us to suppose that Antigone's body is then stretched on the ground. We are left to understand that Haemon, while uttering his lament (1224ff.), has lifted the corpse, so as to extricate it from the noose, and has laid it down."[17] The image exudes phallic symbolism. By enclosing Antigone into the folds of his embrace, Haemon accepts her into himself as if he were a woman, and it is he, not Antigone, who sheds blood. His spurting (Sophocles *Antigone* 1238: *oxeian*) stream recalls the bird's *oxun phthongon* (424), the shrill sound at the loss of a marriage. The repetition of *eunê* (425, 1224) and *lechos* (425, 1225), redundant terms for marriage bed, is too blatant to be accidental. From the first, Sophocles prompts his audience to recall Antigone the bird from the divine dust storm. What the slaves witness fulfills the message sent by Antigone the *teras*. With his stream, Haemon crimsons the woman's cheek in blood. He does not take the blood of her virginity or bestow upon her the promise of children. He falls upon a sword that is "two-edged" (διπλοῦς 1233) in that, by slaying Haemon the son, it slays Haemon the father. Like Deianeira who also falls upon a two-edged sword (ἀμφιπλῆγι φασγάνῳ Sophocles *Women of Trachis* 930), he invades the bridal chamber with the violence of the battlefield.[18] His "nuptials" join him to his bride in a marginality of blood between bride and groom, a rite through which he accepts her as a phallic bride. He takes her as a bloody, deadly groom in a consummation that perverts the *hieros gamos*, the sacred marriage that birthed the cosmos and was ever renewed in marriage beds, for upon it depends life itself:

ἐρᾷ μὲν ἁγνὸς οὐρανὸς τρῶσαι χθόνα,
ἔρως δὲ γαῖαν λαμβάνει γάμου τυχεῖν·
ὄμβρος δ' ἀπ' εὐνάεντος οὐρανοῦ πεσὼν
ἔκυσε γαῖαν· ἡ δὲ τίκτεται βροτοῖς

16. Ann Ellis Hanson ("The Medical Writers' Woman," in *Before Sexuality: The Construction of Erotic Experience in the Ancient Greek World*, ed. David M. Halperin, John H. Winkler, and Froma I. Zeitlin [Princeton, NJ: Princeton University Press, 1990], 325-328; the quotation is found on page 328.

17. As support, Jebb (*Antigone* 217) quotes Sophocles' *Oedipus Tyrannus* 1266 where, after Oedipus finds Jocasta hanging, he is said to cut her down (χαλᾷ κρεμαστὴν ἀρτάνην). Sophocles' specificity in Jocasta's release would appear to preclude, rather than support, such an inference regarding Antigone's situation.

18. For the role of Herakles and Deianeira and sexual reversals in their deaths in Sophocles' *Women of Trachis*, see Rush Rehm, *Marriage to Death: The Conflation of Wedding and Funeral Rituals in Greek Tragedy* (Princeton, NJ: Princeton Univeristy Press, 1994), 77-79.

μήλων τε βοσκὰς καὶ βίον Δημήτριον
δένδρων τ' ὀπώραν· ἐκ νοτίζοντος γάμου
τελεῖθ' ὅσ' ἔστι.

Aeschylus Danaids fr. 44 (Radt)

Holy Sky passionately longs to penetrate Earth.
Passion grips Earth to achieve consummation.
Rain from free-flowing Sky falls
and impregnates Earth. She gives birth for men
to the pasturage of flocks and Demeter's grain
and the fruition of trees. From their moist coupling
is produced all that is.

The Messenger is still reporting when Eurydice turns her back upon the men
and enters the house. He and the Coryphaeus watch, bewildered, as she leaves in
silence. They discuss her leaving in an exchange that is programmatic for the
upcoming scene. In the *exodos*, female silence contrasts with male speech:

Χο.   τί τοῦτ' ἂν εἰκάσειας; ἡ γυνὴ πάλιν
      φρούδη, πρὶν εἰπεῖν ἐσθλὸν ἢ κακὸν λόγον.
Αγ.   καὐτὸς τεθάμβηκ'· ἐλπίσιν δὲ βόσκομαι
      ἄχη τέκνου κλυοῦσαν ἐς πόλιν γόους
      οὐκ ἀξιώσειν, ἀλλ' ὑπὸ στέγης ἔσω
      δμωαῖς προθήσειν πένθος οἰκεῖον στένειν.
      γνώμης γὰρ οὐκ ἄπειρος, ὥσθ' ἁμαρτάνειν.
Χο.   οὐκ οἶδ'· ἐμοὶ δ' οὖν ἥ τ' ἄγαν σιγὴ βαρὺ
      δοκεῖ προσεῖναι χἠ μάτην πολλὴ βοή.

Sophocles Antigone 1244-1252

Coryphaeus:	What do you suppose about that? The woman is gone again,
	before she said a word, good or bad.
Messenger:	I, too, am surprised, but I feed on the hopes
	that, hearing her child's pains, she does not think
	wailing before the city proper, but inside beneath the roof
	she will set forth the grief for her house for her slaves to lament.
	She is not inexperienced in discretion so as to make a mistake.
Coryphaeus:	I do not know. To me too much silence seems
	as heavy as much vain suffering.

It is not clear from the text when Eurydice leaves, perhaps during the Messenger's
philosophizing on Haemon's fate (*Antigone* 1241-1243). But she has heard the
account of her son's suffering. The men are left to discuss her behavior, each
noting her "silence" (1251; 1256). That alone suffices to conclude that Sophocles is
directing his audience's attention to it.[19] Complying, as it were, with funeral

---

19. Does Sophocles stage a so-called Aeschylean silence as has been contended? Elise P.
Garrison ("Eurydice's Final Exit to Suicide in *Antigone*," *The Classical World* 82 [1989], 431)

legislation, Eurydice laments her sons in the house (1302-1304). Whereas Deianeira's nurse brings her words of farewell out from Heracles' bed chamber (Sophocles *Women of Trachis* 920-922), to hear Eurydice's voice, the audience must wait until a man penetrates her inner realm and returns with her words.

Creon enters from the country as the Messenger enters the house. He is attended by his slaves (Sophocles *Antigone* 1320) and is holding Haemon's body (1258).[20] Conspicuously absent for a modern audience is Antigone's body. Its presence would have changed the tenor of the scene, diverting attention away from Creon who now takes center stage. However, theater alone does not account for her absence. Like the slain Athenians of funeral oratory, she has fallen, and her eulogy has been pronounced. She is cast aside because she has played out her part. The Coryphaeus guides the audience in reading what they are watching. Haemon's body makes visual Creon's mistakes and the justice that he learns too late (1270):

καὶ μὴν ὅδ᾽ ἄναξ αὐτὸς ἐφήκει
μνῆμ᾽ ἐπίσημον διὰ χειρὸς ἔχων,
εἰ θέμις εἰπεῖν, οὐκ ἀλλοτρίαν
ἄτην, ἀλλ᾽ αὐτὸς ἁμαρτών.

---

maintains that Eurydice does not depart, as usually thought, on line 1243 or just before it but at 1252 and that she remains in silence as the men discuss her behavior, "the focus of significant dramatic attention while it is in progress." Aeschylean silences surround persons who have experienced catastrophic emotions that cut them off from the ordinary world and confound those around them (Oliver Taplin, "Aeschylean Silences and Silences in Aeschylus," *Harvard Studies in Classical Philology* 76 [1972], 57-58). Eurydice matches the pattern, but "the woman is gone back" (ἡ γυνὴ πάλιν / φροῦδη 1244-1245) seems unequivocal, and the suggestion that "the audience's enthusiastic reaction to a virtuoso messenger's speech" (Garrison, "Eurydice's Final Exit," 435)—itself not demonstrable—drowned out the ἡ γυνὴ πάλιν / φροῦδη is defeated by the spectacle before the audience. The Messenger is not speaking about Eurydice when the audience sees her leave, and when he does speak about her, she has gone. Further, Eurydice's silence in public is one expression of her muteness as a Greek woman while the flight from the public of men is another. She confines her mourning, speech, and body to the house. The playwright could not keep such a woman rooted before men while they discuss her. It savages Eurydice and demeans the very different realm of women that she embodies.

20. The text is inconclusive as to whether Creon is carrying, or merely holding onto, Haemon's body. For Sophocles' original audience, what is meant would be clear from the spectacle. His modern audience does not have that advantage and is left only to interpretation. Having him carry his son's body might convey visually that he has learned something about caring for the dead, while having him hold Haemon's body that the slaves are carrying distances him from the dead. Consistency with the mythmaking together with the effort of carrying even a model and the restrictions that would put on the actor's movements in the episode sufficiently rule out Creon's carrying a body throughout the scene. He is, more than likely, touching the body borne by his servants, an arrangement that befits his failure (Sophocles *Antigone* 1334-1336) even in the final episode to care for anyone but himself. The Coryphaeus, by again pointing out what all in the theater can see, marks not merely the token of Creon's suffering but also his tentative embrace of his dead son.

Sophocles *Antigone* 1257-1260

Here comes the lord himself,
holding in his hands a remarkable memorial,
if it is meet to say, not to another's
ruin but to a mistake that is all his own.

As he beholds the body of his son, Creon at last acknowledges his responsibility for Haemon's death: "O boy, new to life with a new kind of death,[21] aiai, aiai, you died, and you departed because of my bad counsels, not yours" (ἰὼ παῖ, νέος νέῳ ξὺν μόρῳ, / αἰαῖ αἰαῖ, / ἔθανες, ἀπελύθης, / ἐμαῖς οὐδὲ σαῖσι δυσβουλίαις Sophocles *Antigone* 1266-1269).

The Messenger now comes out of the house with news of evils in store for Creon (Sophocles *Antigone* 1277). Aware only of his own suffering (1285), Creon does not foresee the impact of his son's death on anyone else and asks, "What evil is worse than this evil?" (τί δ᾽ ἔστιν αὖ κάκιον ἐκ κακῶν ἔτι; 1281). The Messenger replies with pregnant brevity: "A woman is dead, all-mother of the corpse, a wretched one, just now by newly cut blows" (γυνὴ τέθνηκε, τοῦδε παμμήτωρ νεκροῦ, / δύστηνος, ἄρτι νεοτόμοισι πλήγμασιν 1282-1283). Creon again asks:

τί φής, παῖ, τίν᾽ αὖ λέγεις μοι νέον,
αἰαῖ αἰαῖ,
σφάγιον ἐπ᾽ ὀλέθρῳ
γυναικεῖον ἀμφικεῖσθαι μόρον;

Sophocles *Antigone* 1289-1292

What are you saying, boy? What news are you telling me?
Aiai, aiai,
slaughter on top of destruction—
a woman's death besetting me on both sides.

He does not long remain in doubt. In unison with the Messenger's pronouncement of Eurydice's appearance from the inner recesses of the house (1293), a low, wheeled platform is pushed through the doors of Creon's house. The spectators were accustomed to the *ekkyklêma*, a device for displaying the results of action that transpired inside the house. Only when Eurydice has permanently muted her voice does Sophocles bring her into public view to proclaim in silence her rage. The *ekkyklêma* offers a tableau showing Eurydice lying "near an altar with a sharply whetted knife" († ὀξυθήκτῳ βωμία περὶ ξίφει †1301) clearly extending from her body.[22] The tableau screams in silent reproach at the killer of her sons the thoughts and emotions that this very proper woman could not herself speak in public. The altar is that of Zeus Herkeios, Zeus of the Fence *(herkos)*. Here the master of the

---

21. Sophocles plays on the two senses of "new," namely, "young" and "unheard of, strange." See Liddell, Scott, and Jones, *Lexicon*, 1169 s.v. νέος.

22. The line is corrupt; we follow Arndt's conjecture as printed by Jebb (*Antigone*, 228).

house, enclosed within the protective *herkos* and surrounded by his family and slaves, conducted sacrifices and other rites on behalf of the safety and solidarity of his household. Although tragedy itself speaks of killing by the sword in sacrificial language, Eurydice's bloody slaying of herself at an altar with a sword used as a sacrificial knife collapses the distance between act and imagery. Eurydice has taken her own life as if she were a sacrificial victim (*sphagion*). In doing so, she has corrupted sacrifice into murder and polluted Creon's house at its most sacred place.[23]

Eurydice's death reprises the wedding night and shedding of blood in childbirth even as it repudiates her husband's penetration by a death-dealing, sharp-edged knife.[24] In the pseudo-Hesiodic *Shield,* Creon's wife is called Henioche (83). Sophocles' name, however, announces her role as "Wide-Justice." Eurydice casts her claims for *dikê* (justice, penalty, satisfaction) widely (*eury-*) to encompass Creon's responsibility not only for Haemon's death but also for that of Megareus (Sophocles *Antigone* 1303). Creon is the "child-killer" (παιδοκτόνῳ 1305); she accuses him of murder. "You were denounced" (*epeskêptou*), the Messenger tells Creon, "by the dead woman, with responsibility for the deaths, both then and now" (ὡς αἰτίαν γε τῶνδε κἀκείνων ἔχων / πρὸς τῆς θανούσης τῆσδ' ἐπεσκήπτου μόρων 1312-1313). With *epeskêptou,* Sophocles gives Eurydice a technical term of the law courts for announcing formally the intention to initiate a prosecution for perjury against a witness at a trial.[25] The bride and groom did not exchange vows in an Athenian marriage, and, although Creon has spoken foolishly and cruelly, he has not legally perjured himself. Yet Sophocles wants his audience to consider Creon, the child-killer, a perjurer. We must ask why.

A woman supported the city with sons who would be its defenders. Ideologically, Greek culture characterized the relationship of the mother and son in terms of protecting the community before their household.[26] This is the import of Hecuba's

---

23. The rites of sacrifice (*thusia*) appear to have been governed by the imperative that the victim go to the altar willingly and that in killing the victim, the sacrificers remain innocent of murder. When Eurydice willingly sacrifices herself, she corrupts the ritual death of an animal surrogate into the actual death of a human being. See Froma I. Zeitlin, "The Motif of the Corrupted Sacrifice in Aeschylus' *Oresteia*," *Transactions and Proceedings of the American Philological Association* 96 (1965), 463-508. For the rites of *thusia*, see Jean-Pierre Vernant, "Théorie générale du sacrifice et mise à mort dans la θυσία grecque," in *Le Sacrifice dans l'antiquité, Entretiens sur l'antiquité classique* 27 (1981), 1-21; Walter Burkert, *Homo Necans: The Anthropology of Ancient Greek Sacrificial Ritual and Myth,* trans. Peter Bing (Berkeley and Los Angeles: University of California Press, 1983), 3-12.

24. Loraux, *Tragic Ways,* 15: "a suicide that shed blood was associated with maternity, through which a wife, in her 'heroic' pains of childbirth, found complete fulfillment."

25. Liddell, Scott, and Jones, *Lexicon,* 657 s.v. ἐπισκήπτω, III; A. R. W. Harrison, *The Laws of Athens,* vol. 2, *Procedure* (Oxford: Oxford University Press, 1971), 192-193.

26. The distinction between mother and wife is discussed by Rick M. Newton ("Oedipus' Wife and Mother," *The Classical Journal* 87 [1991], 35-45) in his analysis of Jocasta's shift in attitude toward her husband/son in *Oedipus Tyrannus*.

question to Hector: "Son, why have you left behind bold war and come here?"
(τέκνον, τίπτε λιπὼν πόλεμον θρασὺν εἰλήλουθας; Homer *Iliad* 6.254), and the
lesson of Antigone's *nomos*. A woman's son and her husband, another woman's
son, should be wounded or slain by another man while fighting for the city. It was
the "red badge" that Creon took from Eurydice's sons.[27] One may have died the
death of a sacrificial victim;[28] the other dies the death of a woman in falling upon
his sword. The latter is a man's death for Ajax, but Haemon slays himself as
Antigone's bride. As groom, his house is that facing the audience, but they saw
him leave for another, the bridal chamber of Antigone's cave, where, rather than
taking the woman's blood, he sheds his own like a bride. And for that, Eurydice
denounces Creon for foreswearing the understood oath that obligates a man to a
woman. By virtue of bringing her into his house in marriage, Creon owes Eurydice
the opportunity to realize her procreativity and bring it to fruition in contributing to
house and city. When Menecles could not give his wife a child, he returned her to
her brother's *kyrieia* for him to give out to another husband (Isaeus *Concerning
the Estate of Philoctemon* 7). Creon, by killing Eurydice's children and robbing
them of a marriage bed, has failed in his commitment to her. This is his perjury.

The Messenger calls Eurydice *"pammêtôr* of this corpse" (1282). Translations
such as "real mother" or "true mother" reproduce the Scholiast's understanding:
"the mother in all respects. [The Messenger] emphatically said that up until the
death she was shown to be a mother; after her son's death, she preferred not to
live" (ἡ κατὰ πάντα μήτηρ· ἐμφαντικῶς δὲ εἶπεν, ὅτι καὶ μέχρι θανάτου

---

27. Peleus upbraids Menelaos for coming home unwounded:
    αὐθέντην δὲ σὲ
    μιάστορ' ὥς τιν' εἰσδέδορκ' Ἀχιλλέως.
    ὅς οὐδὲ τρωθεὶς ἦλθες ἐκ Τροίας μόνος;
    κάλλιστα τεύχη δ' ἐν καλοῖσι σάγμασιν
    ὅμοι' ἐκεῖσε δεῦρ' τ' ἤγαγες πάλιν.

    Euripides *Andromache* 614-618

    I look upon you as Achilles' murderer
    and one polluted with his blood.
    You alone came from Troy without a wound
    and your most beautiful weapons in their beautiful cases,
    just as they were over there, you brought back here.

28. Sophocles depends upon his audience's knowledge of the circumstances of Megareus'
death. His allusiveness presupposes a well-known incident, and Greek myths are too detailed for
it not to be accounted for somehow. Whatever his death, it should lend itself to Eurydice's charge
of murder (Sophocles *Antigone* 1305). It is linked in her mind to Creon. Francis Vian (*Les
Origines de Thèbes: Cadmos et Spartes* [Paris: C. Klincksieck, 1963], 213) and Kamerbeek
(*Antigone*, 172) suggest that perhaps Creon had to sacrifice his son Megareus at Tiresias'
bidding. The inference is satisfying in that it balances the death of the one son as a daughter in
a corrupted marriage with the death of the other in an offering corrupted by his being an
unsuitable victim, since, in Athenian sacrificial ideology, it is daughters who are sacrificed. In
each case, Theban Creon substitutes the improper sex.

μήτηρ ἐδείχθη, μὴ ἑλομένη ζῆν μετὰ τὸν τοῦ παιδὸς θάνατον). This is an acceptable reading of the Messenger's meaning, but Sophocles has chosen too unusual a word for its significance to end there. In *Prometheus Bound*, Aeschylus applies *pammêtôr* to Gê, Earth, the true mother of all things (90). *Pammêtôr* connotes the Great Mother Earth, Gaia. Throughout the formative period of the universe, Gaia repeatedly defends her offspring against the aggression of the male attempting to control her children and usurp her procreativity.[29] She conceives the monster Typhaon to overthrow the Olympians and become lord for mortals and immortals in place of Zeus (Hesiod *Theogony* 821-837). The poet of the *Hymn to Apollo* tells how another goddess, Hera, the formidable sister and wife of Zeus, was enraged at Zeus for giving birth to Athena by himself.

πῶς ἔτλης οἶος τεκέειν γλαυκῶπιδ' 'Αθήνην;
οὐκ ἂν ἐγὼ τεκόμην; καὶ σὴ κεκλημένη ἔμπης
ἦα ρ' ἐν ἀθανάτοισιν οἳ οὐρανὸν εὐρὺν ἔχουσι.

Hymn to Apollo 323-325

How did you dare to give birth to gray-eyed Athena alone?
Would I not have borne her? I who am still called yours
among immortals who hold wide heaven?

Hera devises an evil for him by striking Gaia and quickening her to produce Typhaon to be "mightier than Zeus by as much as far-seeing Zeus is mightier than Kronos" (ὅ γε φέρτερος ἔστω ὅσον Κρόνου εὐρύοπα Ζεύς *Hymn to Apollo* 339).[30] *Pammêtôr* said of a mother whose child has been turned into a corpse by a male in mastery over her procreativity evokes the rage of the Great Mother at her subjection to the male in patriarchal marriage.[31] Eurydice *pammêtôr* may owe her origin to Creon's responsibility for Haemon's death in a corruption of the sacred marriage, but the image evokes the goddess's primordial violence in vengeance for her

---

29. See Marylin B. Arthur, "Cultural Strategies in Hesiod's *Theogony*: Law, Family, Society," *Arethusa* 15 (1982), 63-82; Wm. Blake Tyrrell and Frieda S. Brown, *Athenian Myths and Institutions: Words in Action* (New York and Oxford: Oxford University Press, 1991), 15-39.

30. See Jenny Strauss Clay, *The Politics of Olympus: Form and Meaning in the Major Homeric Hymns* (Princeton, NJ: Princeton University Press, 1989), 66-71. In what seems an attempt to resolve the discrepancy in Typhaon's birth (from Gaia or from Hera), a scholion on Homer, *Iliad* 2.783, tells how Gaia, angry at the murder of the Giants, calumniates Zeus to Hera. The latter goes to Kronos who gives her two eggs smeared with his semen and the instructions to bury the eggs in Gaia. From them, Typhaon is born. Hera, later reconciled with Zeus, tells him everything, and Zeus strikes the monster with a thunderbolt.

31. Segal (*Tragedy and Civilization*, 181) considers Eurydice "the grieving mother and 'wide-ruling' (*Eury - Dike*) Queen of the Dead, whose desolation is now spread over [Creon's] entire realm. . . . As a manifestation of chthonic female power and maternal vengeance, she makes the interior spaces of his own house (*mychoi*, 1293) a dark place of corpses (1298-1300)."

motherhood.[32] It is a wrath that draws from the goddess's resentment at what the god did to her and from his having thereby failed to fulfill his obligation. It lashes out at Creon, as it were, from generations of festering rage and crushes him: "O servants, lead me away as quickly as you can, lead me from under foot, who am no more than nothing" (ἰὼ πρόσπολοι, / ἄγετέ μ' ὅτι τάχιστ', ἄγετέ μ' ἐκποδών, / τὸν οὐκ ὄντα μᾶλλον ἢ μηδένα Sophocles *Antigone* 1320-1325). Eurydice does not stop at judging Creon. She exacts payment from him.

When Polyneices and Eteocles died, Creon had no use for the women of his family. He cared for their bodies as he chose. Now, he comes back to the house, holding his son's body. Under the circumstances, the audience might reasonably expect that Creon intends to entrust his son to his mother's care. The expectation is shattered by Eurydice's death. Eurydice has silenced herself; she will not mourn his son for him. This is the *dikê*, the penalty, that Eurydice exacts from Creon. Her death is not the flight from an intolerable situation that was Deianira's (Sophocles *Women of Trachis* 705-722). Eurydice gives Creon the woman he wanted, a silenced woman who refuses to mourn a *philos*, and gains for Antigone the vengeance she prayed for, a silent funeral for Creon. By having Antigone's actor play Eurydice, Antigone, so to speak, takes her own vengeance by again silencing the same voice to a different purpose and effect.[33]

Hearing of Eurydice's death, Creon prays for his own (1329-1330), but he is reminded that he has still a task to fulfill. When the Coryphaeus urges him "to do some of what lies before you" (τῶν προκειμένων τι χρὴ / πράσσειν 1334-1335), he uses a word (*prokeimenôn*) that also denotes laying a corpse out for burial in the *prothesis*. Both corpses, Haemon's and Eurydice's, are now lying forth, but since Creon does not know which one to look at (1344), they are not in the same visual plane. Sophocles keeps the bodies before the audience throughout the *exodos* because they reify Creon's "I killed you. I did it," where his singular "you" refers to either of the dead (ἐγὼ γάρ σ', ἐγώ σ' ἔκανον, 1319).

Where Eurydice is silent in public, Creon plays the woman in lamenting before the city. He sees around himself the ruin he has caused (Sophocles *Antigone* 1298-1299). He is reduced to lamenting his mistakes and bad counsels (1261-1269) and crying for an end to his life (1284-1285, 1308-1309, 1331-1332). He is where he is because he succumbed to the forces of a contest that do not allow any ending before absolute victory and count anything else a defeat. Those in Sophocles' original audience might have feared for themselves in watching the suffering of such a man and, more to the point, the suffering of those around him. Their leaders were motivated by that same contest and long before the time of *Antigone* had been

32. Eurydice as *pammêtôr* may, then, be Sophocles' invention, but the wrath of the primal goddesses at their subordination to Zeus and his rule belongs to panhellenic mythmaking.
33. Charles Segal (*Sophocles' Tragic World: Divinity, Nature, Society* [Cambridge and London: Harvard University Press, 1995], 126-127) points to the correspondence between Antigone and Eurydice.

roaming the Mediterranean in search of victory at the cost of their lives. For all that, Creon seems the same man—the same impious Theban of anti-Athens mythmaking—after his *pathei mathos* (learning by suffering) as before. He leaves, escorted into the house by his slaves, retracing the steps of the women of his family whom he has wronged. It is a visible statement of his reduction by grief into what he most loathes, a woman. He leaves the bodies of his *philoi* for others to care for. When the Coryphaeus pronounces his final advice, it is advice Creon cannot implement:

πολλῷ τὸ φρονεῖν εὐδαιμονίας
πρῶτον ὑπάρχει· χρὴ δὲ τά γ᾽ ἐς θεοὺς
μηδὲν ἀσεπτεῖν· μεγάλοι δὲ λόγοι
μεγάλας πληγὰς τῶν ὑπεραύχων
ἀποτείσαντες
γήρᾳ τὸ φρονεῖν ἐδίδαξαν.

Sophocles *Antigone* 1347-1353

By far is having sense the first part
of happiness. One must not act impiously toward
what pertains to gods. Big words
of boasting men,
paid for by big blows,
teach having sense in old age.

The *ekkyklêma* is drawn inside, and Creon's slaves carry Haemon's body into the house. The chorus exits. The audience stirs. The play is over. But the contest for the prize in tragedy did not end until the end of the third morning with the end of the third and last satyr play.

Before the festival, the council composed a list of names from each of the ten tribes of citizens. These names were placed in ten urns, sealed and stored on the Acropolis. At the beginning of the festival, the urns were brought down and set up in the theater. At this time, the magistrate opened the urns and drew out the name of one man from each urn. These ten men, now designated as judges of the contest, swore to return an impartial decision. With the close of the final satyr play, it was time for them to vote. The judges, weathering the advice shouted down from the slope of the Acropolis, marked their tablets and deposited them in a jar. The magistrate solemnly drew five and, after reading the names, whispered to the herald. The latter, whose voice speaks for the community, proclaimed the victor. Was it Sophocles' head that the magistrate garlanded with the ivy of victory? That can never be known. But for the audience leaving the theater that day, the true victor of Sophocles' *Antigone* was themselves, the *dêmos*, the *polis*, *hoi Athênaioi*.

Bibliography

Adams, S. M. "The *Antigone* of Sophocles." *Phoenix* 9 (1955): 47-62.

———. *Sophocles the Playwright*. Toronto: University of Toronto Press, 1957.

Adkins, Arthur W. H. *Merit and Responsibility: A Study in Greek Values*. Chicago and London: The University of Chicago Press, 1960.

Ahlberg-Cornell, Gudrun. *"Prothesis" and "Ekphora" in Greek Geometric Art*. Göteborg: P. Äström, 1971.

Alexiou, Margaret. *The Ritual Lament in Greek Tradition*. Cambridge: Cambridge University Press, 1974.

Andrewes, A. "The Arginousai Trial." *Phoenix* 28 (1974): 112-122.

Ardener, Shirley, ed. *Defining Females: The Nature of Women in Society*. New York: John Wiley and Sons, 1978.

Arthur, Marylin B. "Cultural Strategies in Hesiod's *Theogony*: Law, Family, Society." *Arethusa* 15 (1982): 63-82.

———. "Politics and Pomegranates: An Interpretation of the Homeric *Hymn to Demeter*." In *The Homeric "Hymn to Demeter": Translation, Commentary, and Interpretative Essays*. Edited by Helene P. Foley, 214-242. Princeton, NJ: Princeton University Press, 1994.

Austin, J. L. *How to Do Things with Words*. 2d ed. Edited by J. O. Urmson and Marina Sbisà. Cambridge: Harvard University Press, 1975.

Bamberger, Joan. "The Myth of Matriarchy: Why Men Rule in Primitive Society." In *Woman, Culture, and Society*. Edited by Michelle Zimbalist Rosaldo and Louise Lamphere, 263-280. Stanford: Stanford University Press, 1974.

Barber, E. J. W. "The Peplos of Athena." In *Goddess and Polis: The Panathenaic Festival in Ancient Athens*. Edited by Jenifer Neils, 103-117. Hanover, NH: Hood Museum of Art, Dartmouth College; Princeton, NJ: Princeton University Press, 1992.

Translations and editions of Sophocles' *Antigone* are listed under the name of the translator or editor.

Barrett, W. S. *Euripides: "Hippolytos."* Oxford: Oxford University Press, 1964.

Barthes, Roland. *Mythologies.* Translated by Annette Lavers. New York: Hill and Wang, 1972.

———. "The Death of the Author." In *Image, Music, Text.* Translated by Stephen Heath, 142-148. New York: Hill and Wang, 1977.

Beazley, John Davidson. *Attic Red-Figure Vase-Painters.* 2d ed. 3 vols. Oxford: Clarendon Press, 1963.

Bennett, Larry J., and Wm. Blake Tyrrell. "Sophocles' *Antigone* and Funeral Oratory." *American Journal of Philology* 111 (1990): 441-456.

———. "What Is Antigone Wearing?" *The Classical World* 85 (1991): 107-109.

Benson, J. L. *Horse Bird and Man: The Origins of Greek Painting.* Amherst: University of Massachusetts Press, 1970.

Benveniste, Emile. *Indo-European Language and Society.* Translated by Elizabeth Palmer. London: Faber and Faber, 1973.

Bernardete, Seth. "Achilles and the *Iliad.*" *Hermes* 91 (1963): 1-16.

——— "A Reading of Sophocles' *Antigone.*" Parts 1-3. *Interpretation: A Journal of Political Philosophy* 4 (1975): 148-196; 5 (1975): 1-55, 148-184.

Boardman, J. "Painted Funerary Plaques and Some Remarks on *Prothesis.*" *The Annual of the British School at Athens* 50 (1955): 51-66.

———. *Athenian Black Figure Vases.* London: Thames and Hudson, 1974.

———. *Athenian Red Figure Vases: The Archaic Period.* London: Thames and Hudson, 1975.

Boegehold, Alan L. "Pericles' Citizenship Law of 451/50 B.C." In *Athenian Identity and Civic Ideology.* Edited by Alan L. Boegehold and Adele C. Scafuro, 57-66. Baltimore and London: The Johns Hopkins University Press, 1994.

Bothmer, Dietrich von. *Amazons in Greek Art.* Oxford: Clarendon Press, 1957.

Bowra, Cecil. *Sophoclean Tragedy.* Oxford: Clarendon Press, 1944.

Bradley, A. C. *Oxford Lectures on Poetry.* 2d ed. London: Macmillan, 1909.

Bradshaw, A. T. von S. "The Watchman Scenes in the *Antigone.*" *Classical Quarterly* 12 (1962): 200-211.

Braun, Richard Emil, trans. *Sophocles: "Antigone."* Oxford: Oxford University Press, 1973.

Bremmer, J. "Scapegoat Rituals in Ancient Greece." *Harvard Studies in Classical Philology* 87 (1983): 299-320.

Brown, Andrew, ed. and trans. *Sophocles: "Antigone."* Warminster: Aris and Phillips, 1987.

Brunk, Richard François Philippe. *Scholia Graeca in Sophoclem ex Editione Brunckiana.* 2d ed. Oxonii: e Typographeo Clarendoniano, 1810.

Burkert, Walter. *Griechische Religion.* Stuttgart: W. Kohlhammer, 1977.

———. *Homo Necans: The Anthropology of Ancient Greek Sacrificial Ritual and Myth.* Translated by Peter Bing. Berkeley and Los Angeles: University of California Press, 1983.

———. *Greek Religion.* Translated by John Raffan. Cambridge: Harvard University Press, 1985.

Burton, R. W. B. *The Chorus in Sophocles' Tragedies.* Oxford: Oxford University Press, 1980.

Buxton, R. G. A. *Sophocles.* Oxford: Clarendon Press for the Classical Association, 1984.

Calder, William M., III. "Sophokles' Political Tragedy, *Antigone.*" *Greece and Rome* 9 (1968): 389-407.

Cameron, H. D. "The Power of Words in the *Seven Against Thebes.*" *Transactions and Proceedings of the American Philological Association* 101 (1970): 95-118.

Caraveli, Anna. "The Bitter Wounding: The Lament as Social Protest in Rural Greece." In *Gender and Power in Rural Greece.* Edited by Jill Dubisch, 169-194. Princeton, NJ: Princeton University Press, 1986.

Caraveli-Chaves, Anna. "Bridge Between Worlds: The Greek Women's Lament as Communicative Event." *Journal of American Folklore* 93 (1980): 129-157.

Carson, Anne. "Putting Her in Her Place: Women, Dirt, and Desire." In *Before Sexuality: The Construction of Erotic Experience in the Ancient Greek World.* Edited by David M. Halperin, John J. Winkler, and Froma I. Zeitlin, 135-169. Princeton, NJ: Princeton University Press, 1990.

Castriota, David. *Myth, Ethos, and Actuality: Official Art in Fifth-Century B.C. Athens.* Madison: The University of Wisconsin Press, 1992.

Charbonneaux, J., R. Martin, and F. Villard. *Classical Greek Art, 480-330 B.C.* Translated by James Emmons. London: Thames and Hudson, 1972.

Clairmont, Christoph W. *Patrios Nomos: Public Burial in Athens during the Fifth and Fourth Centuries B.C.* International Series 161. 2 vols. Oxford: B. A. R., 1983.

Clay, Jenny Strauss. *The Politics of Olympus: Form and Meaning in the Homeric Hymns*. Princeton, NJ: Princeton University Press, 1989.

Collard, Christopher, ed. "The Funeral Oration in Euripides' *Supplices*." *Bulletin of the Institute of Classical Studies of the University of London* 19 (1972): 39-53.

————. ed. *Euripides: "Supplices."* 2 vols. Groningen: Bouma's Boekhuis, 1975.

Collignon, Max. "Cérémonies du marriage." In *Dictionnaire des antiquités grecques et romaines*. Edited by Ch. Daremberg and Edm. Saglio, 1647-1654. Vol. 3. Paris: Librairie Hachette, 1918.

Craik, Elizabeth. *Euripides: "Phoenician Women."* Warminster: Aris and Phillips, 1988.

Culler, Jonathan. *Structuralist Poetics: Structuralism, Linguistics, and the Study of Literature*. Ithaca, NY: Cornell University Press, 1975.

Danforth, Loring M. *The Death Rituals of Rural Greece*. Photography by Alexander Tsiaras. Princeton, NJ: Princeton University Press, 1982.

Danker, Frederic William. *A Century of Greco-Roman Philology: Featuring the American Philological Association and the Society of Biblical Literature*. Atlanta: Scholars Press, 1988.

Davidson, J. F. "The Parados of the *Antigone*: A Poetic Study." *Bulletin of the Institute of Classical Studies of the University of London* 30 (1983): 41-51.

Dawe, R. D. "Some Reflections on Ate and Hamartia." *Harvard Studies in Classical Philology* 72 (1967): 89-123.

Denniston, J. D. *The Greek Particles*. 2d ed. Oxford: Oxford University Press, 1950.

Detienne, Marcel. *Dionysos Slain*. Translated by Mireille Muellner and Leonard Muellner. Baltimore and London: The Johns Hopkins University Press, 1979.

Deubner, Ludwig. *Attische Feste*. Hildesheim: Georg Olms, 1966.

Diels, Hermann. *Die Fragmente der Vorsokratiker*. 6th ed. Vol. 2. Edited by Walther Kranz. Berlin: Weidmann, 1952.

Dodds, E. R. *Euripides. Bacchae*. 2d ed. Berkeley and Los Angeles: University of California Press, 1951.

————. *The Greeks and the Irrational*. Berkeley and Los Angeles: University of California Press, 1951.

Donlan, Walter. *The Aristocratic Ideal in Ancient Greece: Attitudes of Superiority from Homer to the End of the Fifth Century B.C.* Lawrence, KS: Coronado Press, 1980.

Dover, K. J. *Greek Homosexuality*. Cambridge: Harvard University Press, 1978.

DuBois, Page. *Centaurs and Amazons: Women and the Pre-History of the Great Chain of Being*. Ann Arbor: University of Michigan Press, 1982.

———. *Sowing the Body: Psychoanalysis and Ancient Representations of Women*. Chicago: The University of Chicago Press, 1988.

Easterling, P. E. "The Second Stasimon of *Antigone*." In *Dionysiaca: Nine Studies in Greek Poetry by Former Pupils Presented to Sir Denys Page on His Seventieth Birthday*. Edited by R. D. Dawe, J. Diggle, and P. E. Easterling, 141-158. Cambridge: The Editors, 1978.

———. "Character in Sophocles." In *Greek Tragedy*. Edited by Ian McAuslan and Peter Walcot, 58-65. Oxford: Oxford University Press on behalf of The Classical Association, 1993. (First published in *Greece and Rome* 24 [1977]: 121-129).

Edmonds, J. M. *Lyra Graeca: Being the Remains of All the Greek Lyric Poets from Eumelus to Timotheus Excepting Pindar*. 3 vols. Cambridge: Harvard University Press, 1922-1927.

———. *The Fragments of Attic Comedy*. 3 vols. Leiden: E. J. Brill, 1959.

Ehrenberg, Victor. *Sophocles and Pericles*. Oxford: Basil Blackwell, 1954.

Elam, Keir. *The Semiotics of Theatre and Drama*. London and New York: Methuen, 1980.

Fagles, Robert, trans. *Sophocles: The Three Theban Plays*. New York: Viking Press, 1982.

Fisher, N. R. E . "*Hybris* and Dishonour: I." *Greece and Rome* 23 (1976): 177-193.

Flickinger, Minnie Keys. "Who First Buried Polynices?" *Philological Quarterly* 12 (1933): 130-136.

Foley, Helene P. *Ritual Irony: Poetry and Sacrifice in Euripides*. Ithaca, NY: Cornell University Press, 1985.

———. ed. *The Homeric "Hymn to Demeter": Translation, Commentary, and Interpretive Essays*. Princeton, NJ: Princeton University Press, 1994.

Fraenkel, Eduard, ed. and trans. *Aeschylus: "Agamemnon."* 3 vols. Oxford: Oxford University Press, 1950.

Freund, Elizabeth. *The Return of the Reader: Reader-Response Criticism*. London and New York: Methuen, 1987.

Gardiner, Cynthia P. *The Sophoclean Chorus: A Study of Character and Function*. Iowa City: University of Iowa Press, 1987.

Garland, Robert. *The Greek Way of Death*. London: Duckworth, 1985.

————. "The Well-Ordered Corpse: An Investigation into the Motives behind Greek Funerary Legislation." *Bulletin of the Institute of Classical Studies of the University of London* 36 (1989): 1-15.

————. *The Greek Way of Life*. Ithaca, NY: Cornell University Press, 1990.

Garner, Richard. *From Homer to Tragedy: The Art of Allusion in Greek Poetry*. London and New York: Routledge, 1990.

Garrison, Elise P. "Eurydice's Final Exit to Suicide in the *Antigone*." *The Classical World* 82 (1989): 431-435.

Gellie, G. H. *Sophocles: A Reading*. Melbourne: Melbourne University Press, 1972.

Gernet, Louis. *The Anthropology of Ancient Greece*. Translated by John Hamilton, S. J. Nagy, and Blaise Nagy. Baltimore and London: The Johns Hopkins University Press, 1981.

Gill, Christopher. "The Question of Character and Personality in Greek Tragedy." *Poetics Today* 7 (1986): 251-273.

Girard, René. *Violence and the Sacred*. Translated by Patrick Gregory. Baltimore and London: The Johns Hopkins University Press, 1977.

Goff, Barbara. "The Women of Thebes." *The Classical Journal* 90 (1995): 353-365.

Goheen, Robert F. *The Imagery of Sophocles' Antigone: A Study of Poetic Language and Structure*. Princeton, NJ: Princeton University Press, 1951.

Goldhill, Simon. *Reading Greek Tragedy*. Cambridge: Cambridge University Press, 1986.

Gomme, A. W. *A Historical Commentary on Thucydides*. Vol. 2: *The Ten Years' War*. Oxford: Oxford University Press, 1956.

Gould, John. "Law, Custom and Myth: Aspects of the Social Position of Women in Classical Athens." *Journal of Hellenic Studies* 100 (1980): 38-59.

Gouldner, Alvin W. *Enter Plato: Classical Greece and the Origins of Social Theory*. New York and London: Basic Books, 1965.

Grene, David, trans. *Antigone*. In *The Complete Greek Tragedies: Sophocles I*. Edited by David Grene and Richmond Lattimore. Chicago and London: The University of Chicago Press, 1991.

Hamilton, John D. B. "Antigone: Kinship, Justice, and the Polis." In *Myth and the Polis*. Edited by Dora C. Pozzi and John M. Wickersham, 86-98. Ithaca, NY: Cornell University Press, 1991.

Hammond, N. G. L. *A History of Greece to 322 B.C.* Oxford: Oxford University Press, 1959.

Hanson, Ann Ellis. "The Medical Writers' Woman." In *Before Sexuality: The Construction of Erotic Experience in the Ancient Greek World.* Edited by David M. Halperin, John J. Winkler, and Froma I. Zeitlin, 309-338. Princeton, NJ: Princeton University Press, 1990.

Hanson, Victor Davis. *The Western Way of War: Infantry Battle in Classical Greece.* New York and Oxford: Oxford University Press, 1989.

Harrison, A. R. W. *The Law of Athens.* Vol. 1: *The Family and Property.* Oxford: Oxford University Press, 1968; Vol. 2: *Procedure.* Oxford: Oxford University Press, 1971.

Harrison, Jane Ellen. *Prolegomena to the Study of Greek Religion.* 3d ed. Cambridge: Cambridge University Press, 1922.

Harry, J. E. *Studies in Sophocles. University of Cincinnati Studies* 27 (1911): 20-25.

Hathorn, Richmond Y. "Sophocles' *Antigone*: Eros in Politics." *The Classical Journal* 54 (1958-1959): 111-115.

Held, George F. "Antigone's Dual Motivation for the Double Burial." *Hermes* 111 (1983): 190-201.

Henderson, Jeffery. "Women and the Athenian Dramatic Festivals." *Transactions of the American Philological Association* 121 (1991): 133-147.

Herington, John. *Poetry into Drama: Early Tragedy and the Greek Poetic Tradition.* Berkeley and Los Angeles: University of California Press, 1985.

Hester, D. A. "Sophocles the Unphilosophical: A Study in the *Antigone.*" *Mnemosyne* 24 (1971): 11-59.

Hirsch, E. D., Jr. *Cultural Literacy: What Every American Needs to Know.* Boston: Houghton Mifflin, 1987.

Hogan, James C. "The Protagonists of the *Antigone.*" *Arethusa* 5 (1972): 93-100.

Holst-Warhaft, Gail. *Dangerous Voices: Women's Laments and Greek Literature.* London and New York: Routledge, 1992.

Hulton, A. O. "The Double Burial of the *Antigone.*" *Mnemosyne* 16 (1963): 284-285.

Humphreys, S. C. *The Family, Women, and Death: Comparative Studies.* London: Routledge and Kegan Paul, 1982.

Hutchinson, G. O. *Aeschylus: "Septem Contra Thebes."* Oxford: Clarendon Press, 1985.

Immerwahr, Henry R. *Form and Thought in Herodotus*. Cleveland: Press of Western Reserve University for The American Philological Association, 1966.

Jacoby, F. "*Patrios Nomos*: State Burial in Athens and the Public Cemetery in the Kerameikos," *Journal of Hellenic Studies* 64 (1944): 37-66.

Jebb, Richard. *Sophocles: The Plays and Fragments*. Part 3: *The "Antigone."* 3d ed. Cambridge: Cambridge University Press, 1900.

Jenkins, Ian. "Is There Life After Marriage? A Study of the Abduction Motif in Vase Paintings of the Athenian Wedding Ceremony." *Bulletin of the Institute of Classical Studies of the University of London* 30 (1983): 137-145.

Johansen, Holger Friis. "Sophocles 1939-1959." *Lustrum* 7 (1962): 94-288.

Jones, John. *On Aristotle and Greek Tragedy*. London: Chatto and Windus, 1971.

Jordan, Borimir. *Servants of the Gods*. Göttingen: Vandenhoeck and Ruprecht, 1979.

Just, Roger. *Women in Athenian Law and Life*. London and New York: Routledge, 1989.

Kamerbeek, J. C. *The Plays of Sophocles: Commentaries*. Part 3: *The "Antigone."* Leiden: E. J. Brill, 1978.

Kaplan, Louise J. *Adolescence: The Farewell to Childhood*. New York: Simon and Schuster, 1984.

Keuls, Eva C. "Attic Vase-Painting and the Home Textile Industry." In *Ancient Greek Art and Iconography*. Edited by Warren G. Moon, 209-230. Madison: The University of Wisconsin Press, 1983.

———. *The Reign of the Phallus: Sexual Politics in Ancient Athens*. New York: Harper and Row, 1985.

Kirkwood, G. M. *A Study of Sophoclean Drama*. Ithaca, NY: Cornell University Press, 1958.

Kitto, H. D. F. *Form and Meaning in Drama*. London: Methuen, 1956.

Knox, Bernard M. W. *Oedipus at Thebes*. New York: W. W. Norton, 1971 (orig. 1957).

———. *The Heroic Temper: Studies in Sophoclean Tragedy*. Berkeley and Los Angeles: University of California Press, 1964.

———. Introduction to *Sophocles: The Three Theban Plays*, translated by Robert Fagles. New York: Viking Press, 1982.

Kurtz, Donna C., and John Boardman. *Greek Burial Customs*. Ithaca, NY: Cornell University Press, 1971.

Lacey, W. K. *The Family in Classical Greece*. London and Southampton: Thames and Hudson, 1968.

Lang, Mabel. *Herodotean Narrative and Discourse*. Cambridge, MA, and London: Harvard University Press for Oberlin College, 1984.

Lattimore, Richmond. "The Wise Adviser in Herodotus." *Classical Philology* 34 (1939): 24-35.

Lebeck, Anne. *The "Oresteia": A Study in Language and Structure*. Washington, DC: The Center for Hellenic Studies, 1971; distributed by Harvard University Press.

Lefkowitz, Mary R. *The Lives of the Greek Poets*. Baltimore and London: The Johns Hopkins University Press, 1981.

Lesky, Albin. "Zwei Sophokles-Interpretationen." *Hermes* 80 (1952): 91-105.

———. *Greek Tragedy*. Translated by H. A. Frankfort. New York: Barnes and Noble; London: Ernest Benn, 1965.

Lewis, C. S. *Prince Caspian: The Return to Narnia*. New York: Macmillan, 1951. Reprint. New York: Macmillan, 1970.

Lewis, R. G. "An Alternative Date for Sophocles' *Antigone*." *Greek, Roman and Byzantine Studies* 29 (1988): 35-50.

Liddell, Henry George, and Robert Scott. *A Greek-English Lexicon*. 9th ed. Edited by Henry Stuart Jones, with the assistance of Roderick McKenzie; and with the cooperation of many scholars. Oxford: Clarendon Press, 1940.

Linforth, Ivan M. "Antigone and Creon." *University of California Publications in Classical Philology* 15 (1961): 183-260.

Lloyd, G. E. R. *Polarity and Analogy: Two Types of Argumentation in Early Greek Thought*. Cambridge: Cambridge University Press, 1966.

Lloyd-Jones, H. "Sophoclea." *Classical Quarterly* 4 (1954): 91-93.

———. "Notes on Sophocles' *Antigone*." *Classical Quarterly* 7 (1957): 12-27.

Lloyd-Jones, H., and N. G. Wilson. *Sophoclis Fabulae*. Oxford: Oxford University Press, 1990.

———. *Sophoclea: Studies on the Text of Sophocles*. Oxford: Oxford University Press, 1990.

Loraux, Nicole. "Sur la race des femmes et quelques-unes de ses tribus." *Arethusa* 11 (1978): 43-87.

———. *The Invention of Athens: The Funeral Oration in the Classical City*. Translated by Alan Sheridan. Cambridge: Harvard University Press, 1986.

———. *Tragic Ways of Killing a Woman*. Translated by Anthony Forster. Cambridge and London: Harvard University Press, 1987.

―――. "Herakles: The Super-Male and the Feminine." In *Before Sexuality: The Construction of Erotic Experience in the Ancient Greek World*. Edited by David M. Halperin, John J. Winkler, and Froma I. Zeitlin, 21-52. Princeton, NJ: Princeton University Press, 1990.

―――. *The Children of Athena: Athenian Ideas about Citizenship and the Division between the Sexes*. Translated by Caroline Levine. Princeton, NJ: Princeton University Press, 1993.

MacKay, L. A. "Antigone, Coriolanus, and Hegel." *Transactions and Proceedings of the American Philological Association* 93 (1962): 166-174.

Maclean, Norman. *A River Runs Through It and Other Stories*. Chicago and London: The University of Chicago Press, 1976.

Margon, Joseph S. "The First Burial of Polyneices." *The Classical Journal* 64 (1969): 289-295.

McCall, Marsh. "Divine and Human Action in Sophocles: The Two Burials of the *Antigone*." *Yale Classical Studies* 22 (1972): 103-117.

Messemer, Edward J., S.J. "The Double Burial of Polynices." *The Classical Journal* 37 (1942): 515-526.

Miller, Stephen G. *The Prytaneion*. Berkeley and Los Angeles: University of California Press, 1978.

Minadeo, Richard M. "Characterization and Theme in the *Antigone*." *Arethusa* 18 (1985): 133-154.

Monceaux, Paul. "Funus." In *Dictionnaire des antiquités grecques et romaines*. Edited by Ch. Daremberg and Edm. Saglio, 1370-1386. Vol. 2. Paris: Librairie Hachette, 1896.

Müller, Gerhard. *Sophokles: "Antigone."* Heidelberg: Winter, 1967.

Murnaghan, Sheila. "*Antigone* 904-920 and the Institution of Marriage." *American Journal of Philology* 107 (1986): 192-207.

―――. "Penelope's *agnoia*: Knowledge, Power and Gender in the *Odyssey*." *Helios* 13 (1986): 103-115.

―――. "How a Woman Can Be More Like a Man: The Dialogue Between Ischomachus and His Wife in Xenophon's *Oeconomicus*." *Helios* 15 (1988): 9-22.

Mylonas, George E. "A Signet-Ring in the City Art Museum of St. Louis." *American Journal of Archaeology* 49 (1945): 557-569.

Nagy, Gregory. *The Best of the Achaeans*. Baltimore and London: The Johns Hopkins University Press, 1979.

Neuburg, Matt. "How Like a Woman: Antigone's 'Inconsistency'." *Classical Quarterly* 40 (1990): 54-76.

Newton, Rick M. "Oedipus' Wife and Mother." *The Classical Journal* 87 (1991): 35-45.

Nussbaum, Martha C. *The Fragility of Goodness: Luck and Ethics in Greek Tragedy and Philosophy.* Cambridge: Cambridge University Press, 1986.

Oakley, John H. "The Anakalypteria." *Archäologischer Anzeiger* 97 (1982): 113-118.

Oakley, John H., and Rebecca H. Sinos. *The Wedding in Ancient Athens.* Madison: The University of Wisconsin Press, 1993.

Ober, Josiah. *Mass and Elite in Democratic Athens: Rhetoric, Ideology, and the Power of the People.* Princeton, NJ: Princeton University Press, 1989.

Ober, Josiah and Barry Strauss. "Drama, Political Rhetoric, and the Discourse of Athenian Democracy." In *Nothing to Do with Dionysus? Athenian Drama in Its Social Context.* Edited by John Winkler and Froma Zeitlin, 237-270. Princeton, NJ: Princeton University Press, 1990.

Ochs, Donovan J. *Consolatory Rhetoric: Grief, Symbol, and Ritual in the Greco-Roman Era.* Columbia: University of South Carolina Press, 1993.

Ostwald, Martin. *Nomos and the Beginnings of the Athenian Democracy.* Oxford: Oxford University Press, 1969.

Oxenforth, John, trans. *Conversations of Goethe with Eckerman and Soret.* London: G. Bell and Sons, 1901.

Page, D. L. *Further Greek Epigrams.* Cambridge: Cambridge University Press, 1981.

Paolucci, Anne, and Henry Paolucci. *Hegel on Tragedy.* Garden City, NY: Doubleday, 1962.

Parke, H. W. *Festivals of the Athenians.* London: Thames and Hudson, 1977.

Parker, Robert. *Miasma: Pollution and Purification in Early Greek Religion.* Oxford: Clarendon Press, 1983.

Paton, W. R. *The Greek Anthology.* 5 vols. Cambridge: Harvard University Press, 1917.

Patterson, Cynthia. *Pericles' Citizenship Law of 451-50 B.C.* New York: Arno Press, 1981.

———. "*Hai Attikai*: The Other Athenians." *Helios* 13 (1987): 49-67.

Pearson, A. C. *Sophoclis Fabulae.* Oxford: Oxford University Press, 1924.

Pélékidis, Chrysis. *Histoire de l'éphébie attique des origines à 31 avant Jésus-Christ.* Paris: E. de Boccard, 1962.

Pembroke, Simon. "Women in Charge: The Function of Alternatives in Early Greek Tradition and the Ancient Idea of Matriarchy." *Journal of the Warburg and Courtauld Institutes* 30 (1967): 1-35.

Pickard-Cambridge, Arthur. *The Dramatic Festivals of Athens.* 2d ed. Revised by John Gould and D. M. Lewis. Oxford: Clarendon Press, 1986.

Podlecki, Anthony J. "Creon and Herodotus." *Transactions and Proceedings of the American Philological Association* 97 (1966): 359-371.

Preller, Ludwig. *Griechische Mythologie.* Vol. 2, pt. 2: *Die Nationalheroen.* 4th ed. Berlin: Weidmann, 1921; Reprint edited by Carl Robert. Dublin and Zürich: Weidmann, 1967.

Prins, Yopie. "The Power of the Speech Act: Aeschylus' Furies and Their Binding Song." *Arethusa* 24 (1991): 177-195.

Rabinowitz, Peter J. "Shifting Sands, Shifting Standards: Reading, Interpretation, and Literary Judgment." *Arethusa* 19 (1986): 115-134.

Radt, Stefan, ed. *Tragicorum Graecorum Fragmenta.* Vol. 3: *Aeschylus.* Göttingen: Vandenhoeck and Ruprecht, 1985; Vol. 4: *Sophocles.* Göttingen: Vandenhoeck and Ruprecht, 1977.

Reddy, Michael J. "The Conduit Metaphor: A Case of Frame Conflict in Our Language about Language." In *Metaphor and Thought,* 2d ed. Edited by Andrew Ortony, 164-201. Cambridge: Cambridge University Press, 1993.

Redfield, James M. *Nature and Culture in the "Iliad": The Tragedy of Hector.* Chicago and London: The University of Chicago Press, 1975.

———. "Notes on the Greek Wedding." *Arethusa* 15 (1982): 181-201.

Rehm, Rush. *Marriage to Death: The Conflation of Wedding and Funeral Rituals in Greek Tragedy.* Princeton, NJ: Princeton University Press, 1994.

Reinhardt, Karl. *Sophocles.* Translated by Hazel Harvey and David Harvey. New York: Barnes and Noble, 1979.

Reinmuth, O. W. "The Genesis of the Athenian Ephebia." *Transactions and Proceedings of the American Philological Association* 83 (1952): 34-50.

Richardson, N. J. *The Homeric "Hymn to Demeter."* Oxford: Oxford University Press, 1974.

Ronnet, Gilberte. *Sophocle, poète tragique.* Paris: E. de Boccard, 1969.

Rose, H. J. "The Bride of Hades." *Classical Philology* 20 (1925): 238-242.

Rothaus, Richard M. "The Single Burial of Polyneices." *The Classical Journal* 85 (1990): 209-217.

Rouse, W. H. D. "The Two Burials in *Antigone.*" *Classical Review* 25 (1911): 40-42.

Rustin, J. S. *Thucydides. The Peloponnesian War.* Cambridge: Cambridge University Press, 1989.

Saussure, Ferdinand de. *Course in General Linguistics.* Translated by Wayne Baskin, and edited by Charles Bally and Albert Sechehaye in collaboration with Albert Riedlinger. New York, Toronto, and London: McGraw-Hill, 1966.

Schmid, von Wilhelm, and Otto Stälin. *Geschichte der griechischen Literatur.* 2: *Die grieschische Literatur in der Zeit de attischen Hegemonie vor dem Eingreifen der Sophistik.* Münich: C. H. Beck, 1959.

Schroeder, Otto. *De laudibus Athenarum a poetis tragicis et ab oratoribus epidicticis excultis.* Göttingen: Officina Hubertiana, 1914.

Scodel, Ruth. "Epic Doublets and Polynices' Two Burials." *Transactions of the American Philological Association* 114 (1984): 49-58.

Seaford, Richard. "The Tragic Wedding." *Journal of Hellenic Studies* 107 (1987): 106-130.

———. "The Imprisonment of Women in Greek Tragedy." *Journal of Hellenic Studies* 110 (1990): 76-90.

———. *Reciprocity and Ritual: Homer and Tragedy in the Developing City-State.* Oxford: Oxford University Press, 1994.

Seager, Robin. "Elitism and Democracy in Classical Athens." In *The Rich, the Well Born, and the Powerful,* edited by Frederic Cople Jaher, 7-25. Urbana: University of Illinois Press, 1973.

Seale, David. *Vision and Stagecraft in Sophocles.* Chicago and London: The University of Chicago Press, 1982.

Searle, John R. "Metaphor." In *Metaphor and Thought,* 2d ed. Edited by Andrew Ortony, 83-111. Cambridge: Cambridge University Press, 1993.

Segal, Charles. *The Theme of the Mutilation of the Corpse in the "Iliad."* Leiden: E. J. Brill, 1971.

———. *Tragedy and Civilization: An Interpretation of Sophocles.* Cambridge and London: Harvard University Press, 1981.

———. "Sophocles' Praise of Man and the Conflicts of the *Antigone.*" In *Interpreting Greek Tragedy.* Edited by Charles Segal, 137-161. Ithaca, NY: Cornell University Press, 1986.

———. *Sophocles' Tragic World: Divinity, Nature, Society.* Cambridge: Harvard University Press, 1995.

Seremetakis, C. Nadia. *The Last Word: Women, Death, and Divination in Inner Mani*. Chicago and London: The University of Chicago Press, 1991.

Shapiro, H. A. "The Iconography of Mourning in Athenian Art." *American Journal of Archaeology* 95 (1991): 629-656.

———. *"Mousikoi Agones*: Music and Poetry at the Panathenaia." In *Goddess and Polis: The Panathenaic Festival in Ancient Athens*. Edited by Jenifer Neils, 53-75. Hanover, NH: Hood Museum of Art, Darthmouth College; Princeton, NJ: Princeton University Press, 1992.

Shaw, M. "The Female Intruder: Women in Fifth-Century Drama." *Classical Philology* 70 (1975): 255-266.

Siewert, P. "The Ephebic Oath in Fifth-Century Athens." *Journal of Hellenic Studies* 97 (1977): 102-111.

Smyth, Herbert Weir. *Greek Grammar*. 1920. Revised by Gordon M. Messing. Cambridge: Harvard University Press, 1956.

Sourvinou-Inwood, Christiane. "Assumptions and the Creation of Meaning: Reading Sophocles' *Antigone*." *Journal of Hellenic Studies* 109 (1989): 134-148.

———. "The Fourth Stasimon of Sophocles' *Antigone*." *Bulletin of the Institute of Classical Studies of the University of London* 36 (1989): 141-165.

Stadter, Philip A. *A Commentary on "Plutarch's Pericles."* Chapel Hill and London: The University of North Carolina Press, 1989.

Stanford, W. B. *Sophocles: "Ajax."* London: Macmillan, 1963.

———. *The Sound of Greek: Studies in the Greek Theory and Practice of Euphony*. Berkeley and Los Angeles: University of California Press, 1967.

Steiner, George. *Antigones*. Oxford: Oxford University Press, 1984.

Szlezák, T. A. "Bermerkungen zur Diskussion um Sophokles, *Antigone* 904-920." *Rheinisches Museum* 124 (1981): 108-142.

Taplin, Oliver. "Aeschylean Silences and Silences in Aeschylus." *Harvard Studies in Classical Philology* 76 (1972): 57-97.

———. *The Stagecraft of Aeschylus: The Dramatic Use of Exits and Entrances in Greek Tragedy*. Oxford: Oxford University Press, 1977.

———. *Greek Tragedy in Action*. Berkeley and Los Angeles: University of California Press, 1978.

Tod, Marcus N. *A Selection of Greek Historical Inscriptions*. Vol. 2: *From 403 to 323 B.C.* Oxford: Oxford University Press, 1948.

Tompkins, Jane P. "The Reader in History: The Changing Shape of Literary Response." In *Reader-Response Criticism: From Formalism to Post-*

Structuralism. Edited by Jane P. Tompkins, 201-232. Baltimore and London: The Johns Hopkins University Press, 1980.

Turner, V. W. *Schism and Continuity in an African Society: A Study of Ndembu Village Life.* Manchester: University of Manchester Press, 1957.

———. "Liminality and the Performative Genres." In *Rite, Drama, Festival, Spectacle: Rehearsals Toward a Theory of Cultural Performance.* Edited by John J. MacAloon, 19-41. Philadelphia: Institute for the Study of Human Issues, 1984.

Tyrrell, Wm. Blake. "Amazon Customs and Athenian Patriarchy." *Annali della Scuola Normale Superiore di Pisa* 13 (1982): 1213-1237.

———. *Amazons: A Study in Athenian Mythmaking.* Baltimore and London: The Johns Hopkins University Press, 1984.

———. "The Unity of Sophocles' *Ajax*." *Arethusa* 18 (1985): 155-185.

Tyrrell, Wm. Blake, and Frieda S. Brown. *Athenian Myths and Institutions: Words in Action.* New York and Oxford: Oxford University Press, 1991.

Van Gennepp, Arnold. *The Rites of Passage.* Translated by M. B. Vizedom and G. L. Caffee. Chicago: The University of Chicago Press, 1960.

Vermeule, Emily. *Aspects of Death in Early Greek Art and Poetry.* Berkeley and Los Angeles: University of California Press, 1979.

Vernant, Jean-Pierre. "Greek Tragedy: Problems of Interpretation." In *The Structuralist Controversy: The Languages of Criticism and the Sciences of Man.* Edited by Richard Macksey and Eugenio Donato, 273-289. Baltimore and London: The Johns Hopkins University Press, 1972.

———. *Mythe et pensée chez les Grecs: Etudes du psychologie historique.* 2 vols. Paris: François Maspero, 1974.

———. *Myth and Society in Ancient Greece.* Translated by Janet Lloyd. Sussex: Harvester Press; Atlantic Highlands, NJ: Humanities Press, 1980.

———. "Théorie générale du sacrifice et mise à mort dans la θυσίᾳ grecque." In *Le Sacrifice dans l'antiquité, Entretiens sur l'antiquité classique* 27 (1981): 1-21.

Vernant, Jean-Pierre, and Pierre Vidal-Naquet. *Myth and Tragedy in Ancient Greece.* Translated by Janet Lloyd. New York: Zone Books, 1990.

———. *Mortals and Immortals: Collected Essays.* Edited by Froma I. Zeitlin. Princeton, NJ: Princeton University Press, 1991.

Vian, Francis. *Les Origines de Thèbes: Cadmos et Spartes.* Paris: C. Klincksieck, 1963.

Vickers, Brian. *Towards Greek Tragedy: Drama, Myth, Society.* London: Longman, 1973.

Vidal-Naquet, Pierre. *The Black Hunter: Forms of Thought and Forms of Society in the Greek World*. Translated by Andrew Szegedy-Maszak. Baltimore and London: The Johns Hopkins University Press, 1986.

Waldock, A. J. A. *Sophocles the Dramatist*. Cambridge: Cambridge University Press, 1966.

Walker, Henry J. *Theseus and Athens*. New York and Oxford: Oxford University Press, 1995.

Walters, Kenneth R. "Rhetoric as Ritual: The Semiotics of the Attic Funeral Oration." *Florilegium* 2 (1980): 1-27.

West, J. L. *Hesiod: "Theogony."* Oxford: Oxford University Press, 1966.

———. "Tragica VI." *Bulletin of the Institute of Classical Studies of the University of London* 30 (1983): 63-82.

———. *Iambi et Elegi Graeci ante Alexandrum Cantati*. 2d ed. Oxford: Oxford University Press, 1989.

Whitehorne, J. E. G. "The Background to Polyneices' Disinterment and Reburial." *Greece and Rome* 30 (1983): 129-142.

Whitman, Cedric Hubbell. *Sophocles: A Study of Heroic Humanism*. Cambridge: Harvard University Press, 1951.

Wilamowitz-Moellendorff, Ulrich von. *Aristoteles und Athen*. Berlin: Weidmann, 1893.

Wiles, David. "Reading Greek Performance." *Greece and Rome* 34 (1987): 136-151.

Winkler, John J. *The Constraints of Desire*. New York and London: Routledge, 1990.

———. "The Ephebes' Song: *Tragôidia* and *Polis*" In *Nothing to Do with Dionysus?* Edited by John J. Winkler and Froma I. Zeitlin, 20-62. Princeton, NJ: Princeton University Press, 1990.

Winnington-Ingram, R. P. *Sophocles: An Interpretation*. Cambridge: Cambridge University Press, 1980.

Wolff, Hans Julius. "Marriage Law and Family Organization in Ancient Athens." *Traditio* 2 (1944): 43-95.

Wycherley, R. E. *The Stones of Athens*. Princeton, NJ: Princeton University Press, 1978.

Wyckoff, Elizabeth, trans. *Antigone*. In *The Complete Greek Tragedies: Sophocles I*. Edited by David Grene and Richmond Lattimore. Chicago and London: The University of Chicago Press, 1954.

Zeitlin, Froma I. *Under the Sign of the Shield*. Roma: Edizioni dell' Ateno, 1982.

———— . "Thebes: Theater of Self and Society in Athenian Drama." In *Greek Tragedy and Political Theory*. Edited by J. Peter Euben, 101-141. Berkeley and Los Angeles: University of California Press, 1986.

Ziolkowski, John E. *Thucydides and the Tradition of Funeral Speeches at Athens*. Salem, NH: The Ayer Company, 1985.

Index